Teachers' Skills Tests

FOR DUMMIES®

A Wiley Brand

by Colin Beveridge and
Andrew Green

FOR DUMMIES®
A Wiley Brand

Teachers' Skills Tests For Dummies®

Published by:
John Wiley & Sons, Ltd.,
The Atrium, Southern Gate, Chichester,
www.wiley.com

This edition first published 2014

© 2014 John Wiley & Sons, Ltd, Chichester, West Sussex.

Registered office

John Wiley & Sons Ltd, The Atrium, Southern Gate, Chichester, West Sussex, PO19 8SQ,
United Kingdom

For details of our global editorial offices, for customer services and for information about how
to apply for permission to reuse the copyright material in this book please see our website at
www.wiley.com.

The right of the author to be identified as the author of this work has been asserted in accordance
with the Copyright, Designs and Patents Act 1988.

Wiley publishes in a variety of print and electronic formats and by print-on-demand. Some material
included with standard print versions of this book may not be included in e-books or in print-on-
demand. If this book refers to media such as a CD or DVD that is not included in the version you pur-
chased, you may download this material at http://booksupport.wiley.com. For more
information about Wiley products, visit www.wiley.com.

Designations used by companies to distinguish their products are often claimed as trademarks. All
brand names and product names used in this book are trade names, service marks, trademarks or
registered trademarks of their respective owners. The publisher is not associated with any product
or vendor mentioned in this book.

For general information on our other products and services, please contact our Customer Care
Department within the U.S. at 877-762-2974, outside the U.S. at (001) 317-572-3993, or fax
317-572-4002.

For technical support, please visit www.wiley.com/techsupport.

A catalogue record for this book is available from the British Library.

ISBN 978-1-118-66164-2 (pbk), ISBN 978-1-118-67359-1 (ebk), ISBN 978-1-118-67357-7 (ebk)

Printed and bound in Great Britain by TJ International Ltd, Padstow, Cornwall

10 9 8 7 6 5 4 3 2 1

Contents at a Glance

Table of Contents

Chapter 7: Considering the Comprehension Test 133

Part III: Numeracy Skills *157*

Chapter 8: Making Sense of Mental Maths 159

Chapter 9: Stepping up to the Screen: Arithmetic Review 193

Chapter 10: Getting on Top of On-Screen Tests with Tables and Graphs............................211

Introduction

*S*o, you want to become a teacher? Fantastic! Never mind the friends who wittily quote George Bernard Shaw's hilarious (not) 'He who can does. He who can't teaches'. Ignore the steady supply of family members who start presenting you with apples, wry smiles on their faces. Rise above the endless talk of a ridiculous amount of annual leave and the 'clever' comments about a well-paid job where you turn up at 9 a.m. and finish at 3 p.m.

You can pay no attention, because teaching is a great profession and being able to do it well is a real gift. To play a part in watching children and young people develop and learn is a privilege that few jobs provide.

Make no mistake – the work is challenging, uplifting, frustrating and exciting by turns. One day you feel on top of the world, the next you're tearing your hair out and wondering what on earth you've let yourself in for. But we can guarantee that it'll never be dull.

You spend hours marking work, planning lessons and developing the best ways to teach a topic, but when – and yes, this really does happen sometimes – you see your pupils' faces light up when a key concept finally clicks, it's worth every minute.

We know that you're going to make a great teacher – when you get past those pesky Skills Tests. And yes, we've heard all the standard arguments that you don't plan to be a Maths teacher or teach English and so why do you have to revise percentages and fractions or be able to distinguish your pronouns from your prepositions?

Well, here are several reasons:

- You'll be marking books, writing on the board, sending reports to parents, creating resources and doing plenty of other writing as a teacher. You want to look as professional as possible, and so having good English skills is essential.

✔ You'll be responsible for statistics about your classes, working out test percentages and – as you progress through your career – dealing with budgets, analysing data and discovering all manner of places where you need to be moderately sharp with your number skills.

✔ Students pick up attitudes from their teachers. Any outlook that 'numeracy and literacy aren't all that important' is going to rub off on your students. We think that they deserve better than that.

✔ If you don't pass the tests, you don't get into teacher training. No amount of grumbling is going to change that fact, and so you may as well put your energies into studying. (That's the 'it's in the exam!' reason; you'll probably tell pupils that quite frequently.)

We don't plan to turn you into a Maths geek or a literature professor – we couldn't if we tried; all we want to do is help you get through the tests and feel comfortable with the everyday English and Maths you need to be a good, professional teacher.

As you work through the book, you'll find that you get quicker and more accurate with your answers and will go into the test confident of getting the score you need.

Good luck! Let us know how you get on.

About This Book

This book is for you if you're planning to start teacher training and have to pass the Numeracy and Literacy Skills Tests to qualify for your course. We take you through the details of the tests, showing you how to revise in general and what you specifically need to know for these tests.

Andrew is your guide for the literacy side of things, taking you patiently through the tricks of spelling, punctuation and grammar. From him, you discover the following:

✔ Ways to make sense of the madness that is the English spelling system.

✔ How to use your existing knowledge of language and grammar to build new knowledge that you need for the Skills Tests.

✔ Language skills that benefit you for your career as a teacher and for life.

Colin is in charge of numeracy. In his chapters, he shows you:

✔ How to deal with the mental arithmetic test without dissolving into a panic.

✔ How to pull apart word problems and turn them into sums you can do.

✔ How to make sense of complicated graphs and get simple answers from them.

We also provide several sample exams you can use as part of your revision to see how you're getting on, and to give you a flavour of what the tests are like – and the whole book is full of worked examples so you can see both the answer and how to get there!

Foolish Assumptions

Making assumptions is always a risky business, but knowing where we're coming from may put you at ease. So, in writing this book, we assume the following:

✔ You know your basic arithmetic: how to add, subtract, divide and multiply small numbers.

✔ You're able to read and write in English at a basic level. It goes without saying, we hope, that all the rules, guidance and so on that we provide relate to Standard English. Nothing's wrong with colloquialisms and the like in every-day life, but they ain't gonna get ya no points in the Skills Tests.

✔ You want to do well in your Skills Tests as a step to becoming a great teacher!

Icons Used in This Book

Here are the icons we use to draw your attention to particularly noteworthy paragraphs.

Theories are fine and dandy, but anything marked with this icon tells you something practically useful to help you get to the right answer.

Paragraphs marked with this icon contain key points to take away from the book and the essence of each subject.

This icon highlights mistakes that can cost you marks or your sanity, or both! Others have made these errors so that you don't have to.

Beside this icon we provide useful exercises so that you can try out what you discover in a chapter. The more you practise, the easier the actual test is sure to be.

If you prefer you can safely skip anything marked with this icon without missing out on the main message. But you may find the information useful for a deeper understanding of the subject.

Beyond the Book

For a more realistic experience, visit www.dummies.com/go/teachersskillstests to access audio versions of the spelling and mental arithmetic questions, similar to those used for the actual tests. You can also check out this site for the latest updates on changes to the tests. Why not also visit www.dummies.com/cheatsheet/teachersskillstests for more quick and easy tips on how to brush up on your test-taking skills, giving you the confidence you need to sail through your Literacy and Numeracy tests.

Where to go from Here

Head to Chapter 2 for an explanation of what you're likely to find in your Literacy and Numeracy tests. If you're in a hurry to see where you are, you may want to jump straight to the timed tests in Chapters 12 and 13. On the other hand, if you have plenty of time before the exam, you may prefer to start with Chapter 3 and set yourself up with a detailed study plan.

You can also use the index and Table of Contents to find the areas you want to study. This book is a reference – keep it with your study gear and turn to it whenever you have something you want to look up!

We wish you the very best in your Professional Skills Tests, and hope this book helps you to pass the exams in style! Good luck – both with the exams and with your career as a teacher.

Part I
Getting Started with the Skills Tests

getting started
with
teachers'
skills tests

In this part . . .

✔ Learn to leap through the right hoops to become a teacher.

✔ Find out exactly what you need to know to sit and pass the Skills Tests.

✔ Sit down and study: perfect your revision technique and get mentally prepared.

✔ Keep yourself calm, stay motivated and succeed!

Chapter 1

Receiving Your Ticket to the Classroom

● ●

In This Chapter

▶ Exploring your options for training as a teacher

▶ Understanding the need for the Skills Tests

● ●

*L*ike just about anything worthwhile in life, becoming a teacher takes work and needs you to fulfil several requirements. One of these, whether you like it or not, is that you have to pass your Professional Skills Tests.

You may be a superb sports coach, a maestro in the music studio, an excellent exponent for English literature or a genius in the geography classroom. You may be able to inspire your pupils with enthusiasm for equilateral triangles, devotion to design technology or passion for the painting processes of Jackson Pollock. You may, in other words, be God's gift to the teaching profession, but without passing your Skills Tests you aren't going to reach even the first rung of the teaching ladder.

In this chapter, we lead you through a quick tour of the paths that you can take to become a teacher, providing information about what's required of you along the way. We also explain why you have to pass the Professional Skills Tests before you can enter a course of Initial Teacher Education (ITE).

Tracing the Routes to Becoming a Teacher

As the rather unpleasant saying goes, 'there's more than one way to skin a cat'. Likewise, you have more than one way into the teaching profession (and fortunately they're all less messy and less damaging to the poor felines). Your task is to find the way that best suits you and your circumstances. If you've yet to make that decision, this section can help.

Passing the early stations en route to Teaching Central

No matter which route you take to becoming a teacher – and we outline plenty in this section – you encounter a number of common stops along the way:

- ✓ **GCSEs:** Having a Grade C or better at GCSE (or equivalent qualifications from other countries) in English and Maths has long been a pre-entry requirement for teacher-education courses.

- ✓ **Professional Skills Tests:** You're reading this book, of course, because you need to pass the Literacy and Numeracy Skills Tests to be accepted onto a teacher-training course.

- ✓ **A degree:** To be a teacher, you require a university degree. You either need to hold a degree in advance of deciding that you want to become a teacher, or to earn one as part of your ITE.

- ✓ **Qualified Teacher Status (QTS):** To achieve QTS, you have to demonstrate to the university or school leading the training that you meet the Teaching Standards established by the Department of Education. At that point, the university or school recommends you for QTS to the Teaching Agency (TA), which is the body that awards the status (check out the Teaching Standards at https://www.gov.uk/government/publications/teachers-standards).

To look into all the available options for becoming a teacher in more detail than we have space for, visit the TA website at http://www.education.gov.uk/get-into-teaching/teacher-training-options.aspx

The information and guidance we provide in this chapter is solid. But your best course of action before making any decisions is to check with the universities and programmes that you're considering and make sure that you know the rules, regulations and requirements specific to them.

Pursuing an undergraduate degree

If you don't have a university degree and you want to train as a teacher, you can pursue a degree and work towards QTS (which we define in the preceding section) at the same time at university.

Two types of undergraduate qualification can lead to QTS:

- **Bachelor of Arts (BA)/Bachelor of Science (BSc) courses with QTS:** These courses provide an honours degree in a particular academic subject (such as English, Maths or Physical Education) alongside working towards QTS. Regular assessed school placements spread over the duration of the degree programme allow you to explore the *pedagogic* (that is, the theoretical and practical) approaches appropriate to the teaching of the academic subject in the school context.

- **Bachelor of Education (BEd) courses:** These programmes are honours courses in education. They're available for primary and secondary education, but given the usual requirement for secondary teachers to possess degree-level knowledge in a particular National Curriculum subject, BEd qualifications (which don't provide such a specialist focus) are much more common for primary education.

These two courses typically take three or four years to complete.

As with other undergraduate courses, you apply for entry to these programmes via the Universities and Colleges Applications Service (UCAS) at www.ucas.ac.uk.

Taking a postgraduate path

You have two options available if you have a degree in hand and decide that teaching is for you:

- ✔ **University-based training:** Led primarily by university and academic tutors.

- ✔ **School-based training:** Led primarily by a Training School.

These models involve a close partnership between universities and schools, because a balance of academic learning about education and pedagogy and practical application of these subjects through classroom experience is important. Teachers working in schools and university lecturers in education provide different but complementary perspectives on the work of the teacher.

Theory without practice can be abstract and unrealistic, and practice without understanding of the underpinning theory runs the danger of being simplistic and will not provide you with a detailed understanding of the complex processes at work in the classroom.

University-based routes

Postgraduate routes into teaching via a higher education institution (HEI) generally allow you to obtain a *Postgraduate Certificate in Education* (PGCE) with recommendation for QTS.

HEI-based PGCE routes are becoming increasingly rare because policy now favours school-based routes. As a result, numbers of training places allocated to universities for PGCE provision have been cut significantly. Check out the later 'School-based routes' section for the other ways of obtaining a PGCE.

A PGCE is an academic qualification that's often studied for and assessed alongside QTS. It allows students to explore philosophies and purposes of education, theories of how teachers teach and learners learn, the history of academic subjects and the ideas underpinning subject pedagogies.

PGCEs are awarded in two forms, though both require that you've already completed your first degree (usually in the subject you want to teach):

- ✔ **Professional level:** PGCEs at this level are assessed according to undergraduate criteria.

- ✔ **Masters level:** PGCEs at this level are assessed according to postgraduate criteria and carry Masters-level credits. These credits can be really useful if you want to go on to complete a full Masters in Education at a later date.

Check out carefully with your university whether the PGCE you're interested in carries Masters-level credits or not, because it can obviously have an impact on potential employers.

Strictly speaking, you don't *have* to have a PGCE; QTS is all that's required in order to work in schools in the UK. But many employers like to see that you also have the PGCE, which is seen as adding some academic rigour to the practicalities of QTS.

To gain access to most programmes you need a good honours degree (2:2 or higher), although the TA has sought to 'raise the bar'. In many cases a 2:1 or higher is now required, and in all subjects degree classification has a direct impact on levels of funding (see the nearby sidebar 'Show me the money!' for more on funding).

Also, with limited numbers of university-based PGCE places now available, admissions tutors can (and will) be much more selective. Entry criteria for PGCE programmes are, therefore, likely to become higher.

Show me the money!

The good news is that funding of up to £20,000 is currently available (depending upon subject and degree qualification) for a variety of university-based and school-based postgraduate routes into teaching. For more information, take a look at http://www.education.gov.uk/get-into-teaching/funding/postgraduate-funding.

Overseas qualifications

If you qualified at an overseas university, you can still apply for any of the routes outlined here. Check out whether your degree and other entry qualifications (for example, GCSE English and Maths) are considered equivalent by referring to UK NARIC, the national agency responsible for providing information and advice about how qualifications and skills from overseas compare to the UK's national qualification frameworks.

The TA claims that an A-level in the target subject plus any degree is enough to gain entry into a postgraduate programme, but the reality is that most HEIs have much higher benchmark entry criteria. So, if your dream is to become an English teacher but you have a first degree in Forensic Science, you're unlikely to gain a place.

PGCE programmes are available in full-time (FT) and part-time (PT) routes. FT routes take one year and PT routes up to two years. Please check carefully with individual HEIs, though, because not all HEIs are allowed to offer all subjects and only some subjects are available on a PT basis.

HEIs operate according to strict target numbers, and so early application for PGCE courses is advisable.

You have to apply for all PGCE courses via UCAS TT. See the website at `http://www.ucas.com/how-it-all-works/teacher-training` for further details about the application process.

School-based routes

As well as the university-based routes we outline in the preceding section, you also have a variety of school-based routes into the teaching profession.

School-based routes are open only to individuals who already hold a university degree.

School Direct

A new major route is School Direct (SD). Typically a one-year programme (though some schools may opt to offer part-time alternatives), SD exists for primary and secondary levels. The route is available to high-quality university graduates and leads to the award of QTS if you complete it successfully.

Training is led by a Training School, but a partner university is also involved in the programme. No fixed rules apply about how this arrangement must work in practice.

Some schools adopt a model in which, as a student, you're released for blocks of academic study at the partner university, where you prepare for a PGCE (we define the PGCE earlier in this chapter in 'University-based routes'). In other cases, the academic programme supplements the school-based one but doesn't lead to the award of a PGCE. Other schools develop bespoke relationships with universities in which teaching by university staff takes place in local clusters of schools or even in a single centre. Again, this arrangement may (or may not) lead to the award of a PGCE.

As you can see, a lot depends upon the nature of local partnership and assessment arrangements negotiated between the Training School and the partner university. The only way to be certain is to approach your chosen provider and ask!

School Direct exists in two versions:

- ✔ **SD Training:** see details above.

- ✔ **SD Salaried:** arrangements for application remain the same, but this route is normally open only to candidates who have three or more years' experience in work. Note, though, that this work can be in any field – it doesn't have to be in education. Successful applicants will receive a salary from their Training School – the clue's in the name! As with the SD route, places offered on this route also lead, if completed successfully, to the award of QTS and may carry the PGCE.

Funding of up to $20,000 for the SD Training route is currently available depending upon subject and degree qualification. For information, check out http://www.education.gov.uk/get-into-teaching/funding/postgraduate-funding.

Application for School Direct places is also made via UCAS TT. For full details see http://www.ucas.com/how-it-all-works/teacher-training.

School-centred Initial Teacher Training

School-centred Initial Teacher Training (SCITT) programmes are generally completed in a year (see http://www.education.gov.uk/get-into-teaching/teacher-training-options/school-based-training/school-centred-training for details). They lead to the award of the all-important QTS and some also to the PGCE.

As with the SD routes in the preceding section, SCITTs have to involve universities, but the relationship is somewhat different, because the route has to be validated by a partner university. So, although this route is primarily – as its name gives away – school-centred, the responsibility for assessment remains with the university.

The extent to which students following SCITT routes receive taught input from the validating university varies, and so check this aspect out carefully before you apply to make sure that the programme does what you want it to do.

Details of possible funding are available via the TA website (http://www.education.gov.uk/get-into-teaching/funding/postgraduate-funding) and application for SCITTs is generally made via UCAS TT (see http://www.ucas.com/how-it-all-works/teacher-training) – though look into this carefully, because it's not always the case.

Teach First

Teach First has a particular social and educational mission to work with schools operating in socially disadvantaged areas. As such, the schools it works with often provide very challenging (though potentially very rewarding) experiences.

To enter the Teach First school-based route into teaching, you need a minimum of a 2:1 degree or 300 UCAS points. (UCAS points are awarded for A-level grades and/or other post-age-16 qualifications.)

Teach First advertises a UCAS tariff in its entry criteria because so many of its applicants have yet to graduate. The 300 UCAS point indicator is, therefore, a benchmark for pre-graduation applicants. Participants (that's what Teach First calls students on its programme) who don't go on to obtain a 2:1 or a First Class degree are usually required to withdraw from the programme.

Teach First operates in ten regions:

- ✔ East Midlands
- ✔ Greater London
- ✔ Kent & Medway
- ✔ North East
- ✔ North West
- ✔ South West
- ✔ South Coast
- ✔ Teach First Cymru (Wales)
- ✔ West Midlands
- ✔ Yorkshire & The Humber

As an applicant you apply centrally to Teach First, indicating the region in which you want to work, though there's no guarantee regarding the region in which you'll be placed.

Teach First has no fees and offers an initial contracted period of two years: the first year paid as an unqualified teacher, the second year paid as a qualified teacher, assuming that the award of QTS is made at the end of the first year.

The programme begins with a Summer Institute that's HEI-based. Here you receive an intensive introduction to Professional Studies and Subject Studies in the area in which you're training to teach. All accommodation, travel and food costs for the period of the Summer Institute are paid, and so you don't need to worry about that!

Teach First operates its own assessment and admissions procedures: check out `graduates.teachfirst.org.uk`.

Getting qualified: Teachers without QTS

If you're already an experienced but unqualified teacher or an overseas trained teacher (OTT) who now wants to gain QTS, several options are designed specifically for your situation.

Unqualified UK teachers

If you're working unqualified in schools (maintained or independent) or in other related educational roles, you can take one of several specially designed routes to QTS:

- ✓ **Assessment Only (AO):** This programme is for teachers who can demonstrate that they've already met in full the requirements of the Teaching Standards. In this case, no formal ITE is required, but you still need to pass the Professional Skills Tests. You have to apply for AO routes directly to an 'accredited provider' – generally university-based programmes (see the earlier section 'Taking a postgraduate path').

- ✓ **Assessment-based route:** This option (different from the above in spite of its similar name) is for candidates for entry to teaching who require some, but a minimal amount of, additional training in order to meet the requirements of the Teaching Standards. This process is administered by the University of Gloucestershire, to which you need to apply (see http://www.glos.ac.uk/courses/teachertraining/Pages/qts.aspx).

Before considering application for this route, check the TA website (www.education.gov.uk/get-into-teaching) for current details, because not all phases of education and not all subjects are always available. And, yes, you do need to pass the Professional Skills Tests (there's no escape!).

Overseas experience

If you've been a teacher in a country other than the UK, your path to QTS depends upon where you previously taught:

- ✓ **European Union (EU):** If you're a teacher qualified in an EU state, your QTS is recognised automatically.

 ✔ **Australia, Canada, New Zealand and United States:**
 If you're a qualified teacher from one of these countries,
 you can apply directly to the TA to have your QTS recognised in the UK (subject to meeting Border Agency
 requirements in terms of right to reside and right to work
 in the UK).

 ✔ **Other countries:** If you trained in any other country outside the EU, the Overseas Trained Teacher Programme
 (OTTP) allows you to work in the UK for up to four years
 on an unqualified basis while gaining your QTS after you
 find a UK school to employ you. Known as Employment
 Based Initial Teacher Training (EBITT), the length of
 your training programme is determined by your EBITT
 provider.

You need to take the Professional Skills Tests only if you fall
within the third category listed above.

Introducing the Professional Skills Tests

Before meeting the conditions for acceptance on an Initial
Teacher Education (ITE) course to become a teacher, you
need to pass the Professional Skills Tests in Literacy and
Numeracy (for a complete description of these tests, turn
to Chapter 2).

Professional Skills Tests have long been part of the landscape
of teacher education, but as a candidate who wants to undertake teacher-education programmes you now have to pass
these tests upfront. In other words, the tests are a pre-entry
requirement.

Therefore, you no longer have the luxury of time and multiple
opportunities to pass these tests. All offers to take up places
on teacher-education programmes are conditional on the
successful pre-course completion of the Professional Skills
Tests: no pass, no place.

Taking the tests despite having the relevant GCSEs

Most people entering the teaching profession have already gained GCSEs (or equivalent qualifications from other countries) in English and Maths. In fact, proving that you have a Grade C or better at GCSE level in these subjects has long been a pre-entry requirement for teacher-education courses. Despite having these qualifications, however, and even if you have a degree or a PhD in English or Maths, you still have to take your Professional Skills Tests.

The reality is that even if you went straight to university from school and from there are now seeking to go straight into teacher education, five years have passed since you did your GCSEs. Taking into account gap years, employment, parenting and so on, for many people much longer periods have elapsed. After such a gap, being asked to undergo a new test of your abilities is quite reasonable.

Understanding why you have to do the tests

The rationale for the Professional Skills Tests is clear. Whether you aim to teach at primary or secondary level, and whatever your specialist subject, you need to be an effective and accurate user of language and numbers.

All teachers have to engage in the teaching of reading and writing to some extent. If you're a budding biology teacher who wants your pupils to be able to spell 'photosynthesis', you have to teach them (we cover spelling in Chapter 4). If you're a food-tech teacher and you want your pupils to write in particular forms and styles, that's down to you.

Plus, think about the many occasions when teachers have to use language in other aspects of their jobs: writing letters to parents, composing end-of-year reports, speaking at consultation evenings and so on. Turn to Chapters 5, 6 and 7 for all about punctuation, grammar and comprehension, respectively.

In addition, teachers (yes, even English teachers) need to be numerate – how else do you expect your pupils to read statistical data in non-fiction texts or present numerical material in their own writing if you don't teach them? As with English, teachers also need to use numeracy outside the classroom: working out examination results, analysing school and national performance data, and so on. We discuss the Numeracy parts of the tests in Part III of this book: mental arithmetic (Chapter 8), general arithmetic (Chapter 9) and statistics (Chapter 10). We supply useful numeracy practice questions in Chapter 11.

Don't forget that your literacy and numeracy abilities also impact on pupils and teaching colleagues. Teaching is a collaborative endeavour, and unless all teachers of all subjects reinforce the importance of, and demonstrate the effective use of, language and numbers, pupils' education is bound to suffer.

Like any policy or code of practice, weak performance by individuals has a knock-on effect. Accurate and creative use of language and numbers is important not only for effective communication, but also because your example as a teacher rubs off on your pupils. If you don't use these key skills accurately and confidently, and explicitly reinforce how important they are, the result is an adverse impact on the children you teach. If you don't value literacy and numeracy in your work, how can you expect them to do so?

Therefore, literacy and numeracy are vitally important for teachers and you can see why the authorities require you to show that you possess the basic skills in these areas. But you don't have to do so alone: we're here to help prepare you for the tests. As well as the specific chapters we reference earlier in this section, you may want to take a look at Chapter 2, where we describe the tests in detail, and Chapter 3, in which we provide some invaluable test strategies. We also supply timed tests for you to practise: on literacy in Chapter 12 and numeracy in Chapter 13. Try these out before you take the tests and nothing is going to surprise you on the day.

Chapter 2

Scoping out the Skills Tests

. . . .

In This Chapter

▶ Running through the practicalities

▶ Reading about the literacy test

▶ Counting down to the numeracy test

. . . .

*A*s part of the government's drive to improve the calibre of applicants to teacher training, it has introduced tests in numeracy and literacy at the start of your course, replacing the old tests (which you were able to take at any time during your course). The new tests are also designed to be harder (sorry, 'more rigorous') than the old versions: you need to get at least 18 out of a possible 28 marks (about 63 per cent) to pass.

Until 2012, you were allowed to take the Skills Tests as many times as you wanted until you attained the pass mark, but this arrangement has been replaced with a three-strikes-and-you're-out policy. If you fail either of the tests three times, you have to wait two years before you can apply for teacher training again. Your first attempt at each test is free, but if you need to take either paper again you're charged a fee – currently £19.25 – when you book. So now you know the official cost of failure!

In short, getting through the Skills Tests is significantly more difficult than in the past. The good news, however, is that we give you all the information and practice you need to get your literacy and numeracy up to speed so that you can succeed at the tests with minimal stress. In this chapter, we run through the Skills Tests in general and also focus on the Literacy and Numeracy tests individually.

Discovering the Test Basics

A bit of organisation can really improve your chances of getting through the Skills Tests without a panic attack. We're not talking about organising your notes (although that helps) – we mean booking your test as early as you can, showing up in the right place ahead of time and making sure that you're set up for doing the test.

The more confident you can be about showing up in the right place at the right time and avoiding test-day hassles, the more you can concentrate on just getting the answers right!

Arranging your test

To get you used to the bureaucracy you need to master as a teacher, you have to apply for the various elements of teacher training in a specific order. Here's how the process goes:

1. **Arrange your Skills Tests for a date after you plan to apply for your course, but before you plan to start training.**

2. **Submit your application(s) for teacher training.**

3. **Study for, and pass, your Skills Tests.**

4. **Succeed at your initial teacher education (ITE) interview.**

5. **Start your course.**

You register for your tests online (you can find all the links you need at www.education.gov.uk – search for 'Skills Tests registration' and you're taken to the right page).

Ensuring a level playing field

If you've been assessed as having dyslexia or dyscalculia, if you're hard of hearing or visually impaired, or you have any other circumstances that may affect your performance in the exam, you may be entitled to extra time for the paper or to special arrangements. Make sure to mention these issues when you apply for the test.

When you sign up, make sure that the details you provide match the details on your application and your ID – you don't want to get turned away because you write that your name is Tony but your passport says Anthony!

You also need to ensure that the email address you provide is one that you check regularly – all teacher-training-related correspondence comes to it and you don't want to miss anything!

Showing up (it's a good idea!)

You take your tests at a Pearson Professional Centre – a dedicated testing centre that's similar to the one where you take a driving theory test.

You need to bring some documentation with you:

- ✔ Evidence of your application – a copy of your application form or your confirmation of receipt does the trick.

- ✔ A copy of your test booking email.

- ✔ Two forms of ID, including a passport, driving licence, European national ID card or student card. If you have only one of these forms, you can also use a bank card or Armed Forces ID, as long as it's signed and valid.

The test centres do *not* provide childcare – if you're responsible for children, you need to arrange for alternative care while you're taking the test.

Taking the test

You don't have to bring anything with you for the test. In fact, the less you bring, the better: the test centres don't let you take *anything* to the computer where you're doing the exam. As well as the obvious things, such as notes and calculators, this rule includes phones, jackets, bags and drinks. We've even heard of people being asked to leave their watches behind – presumably in case knowing the time would confer some kind of unfair advantage!

You can consult a list of rules at www.education.gov.uk, most of which are common sense: be nice to the staff, don't cheat, don't talk to anyone in the exam, don't disturb anyone and don't confuse the test centre with a canteen – you're not to eat or drink in the exam.

You take the test on one of the centre's computers. The questions ask you to type in answers, click boxes to indicate which statements are true or click an element of a graph or table with a particular property.

Each test typically takes about 45 minutes, and you need to pick up about two-thirds of the available marks to record a pass.

Don't worry about tests being interrupted for any reason (such as fire alarms), because it happens very rarely – and it's not under your control, in any case. Focus on studying instead! The test centres have procedures in place for suspending tests so that you can resume them after any incident is resolved, or for rearranging your test if resuming isn't possible.

After you finish the test, you're told pretty much straight away whether you passed or not. That's all the information you get – you aren't told your score.

Limbering up for Your Literacy Test

In total the Literacy test lasts for only 45 minutes, and so it's a pretty concentrated test of your abilities with the English language. In that time it covers spelling, punctuation, grammar and comprehension, using spoken and written word forms. Anything, in other words, to do with words!

The content of the test relates to you and your future as a teacher in two general ways:

✔ **The materials for the test always draw on issues and texts directly related to the world of education, so they're highly relevant to your professional work as a teacher.**

No matter what phase or what subject or subjects you're training to teach, the material relates in some way to what you're going to be doing.

> ✔ **The literacy skills the tests deal with are essential to your everyday work as a teacher.**
>
> Correct use of language and the ability to respond accurately to written and spoken language are fundamental to good teaching and learning. Day in, day out you'll be using spoken and written language – it's the currency of the classroom and without it you're bankrupt, because without it nothing can take place.

All teachers, no matter what they teach, have a responsibility to make themselves clearly understood. What's the good of knowing everything about your subject if you're incapable of conveying it accurately in language? You owe it to your pupils to be accurate in your use of language at all times. Parents and carers, your head of department and head teacher quite rightly expect the highest standards of you in your use of language.

The Literacy test always comes in four parts, but the precise number of marks available differs from test to test, because of the variation in how many marks are available for the grammar and comprehension sections:

> ✔ The spelling test is always worth 10 marks. You have to listen to 10 sentences and in each one you're asked to spell one word.
>
> ✔ The punctuation test is always worth 15 marks. You're faced with a text into which you have to add 15 missing marks of punctuation.
>
> ✔ The grammar test is worth between 10–12 marks (the number of marks varies from one test to another). This test is multiple choice and text-based, and you have to select the correct options to insert into the passage.
>
> ✔ The comprehension test is again worth from 10–12 marks (the number varies from test to test). This test is based on a short (600–700 word) but complex passage to which you have to complete a variety of responses.

Given that you have only 45 minutes to complete all four sections of the test, you need to go in with a plan of action clearly set out in your head. Use the trial tests that are available online and in this book (see Chapters 4–7) to help you work out how long you want to spend on each section of the test. Doing so allows you to judge your progress through the test carefully, making sure that you're spending long enough, but not too long, on each section.

Also, allow time at the end of each test section to check over your answers before moving on – especially with the spelling section, to which you can't return after you decide to continue to the next part of the test.

Succeeding at the spelling section

You need to complete this section of the test first: it's the only one to which you can't return and so understanding exactly what's asked of you is important, as is making sure that you don't miss out on essential marks.

The words you're required to spell are always identified by a blank box at the point at which they appear in a sentence. This is really helpful, because it provides a key context for the word, which can help you when deciding upon its spelling. The audio-recording doesn't read the whole sentence, only the word that you're required to spell.

You're allowed to listen to each word as many times as you need to before committing to your answer, which you complete by typing into the box on the test page.

After you type your response into the box, read the sentence as a whole to check that the word you've keyed in makes sense in context.

The guidance for the spelling section of the test indicates that all words tested carry 1 mark. The words you have to spell are words you can reasonably be expected to know for the fulfilment of your role as a teacher. They aren't obscure or technical but relate to the general professional roles of all teachers. The conventions of UK English – as opposed to American English! – spelling are used on all occasions with the sole exception of -ise/-ize, -ising/-izing, -isation/-ization, etc. Although both are acceptable, it is probably best to be consistent throughout the test – use either -ise or -ize all the time, rather than switching from one to the other and back again!

Test technique is important. Don't spend long periods of time racking your brains over one word that you can't spell. You haven't got the time, and doing so only panics you. If you can't think of the spelling quickly, move on to the next one. You can always return to tricky ones before moving on to the next section of the test.

You can return to answers while you remain in the spelling section of the test, and so checking back over all your responses before submitting the page is well worthwhile, because after you've done that you can't go back. Not ever. The door is closed, the window is bolted and the train has pulled out of the station: that's the point of no return!

Alternative provisions are made for candidates with hearing impairments for whom the use of headphones would be a problem. If this applies, a multiple-choice format for questions is adopted. Instead of listening to the word to be spelled, four options for spelling the word – including three with common possible mistakes – are provided and the correct option needs to be selected.

We cover strategies to help with the demands of spelling in Chapter 4.

Preparing for the punctuation section

In this section of the test you're given a passage of text – usually between 150–200 words long – containing 15 errors in punctuation. Most of these errors are in the form of omissions – that is, punctuation that you have to insert. Some errors, however, can involve slight textual amendments (for example, changing a lower case letter for an upper case letter where one's required). Each insertion carries a single mark.

You *never* have to remove incorrect punctuation; you only ever have to insert punctuation or make slight textual corrections to remove errors.

Punctuation is an art, not a precise science, and so the guidance for the tests states that you should limit your insertions and changes to 'unequivocal errors'. In other words, don't insert punctuation in issues of stylistic interpretation (for example, by resetting text into a bullet-pointed list or changing commas for brackets or dashes).

The test is designed to cover every aspect of punctuation, which the test specification defines as follows:

- ✔ **Main punctuation for marking units of meaning:** Paragraphing, full stops and commas.

- ✔ **Other punctuation for marking units of meaning:** Colons, semi-colons, question marks, exclamation marks, brackets (and other parentheses).

- ✔ **Punctuation to mark the status of language:** Speech marks and quotation marks.

- ✔ **Punctuation within words:** Hyphens, apostrophes and capital letters.

You can find details about the usage of all these aspects and exercises to help you practise their use in Chapter 5.

Grappling with the grammar section

In this section of the test you're expected to complete a passage of text by making insertions at identified points from a set of multiple choice options. Each insertion is worth a single mark.

According to the guidance, you aren't being tested for your knowledge of *syntax* (which is the positioning and relation-ship of words in a sentence, and not a financial levy for bad behaviour!); instead you're looking for the selection that best fits into the text at the point identified. The object is to achieve clarity of expression by picking the option that fulfils this aim most effectively.

These passages are selected because they reflect the formal and professional nature of teaching, and you should therefore avoid answers that seem too colloquial.

Pay particular attention to the following:

▸ **Use of Standard English:** For example: sentence boundaries, sentence fragments, textual cohesion, agreement of subject and verb, inappropriate or incomplete verb forms, errors with prepositions, mistakes in comparative/superlative forms (e.g. fat, fatter, fattest; or rapidly, more rapidly, most rapidly), and so on.

▸ **Unambiguous use of language:** For example: incorrect verb tenses, vague references, incorrect participles, incorrect auxiliary verbs, confusion of vocabulary.

▸ **Professionally suitable language:** For example: inconsistent tone, inappropriate register, shift in person/perspective, unnecessary repetition, unnecessary conjunctions and so on.

Chapter 6 contains more details and explanations.

Understanding the comprehension section

This section requires you to work with a single, complex passage of text of between 600–700 words. These texts are suitably demanding and comparable to publications in the educational press or documents published by government agencies.

The comprehension test requires you to be able to identify the salient points of the texts, to infer and deduce meaning, to distinguish facts from opinions, to decide relative importance, to present material from the original in different forms, to retrieve information accurately, to synthesise material from across the text, and to provide evidence to support or deny particular points of view. Each correct response is awarded 1 mark.

The required responses come in nine sorts:

▸ **Categorising statements:** You 'drag and drop' the identified statements into appropriate categories.

▸ **Complete bullet-point lists:** You have to select the most appropriate statements from a list of options in order to create a bulleted list for particular functions.

✔ **Information sequencing:** You identify the order in which a sequence of statements should appear.

✔ **Present main points:** You have to select from a list of statements a given number that most accurately reflect the content of the text.

✔ **Matching summaries to text:** You select the statements from a list of options that most accurately reflect the meaning of the text.

✔ **Meanings of words and phrases:** You select from multiple-choice options the best alternatives for selected words and phrases in the original text.

✔ **Evaluate statements about the text:** You have to evaluate how far given statements are true about the source text or the extent to which they're supported.

✔ **Selecting headings/sub-headings:** You're asked to select the most appropriate headings/sub-headings for use in organising material from the source text.

✔ **Audience/readership:** You may be asked to rank how important and/or useful the source text would be to particular groups of readers.

We provide more information in Chapter 7.

Nailing down the Numeracy Test

The Numeracy test is a relatively short assessment of your ability to deal with the fundamentals of arithmetic and apply mathematical thinking to real-life situations. In practice, that means solving problems with graphs and/or numbers in them.

The test-setters claim that these questions are the kinds of problems you'll need to deal with in your day-to-day life as a teacher; although we suspect you'll struggle to find (say) a drama teacher who uses box-and-whiskers plots (see the later section 'Dealing with data' for a definition) on a daily basis, or indeed ever. Even maths teachers don't use them that often.

Nevertheless, as you rise through the ranks as a teacher and become more heavily involved in the administration side of things, you'll need to be able to deal with students' performances, department budgets and the like. That means that you need a solid level of mathematical reasoning, and you need to be able to handle data competently – so, honestly, this test is far from a waste of time.

Even if that hasn't convinced you and you still think the test is pointless: hard cheese. The rules say that if you want to train to be a teacher, you need to pass the Numeracy test within your first three attempts, whether you think it's worthwhile or not.

Your Numeracy test is in two parts: a mental arithmetic section, in which 12 questions come at you through headphones, followed by an on-screen test where you have to answer 16 questions, generally word problems and questions involving graphs and/or tables.

Thinking about the mental arithmetic section

In this section of the test, you listen to questions through a headset. You hear each question twice, and then have 18 further seconds to type in your answer. When that time is up, you hear the next question; you can't go back and change your answer after the test has moved on.

You do have access to a small whiteboard and pen to make notes and do your sums – it's not *strictly* mental arithmetic – but you don't have access to a calculator in this part of the test.

With that in mind, the questions don't involve crazy-hard sums – you do need to know your times tables very well, however, as well as quick and reliable methods for multiplication and division.

Typically, you need to answer questions on the following topics:

> ✔ **Clock work:** A typical question may ask how many half-hour classes 28 ten-minute interviews would require.

> ✔ **Conversions:** You may well need to convert money from one currency to another, or between different measurement systems. One regular question involves converting between miles and kilometres.

✔ **Fractions and decimals:** You need to be able to work with fractions, as well as multiply and divide by decimals.

✔ **Percentages and ratios:** You may need to split a number or an amount into a given ratio, find a percentage of a value, or give the sale price of an item after it's reduced by a certain percentage.

✔ **Weights and measures:** Often, you're asked about speed, distance and time, or about how much of an ingredient you'd need for a particular science experiment.

✔ **Working with money:** For example, you may need to work out a total sponsorship amount and split it between several charities.

Practise converting quickly between decimals, fractions and percentages. This kind of question comes up all the time, and being able to say 'that's easy!' about one of the questions really builds your confidence.

Although being quick and accurate with your maths is obviously vital in this part of the test, you also need good mental strength. It's easy to get knocked off your stride by a hard question or when you grow frustrated when time runs out for a question. You can't afford to let that kind of thing get to you: forget what's gone and get on with the next question.

Worrying about the previous question doesn't help you get the point for the question you're working on now. In the test, just do one thing at a time.

If you want to improve your mental arithmetic, Chapter 8 is a great place to start: we supply detailed instructions on how to tackle questions, as well as some sample tests.

Managing maths questions on the screen

In the on-screen part of the Numeracy test you're given 16 questions to answer, one at a time, on the screen.

Answering the questions may require you to click on the correct option, select which of several statements are true or type in a number. You can flick back and forth between questions and 'flag' anything you want to come back to later if you have time; if you realise you've made an error, you can go back and correct it.

You also have access to a calculator, which is part of the testing package. It's not a very *good* calculator (it can quite often misinterpret what you mean, unless you're very careful), and you need to exercise some common sense when it gives you an answer (you need to ask yourself 'does that *look* about right?' every time) – but it certainly helps with some of the trickier questions.

You can practise the tests and get used to using the system online at www.education.gov.uk – make sure that you're comfortable with the calculator and the controls before you take the test! We also provide extra sample on-screen tests for you in Chapter 11.

Dealing with data

The vast bulk of the Numeracy test is about reading, interpreting and analysing graphs and tables. A good deal of it is common sense – 'say what you see' was good advice on TV's *Catchphrase* and it's good advice in the Numeracy test!

You need to know about quite a few different graphs, ranging from the fairly simple to the quite complex. Here are some of them, in order of complexity:

- ✔ **Bar charts:** These graphs are the ones you see most often in everyday life – they look like a photo of skyscrapers (sometimes like Colin's photos of skyscrapers: he can never get the camera the right way round, so they end up sideways).

- ✔ **Line graphs:** As you'd expect, line graphs consist mainly of lines (or, sometimes, curves). Across the bottom of the graph, you generally have time; the line goes up and down to show the value of what you're measuring at each given time.

- ✔ **Scatter graphs:** These graphs are a close cousin of line graphs, although they normally show a relation between two different variables – for instance, students' scores in two different exams, or their ages and heights. Each observation is marked with a symbol somewhere on the grid.

✔ **Pie charts:** These graphs aren't as difficult as you remember (but just as delicious)! They use pie-shaped slices of different sizes. In the Numeracy test, you're usually given percentages rather than angles, and you normally just have to convert between numbers and percentages.

✔ **Cumulative frequency plots:** These are a bit more of a challenge: they're like line graphs, but show you the 'total so far' at each point on the bottom axis. You can use them to find things such as the median and interquartile range (check out the nearby sidebar 'Averages and measures' and Chapter 9 for more on these terms).

✔ **Box-and-whisker plots:** These graphs are notorious, but not for any good reason: they simply show the highest and lowest measurements, as well as the quartiles and the median (again, check out 'Averages and measures' and Chapter 9).

In some cases, you have to work out the data you need from a graph or table – for instance, you may need to read a bar chart to find the values you need to average. At other times, you may need to spot a trend from a graph – whether it's increasing or decreasing. If it's changing by the same amount each time, you may need to predict a future, past or missing value based on the trend.

We take you through all you need to know about graphs and tables in Chapter 10.

Wading through word problems

As well as the on-screen questions that involve reading and interpreting data in graph or table form (which we describe

Averages and measures

The median and the quartiles are examples of *statistics* – numbers that summarise a set of data. You need to be comfortable with the three major kinds of average (mean, median and mode) as well as measures of spread

such as the range and interquartile range.

Flip to Chapter 9 to brush up on these statistical terms.

in the preceding section), the testers usually throw in two or three wordy questions that are nothing to do with data. The on-screen word problems are, generally, just more complicated versions of the mental arithmetic questions. They may involve more steps, or more difficult calculations, than the quick-fire round does.

Typical word questions look at the following:

✔ **Ticking off the time:** You may need to figure out when a parents' evening will end, split over several days with breaks.

✔ **Travelling in style:** Conversions between different units, speed–distance–time questions, fuel costs and 'when should you set off?' are all commonplace.

These questions don't make up a huge proportion of the on-screen test – normally two or three out of the 16 marks – but they can be the difference between passing and failing!

To help make sure that you're on the right side of that line, check out Chapter 9 on general arithmetic.

Chapter 3

Studying to Succeed

● ●

In This Chapter

▶ Getting yourself set physically

▶ Being exam-ready mentally

▶ Excelling with exam technique

▶ Improving your skills each and every day

● ●

Don't worry if you're not looking forward to studying (we know that feeling!), because in this chapter we describe how you can make things easier for yourself. You don't have to enjoy studying, but we won't tell anyone if, after reading this chapter, you suddenly find yourself thinking, 'this isn't so bad after all'. We show you how to make the whole experience a bit less intimidating, a lot less stressful and (whisper it) more enjoyable. Like most things, success boils down to preparation and being positive – and we help you on both these fronts.

We describe a few ideas about setting up somewhere to work, where you can be comfortable and concentrate with as few distractions as possible, and where everything you need is to hand. When you're comfortable, calm and ready to work, learning becomes a million times easier. (Yes, a million times. We checked.) We give you some top tips about calming yourself down and shutting off the little voice that says 'can't' – because when you start believing you can do it, you're halfway to success.

We also provide a few techniques to control your nerves on test day and some approaches for taking exams so that you can squeeze every last mark out of the paper. We delve into the nitty-gritty of preparing for exams, picking out the preparation techniques that we find most helpful.

Don't attempt to use them all at once, otherwise you'll probably end up being late for your Skills Test – try a few and see what works for you.

Setting Yourself up Physically

The key to studying successfully is to prepare yourself properly. When you have all the tools you need and a space to study in, getting everything under control is much easier. We also give you some ideas on taking good notes so that you can revise easily from them later on.

Compiling your tools of the trade

Luckily, neither literacy nor numeracy requires a great deal of equipment – you can do a lot of the work with just paper, a pencil and this book.

That said, here are a few things that make studying easier:

- ✔ **A notebook:** If you keep a single, special notebook for each subject, finding the notes you take is much easier – as is picking up from where you reached the last time you did some studying.

- ✔ **Felt tip pens:** Using colour to take notes really helps you to remember what's going on – even if you just use colours to highlight the most important points, you're able to find those sections at a glance.

- ✔ **A calculator:** Although the mental arithmetic test is a non-calculator paper, being able to check your work as you go along and find your mistakes is great while you're studying. Plus, you may well need a calculator while revising on-screen maths.

- ✔ **A dictionary:** This is useful in two ways:

  - When you're reading and need to check out the meaning of a word.

  - When you're trying to spell a word and you want to see whether you've got it right.

You can't use a dictionary in the Skills Test itself, of course, but while you're studying these habits are great to settle into.

✔ **A thesaurus:** Although the Skills Test doesn't require
you to write, a thesaurus is great for helping you expand
your vocabulary, which really helps in preparation for
all sections of the test and for your professional role as a
teacher. The more confident you are in the use of a wide
variety of language, the better.

Creating a space of your own

No rule says that you must study at a desk, at home or even
indoors: a change of scenery can often do you good by putting
you in a different frame of mind and providing some inspira-
tion. We're big fans of picking up our stuff and heading to the
coffee shop or the park when we're stuck; more often than not
it can jolt you out of a rut.

The thing is, you can study wherever you want to, and you
can experiment to find the situation that works best for you.
Try out several places if you need to: you can go to your local
library, spread out on your bed, monopolise the kitchen table
or even try out the sofa, half-distracted by the telly.

When you have a space and time that works for you, tweak it
to make it better still. Here are some ways you can make your
workspace better for studying:

✔ **Minimise distractions:** Focusing is difficult when you're
constantly being distracted by phones, Facebook, email
and the like. Perhaps you find that putting on background
music helps (as long as it doesn't distract you), or consider
downloading some white noise (try `simplynoise.com`)
or noise-reducing headphones to drown out the outside
world.

If you have housemates or family who continually demand
your attention, you may need to ask them nicely to leave
you alone until you're done. And if all else fails, you can
always leave them to it and take yourself off to a more
conducive place to study.

✔ **Maximise comfort:** If you're physically uncomfortable when
you study, relaxing mentally is extremely hard. If your brain
is thinking 'this chair is really uncomfortable', it's not thinking about how to spell 'uncomfortable'. Do all you can to
make your workspace welcoming and cosy – make sure

that you can sit up straight (see Chapter 14 for more on the importance of posture), stay at the right temperature and have a drink.

✔ **Keep it tidy:** Some people are happier than others to work in the middle of a mess, but an untidy desk can be a distraction. We suggest spending a few minutes at the end of a study session putting everything in its place.

Maintaining good notes

When we start working with students, we can usually tell how interested they are in learning by taking a look at their note-book or exercise book. Although not a foolproof rule (some of the brightest students have practically illegible handwriting), the neater – and more attractive – you make your notes, the easier you can read them, the easier you can see what you've done and the easier you can pick up on mistakes.

Decide whether you prefer to keep your notes on a computer, in a notebook or on loose paper – but find a system that works for you and stick with it!

One of the best things you can do is keep a vocabulary book in your notebook or on your computer. Whenever you come across a word, a spelling or an idea that you don't know or quite understand, write down the word on one side of the page and its definition on the other side.

Cue cards are an excellent way to improve your vocabulary. Write the word on one side of a card and the meaning on the other. Run through the cards every so often until you can rattle off the definition without thinking.

Preparing Yourself Mentally

Mental preparation is just as important as physical. Common sense tells you that you can't pass an exam if you don't turn up physically; well, the same applies to turning up mentally prepared with a clear, focused and calm mind.

In this section, we help you to clarify your reason for taking the exam and provide some tips on keeping the panic-demons at bay.

Inspiring yourself to stay motivated

Colin never thought that he could run a marathon – until he decided to do so to raise money for charity, in memory of his grandmother. As soon as he had a *reason* to train properly, he committed fully and got on with it.

Studying for a reason

Being properly motivated is a great boost to being successful at exams. Reminding yourself every now and again of the reason why you're studying really motivates you to get the books out when you're struggling.

Whatever it is, you *are* studying for a specific reason and so spend some time getting it clear in your mind. Write it down in your own words and stick a note of it somewhere you can see it.

 For example, you can write 'I want to inspire students' in felt tip on a bit of paper and stick it behind your desk, or make your screensaver a picture of students happy with their exam results. Perhaps you can carry it on a card in your wallet or purse so you can see it when you're out and about, recite it as a mantra, or turn it into a song to the James Bond theme tune – anything that reminds you of exactly why you're learning all this stuff.

Keeping your head on straight

Colin used to suffer from debilitating panic attacks when out shopping. He got short of breath, his head felt like it was full of cotton wool and he just stood there, blocking the door to the supermarket until the feeling eventually passed.

It's a horrible experience, not to be wished on anyone, but a lot of people have exactly the same experience when faced with maths questions, exams or both. Luckily, Colin had help from some counsellors who showed him how to calm down and get his shopping done without getting in everyone's way. The approach boils down to three things:

- ✔ **Posture:** How you position your body makes a huge difference to how you feel. If you stand or sit up straight, you breathe better, feel more confident and can fool your brain into thinking about the task at hand, instead of how unpleasant it is.

- ✔ **Oxygen:** Your brain doesn't function well without enough oxygen (water is good, too). Breathing deeply helps to calm you down and get you thinking – have a look at Chapter 14 for more details.

- ✔ **Positive self-talk:** Saying encouraging things to yourself is a great idea. If you're encouraging a friend to study, you don't tell her that she's stupid and is never going to get the hang of it (at least, we hope you wouldn't, otherwise teaching is probably not the career for you!). Therefore, don't bully yourself that way. Check out Chapter 14 where we provide more info.

POPS – posture, oxygen and positive self-talk – are fantastic tools for when you need to calm down quickly. Take a few moments to breathe and tell yourself 'I can do this' if you find yourself blanking in an exam – or anywhere else for that matter.

Acing your Exam: Tips for Exam Technique

Just knowing your stuff isn't enough to do well in an exam. Being knowledgeable is just one leg of the trousers . . . and you don't want to go into an exam half-dressed (it distracts the other students). A solid exam technique behind you helps you to feel more confident.

You need to prepare for the exam. Ask yourself questions such as the following:

- ✔ What are the test setters likely to ask?

- ✔ How long will I have?

- ✔ How many sections are in the test? Do they carry equal marks?

- ✔ How long should I be spending on each section? Will I be rushing, or will I have plenty of time to check?

- ✔ How will I keep calm and focused in the exam situation?

In other words, go into the test with your plan all worked out. If you're confident that you know how you're going to approach the test, you're much more likely to do better.

Nobody likes nasty surprises. The more practice you get with past papers, the better prepared you're likely to be. You can get hold of past papers free of charge from the Skills Test website at `http://www.education.gov.uk/schools/careers/traininganddevelopment/professional/`.

Although we're risking the Teacher Secret Police coming after us, here we reveal the highly classified details of exam technique:

✔ **Control your nerves:** Freezing up in an exam isn't a good thing. Use the techniques we describe in the earlier 'Keeping your head on straight' section to help: sit up straight, take a deep breath and tell yourself 'I can do it!'.

✔ **If you can, read the paper all the way through:** If you prepare well, you know roughly what the test entails – but reassuring yourself that this test isn't different from the ones before is always a good idea. Reading through the questions first also gives your brain a chance to start its wheels turning on some of the harder questions – your subconscious can begin work on those while you rattle off the easy ones . . . which you can also pick out while you read through the paper.

✔ **Where possible, pick the low-hanging fruit first:** If you have any doubt about finishing on time, *do the quick, easy questions first.* You don't want to get to the end of the exam and realise that the last two questions are straightforward and you could've answered them if you hadn't puzzled over a hard one you ended up guessing. Doing some easy questions first also gives you a good solid base – if you can pick up easy marks early on, your confidence grows and you have a little longer for the harder questions.

✔ **Don't dilly-dally:** Don't spend too long on one question. If you get bogged down or stuck, flag the question, go on to the next question and come back to the hard one later on if you have time. Spend time on marks you can definitely get. This approach also gives your mind some time to figure things out while you think about the next question – quite often, you come back to the hard question and say 'Oh! It's easy!'.

> ✔ **Sprint to the finish:** If you start to run out of time, stay calm and figure out how to use your last few minutes most productively. It's better to give a sensible-looking answer than no answer at all!

Read the question carefully and make sure that what you write down really does answer the question.

Revising for Success

The best way to get good at something is to do it repeatedly. To improve at chess, you play lots of chess, until it makes sense; to get good at knitting, you do lots of knitting, until it makes sense; to become expert at eating chocolate, you need to stuff your face day and night (though perhaps that's not the healthiest of examples!). Guess what: the best way to get good at maths and literacy is to do them repeatedly.

To add to the suggestions we provide throughout this chapter, here we divulge some maths- and literacy-specific tips.

As a basic principle in revision, if you're always getting answers right you aren't being challenged enough. Getting things wrong is a sign that you're pushing yourself and is a key step on the way to getting them right the next time.

Keep a list of mistakes – not to beat yourself up with, but as a useful list of things to check if you end up with the wrong answer. After a while, you get so used to asking yourself the following sorts of things that it becomes second nature: 'Have I multiplied the right things together? Should I start a new sentence here or use a semi-colon? Is that decimal point in the right place? Should that be a double consonant?'

Mastering maths

Doing lots of maths is a giant step towards getting good at maths. But simply writing out '1 + 1 = 2' over and over again isn't going to help you in the slightest.

If you want to get better at maths, here are three main areas that we suggest you focus on:

✔ **Master the basics:** Spend some time at the start of each study session checking that you can do the fundamentals properly, such as multiplying and dividing with various sizes of numbers and working with fractions and percentages – in other words, the sums that are going to come up repeatedly in the paper (flip to Chapter 8 for more details). The more quickly and reliably you can do these sums, the better you'll do.

✔ **Stretch yourself:** Ideally, always be working on material that's just a little harder than you're comfortable with – so you come out of each session just a little bit further on. You'll be surprised how quickly you advance.

✔ **Check your work:** Get into the habit of figuring out what mistakes you've made (everyone does) and putting them right. You're bound to make errors in the exam, but if you've had practice in spotting them and correcting them, you're able to rescue a few marks on the big day.

Limbering up at literacy

To do well in your Literacy test and become a good reader and writer, you need to get reading and writing. The only way to improve your skills in spelling, punctuation, grammar and comprehension is to use them over and over and over (we provide loads of useful tips in Chapters 4 to 7, respectively).

Here are three things that you can do pretty much anywhere to get better at literacy and keep your verbal muscles flexing:

✔ **Spell your way through the day:** No matter where you are or what you're doing, you can always take a second or two out to have a go at your spellings. Look around at what you see and spell the names of the objects. What are you doing or thinking about? Try spelling it out. Then check it in the dictionary you're no doubt now carrying in your pocket.

Don't only go for simple words: try out more challenging ones. Familiarity breeds confidence, and the more you spend time spelling, the more confident you become.

✔ **Question your reading:** Whenever you're reading something – and everyone spends a surprisingly large amount of time doing that – set yourself tasks and questions of the sort you'll face in the literacy test. For example:

- Summarise your reading into a set of key points.

- What sub-titles would you insert into what you're reading, and where would you put them?

- Who's the intended audience of the text you're reading and how do you know?

- Is what you're reading constructed logically and helpfully for the person doing the reading?

- Rephrase what's being said in a different way.

✓ **Join the grammar police:** The world of words around you is littered with errors, such as 'Apple's' or 'Potatoe's' advertised in the grocer's window and missing possessive apostrophes. When you're listening to the radio or watching the TV, think about whether subjects and verbs agree. When you're looking at a text, look for places where sentences aren't punctuated properly.

If you're in any doubt, use the guidance in Chapters 5 and 6 to help you. Language use is an art not a science, and people do all sorts of creative things with language that aren't technically accurate, but for the purposes of acing your Skills Test, become a pedant!

Playing games for revision

Unfortunately, not many games or apps are aimed at adult learners, which is a real shame because being motivated to learn something as part of a bigger storyline is normally better than learning it for its own sake.

However, you can make your own games. Here are some ideas:

✓ **A simple quiz:** Find a friend who's also studying and set each other questions (of course, only ask questions you can answer yourself!). As a variation, make your own version of Trivial Pursuit with questions in several categories.

✓ **A mathematical maze:** A student of Colin's used to put a yellow sticky note on every door in her house: before she allowed herself to go through the door, she had to ask and answer the question correctly.

Don't put too difficult a question on the toilet door!

✔ **A word chain:** If you have a spare couple of minutes, try building a word chain in a set time limit. Start by seeing how many four-letter words you can build into a chain by substituting one letter at a time (for example, KING → KIND → FIND → FOND → FORD → WORD and so on). Or build a chain where each four-letter word has to begin with the last letter of the word before (for example, KING → GROW → WIND → DATE → EVER → RACK and so on).

Then build in more challenge: perhaps do it with five-letter words. Or develop chains where each successive word has to begin with the last letter of the previous word, but also has to be one letter longer (for example, KING → GIVEN → NOBODY → YELLING → GOVERNOR and so on). This kind of thing really livens up your brain as regards working with words.

✔ **Concentration:** Make up a set of cards (an odd number of pairs is good); on half of them write questions; on the other half write the answers. Place them face down on the table and shuffle them around. Then turn over a pair at a time, trying to match questions with answers. (It's more effective than you'd think!)

Shopping for exam success

You have to do these tests because numeracy and literacy are so much a part of your everyday life and work as a teacher. Therefore, look everywhere you possibly can for chances to practise in your everyday life.

Here are some suggestions from the high street:

✔ In the supermarket, try to figure out your approximate bill before you get to the checkout.

✔ Work out how to spell 'mulligatawny' soup before you get to the shelves to buy it. Don't choose tomato soup just to make the spelling easier! If you want mulligatawny, you need to earn it!

✔ When you buy something with a percentage discount, work out how much you save.

✔ When you say to yourself a phrase such as 'I have bought bread and butter', explain why you opted to use the present perfect tense.

✔ When you're planning to travel somewhere, work out what your average speed will be (in miles per hour *and* kilometres per hour), and then try rephrasing the question in two or three different ways.

✔ When you spot a graph in the newspaper, see what information you can gather from it, and then read the text surrounding the graph and check your comprehension.

Maths and literacy are required everywhere – and the more you can find and play with them, the better! Doing so creates a great habit that makes the Skills Tests a whole lot less stressful.

Treating yourself for motivation

We don't know about you, but being bears of very little brain we find it hard to keep our noses to the grindstone at times. If we really want to get something done, the idea of a reward usually helps. One of the ways Colin got over his fear of supermarkets was by realising that supermarkets contain pastries to purchase and eat; if he did the unpleasant chore, he gave himself a moderately-tasty apple turnover. For Andrew, the idea of a well-deserved pint of real ale at the end of a long day's study never does any harm!

Your brain is probably more sophisticated than ours, but we bet it responds well to giving yourself rewards when you do something good! At the end of every study session, make sure that you have something more pleasant lined up, whether it's your favourite TV show, some chocolate or a walk in the park.

Part II
Literacy Skills

Top Five Ways this Part will Leverage Your Literacy Skills

✔ Obveously it's very importunt that teechers can spel correckly. and that they can communikate well threw they're riting. This part of the book will help you make sure your spelling strategies are up to scratch.

✔ It is terrible if youre trying to read something and there is no punctuation if there isnt how do you know where one sentence ends and the next begins its really annoying. We'll help you out with punctuation and grammar too.

✔ Master a set of strategies that are about more than words and letters. This is great professional learning that enhances your professional credibility.

✔ Come to terms with comprehension and the types of questions the Skills Tests will throw at you.

✔ Optimise your problem-solving skills when it comes to language. Your pupils, their parents and others you'll communicate with in the course of your job as a teacher will expect you to be getting this kind of stuff right.

Go to www.dummies.com/go/teachers professionalskillstests for free audio practice tests.

In this part . . .

- ✔ Be successful in your spelling and learn to spell well.
- ✔ Eye the dots – punctuate perfectly.
- ✔ Get to grips with grammar and get top marks.
- ✔ Get cracking with your comprehension: learn to understand what you've read.

Chapter 4

Falling Under the Spell of Spelling

A key part of being a successful teacher is the ability to spell. You need to be able to spell out things clearly to pupils and cast a spell over them during lessons (though not literally: the National Curriculum frowns on potions and cauldrons in the classroom!). But in this chapter we're thinking specifically about word spelling.

One of the major elements of the Key Skills Tests is accurate spelling. The ability to spell well obviously comes into play in conjunction with the audio-based spelling section of the Literacy test, which tests your spelling directly. But a strong grasp of spelling is also important to succeed in the comprehension section of the Literacy test: for example, you need to distinguish between word meanings, which can depend on your spelling as well as reading abilities. (Chapter 7 provides a complete review of this section of the test.)

In this chapter, we describe a number of approaches that help you assess and improve your spelling (including separating words into parts and identifying useful patterns). We also provide five practice tests that mimic the spelling section of the Literacy test.

Breaking Words Up

Lots of things in life seem difficult and intimidating if you look at them as a whole: the Sunday broadsheets, Russian novels . . . John McCririck. But if you break them down into smaller parts, you can see a way to approach them. For example, marathon runners don't look at all 26 miles in one go; they concentrate on running the first mile, the second and so on as they aim to complete the race.

The same approach applies to spelling. Often if you try to spell a complicated word whole you can make a mess of it, and so you need to look at how you can break words down into smaller units to make the task easier. You can do so in several ways, as we describe in this section.

Sounding off! Finding out about phonics

You've probably come across phonics. In primary and secondary schools around the country, phonics forms a large part of the government's strategy to improve literacy, and so you're going to hear a whole lot more about it!

Simply put, *phonics* is the relationship between sounds and the letters that correspond to them, and you can put it to work in order to improve your spelling skills. When trying to spell a difficult word, *sounding it out* – turning each unit of sound into a corresponding letter or letters – is a useful technique.

Here's an example: imagine a feline mammal, possibly ginger in colour and with thick soft fur. A cat, in fact (but not in a hat). Well, the word CAT is constructed of three individual units of sound (or *phonemes* for the technically inclined). Sound it out to yourself now: C-A-T; C-A-T; C-A-T.

Never mind the shame and the fact that your partner, your children or those people on the train are now looking at you in confusion, pity and perhaps even with a growing sense of fear. We're talking about passing your Professional Skills Tests here and sounding out words really helps. Strange looks are a small price to pay! Say it out again: C-A-T.

So, if you want to write about that adorable ginger puss, you're going to write 'cat'.

Straightforward so far. But in some cases, individual sounds aren't represented by single letters, but by combinations of letters. In the word THINK, for example, the initial sound of the word is represented by 'th'.

You can break down every word in English in this way. All you need to know is the different possible ways of writing each sound.

Figures 4-1 (for consonants) and 4-2 (for vowels) contain the sounds (phonemes) found in the English language and the various ways in which you can write each one (graphemes).

24 Consonant Phonemes / Graphemes

Phoneme (sound)	Examples	Graphemes (written patterns)	Phoneme (sound)	Examples	Graphemes (written patterns)
/ b /	banana, bubbles	b, bb	/ s /	sun, mouse	s, ss, ce, se, c, sc
/ c /	car, duck	c, k, ck, q, ch	/ t /	turtle, little	t, tt
/ d /	dinosaur, puddle	d, dd	/ v /	volcano, halve	v, ve
/ f /	fish, giraffe	f, ff, ph, gh	/ w /	watch, queen	w, wh, u
/ g /	guitar, goggles	g, gg	/ x /	fox	x
/ h /	helicopter	h	/ y /	yo-yo	y
/ j /	jellyfish, fridge	j, g, dge, ge	/ z /	zip, please	z, zz, ze, s, se
/ l /	leaf, bell	l, ll, le	/ sh /	shoes, television	sh, ch, si, ti
/ m /	monkey, hammer	m, mm, mb	/ ch /	children, stitch	ch, tch
/ n /	nail, knot	n, nn, kn	/ th /	mother	th
/ p /	pumpkin, puppets	p, pp	/ th /	thong	*th*
/ r /	rain, write	r, rr, wr	/ ng /	sing, ankle	ng, n

Figure 4-1: Consonant graphemes.

Think of a variety of words you may want to spell – some simple, some more complicated. Working with the information in Figures 4-1 and 4-2 helps you to work out the various possibilities for spelling these words, using phonics.

20 Vowel Phonemes / Graphemes

Needs to be at least one of these vowel sounds in every word (one per syllable)

Phoneme (sound)	Examples	Graphemes (written patterns)	Phoneme (sound)	Examples	Graphemes (written patterns)
Short Vowel Sounds... /a/	apple	a		/oo/	m<u>oo</u>n, scr<u>ew</u>	oo, ue, ou, ew, u-e
/e/	elephant, br<u>ea</u>d	e ea	Other Vowel Sounds... 'oo'	b<u>oo</u>k, c<u>ou</u>ld	oo, u, ou
/i/	igloo, g<u>y</u>m	i y	/ou/	h<u>ou</u>se, c<u>ow</u>	ou, ow
/o/	<u>o</u>ctopus, w<u>a</u>sh	o a	/oi/	c<u>oi</u>n, b<u>oy</u>	oi, oy
/u/	<u>u</u>mbrella, w<u>o</u>n	u o	'r' Controlled vowels... /ar/	st<u>ar</u>, p<u>ar</u>t	ar, a
Long Vowel Sounds... /ae/	r<u>ai</u>n, tr<u>ay</u>	ai, ay, a-e, a	/or/	f<u>or</u>k, b<u>oar</u>d	or, aw, a, au, ore, oar, oor
/ee/	tr<u>ee</u>, m<u>e</u>	ee, ea, ie, y, e, ey	/er/	h<u>er</u>b, n<u>ur</u>se	er, ir, ur, ear, or
/ie/	l<u>igh</u>t, k<u>i</u>te	igh, i-e, y, i, ie	/air/	ch<u>air</u>, p<u>ear</u>	air, ear, are
/oa/	b<u>oa</u>t, b<u>ow</u>	oa, ow, o, o-e	/ear/	sp<u>ear</u>, d<u>eer</u>	ear, eer, ere
/ue/	t<u>ube</u>, em<u>u</u>	u-e, ew, ue, u	'schwa' unstressed vowel close to /u/ as in teach<u>er</u>, th<u>e</u>, pict<u>ure</u>		

Figure 4-2: Vowel graphemes.

Although phonics can give you the range of possible combinations of letters for spelling a word, you still need to identify which is correct. So, although a useful tool in spelling, you have to use phonics in combination with other methods.

Making pronouncements on syllables

Dividing words into syllables is a useful way to break them down into their component parts and improve your ability to spell unfamiliar words correctly.

A *syllable* is a unit of pronunciation spoken without interruption and always centred on a vowel. A syllable may be a vowel (or combination of vowels) on its own or consist of a vowel (or combination of vowels) preceded by, succeeded by or surrounded by a number of consonants. Syllables aren't of uniform length, but always represent a unit of pronunciation.

Examples

The word AGO has two syllables: 'A' and 'GO'. The first syllable (A) consists of a single vowel; the second syllable (GO) consists of the vowel 'O' preceded by the consonant 'G' to create a single unit of pronunciation (GO).

Counting up your vowel sounds

You encounter vowel combination beauties called *diphthongs* (two vowel sounds that combine within a single letter or combination of letters to create one sound unit: for example, LOW, LOIN and LAIR) and *triphthongs* (where three vowel sounds combine in the same way to create one sound unit: for example, as in the words, FIRE, HOUR and EMPLOYER.

Here are a couple of more complicated examples. The word UNIVERSE consists of three syllables 'U', 'NI' and 'VERSE'. The first syllable is the sole vowel 'U', followed by a second syllable – the consonant-vowel combination 'NI' – and a final long combination 'VERSE' centred on the first 'E'.

Now consider the two-syllable word TREEHOUSE. The first syllable is 'TREE', the long 'e' sound being created by doubling 'EE'; the second syllable is 'HOUSE', which uses a different kind of vowel combination 'OU', technically known as a *diphthong* (see the nearby sidebar 'Counting up your vowel sounds').

A syllable test

A failsafe test exists for knowing the number of syllables in a word. (If you're on a commuter train, you now need some elbow room. So if you haven't already scared everyone off by chanting 'C-A-T, C-A-T, C-A-T' from the preceding section, you may want to move to a less crowded area of the carriage.)

Hold your hand flat just beneath your chin, so that when you open your mouth wide your chin touches your hand. When you speak a word, the number of times your chin hits your hand is the number of syllables in the word. Say CAT; come on, don't be shy. Your chin hits your hand once because CAT has a single syllable. Now say AGO and notice that your chin hits your hand twice. Say UNIVERSE and your chin meets your hand three times.

This test always works and really helps in breaking words down into their constituent parts, so that you can work on spelling individual syllables as you construct the spelling of more complex words.

Here are a few more complex words to try. Use the lines or a separate sheet of paper to work out the number of syllables in each of these words:

quite _____

quiet _____

underneath _____

wonderfully _____

Answers: quite = one syllable; quiet = two syllables; underneath = three syllables; wonderfully = four syllables.

Getting to the roots

As well as using their sounds (as we discuss in the two preceding sections), you can also unlock the correct spelling of complex words by thinking about their units of meaning.

Root words

Often, longer words are constructed around a *root word*, with resulting families of words. Here are some examples, with the root element of the word in bold type:

- ✔ **manage: manage**r, **manage**ment, **manage**able, un**manage**able, **manage**rial, **manage**d, **manag**ing

- ✔ **trust: trust**ing, **trust**worthy, un**trust**worthy, mis**trust**, **trust**ed, dis**trust**

- ✔ **happy:** un**happy**, **happ**iness, un**happ**iness, **happ**ily

- ✔ **structure: struct**ural, con**struct**, de**struct**ible, recon**struct**, decon**struct**, de**struct**ive, super**structure**

Now try it yourself. Perhaps add more words using the identified root words to the families of words above, or create some new word families of your own.

Prefixes and suffixes

In order to construct words from the root, you have to add a variety of beginnings and endings before and/or after the root word – some are only a single letter long, some more substantial:

> ✔ **Prefix:** Any addition *before* a root word.
> ✔ **Suffix:** Any addition *after* a root word.

Identifying prefixes and suffixes is especially useful in the listening test component. Keep your ears wide open for familiar elements of words and structure your thinking around them. INCONSIDERABLE is a mouthful on its own, but as a familiar root word CONSIDER with a prefix ('IN') and a suffix ('ABLE') it becomes a lot more straightforward.

To give yourself the best chance of succeeding on the Literacy test, memorise the spelling of frequently occurring prefixes and suffixes and their meanings, like the ones in Tables 4-1 and 4-2.

Table 4-1	Common Prefixes to Remember	
Prefix	**Definition**	**Example**
anti-	against	anticlimax
de-	opposite	devalue
dis-	not; opposite of	discover
en-, em-	cause to	enact, empower
fore-	before; front of	foreshadow, forearm
in-, im-	in	income, impulse
in-, im-, il-, ir-	not	indirect, immoral, illiterate, irreverent
inter-	between; among	interrupt
mid-	middle	midfield
mis-	wrongly	misspell
non-	not	nonviolent
over-	over; too much	overeat
pre-	before	preview
re-	again	rewrite
semi-	half; partly; not fully	semifinal
sub-	under	subway

(continued)

Table 4-1 *(continued)*

Prefix	Definition	Example
super-	above; beyond	superhuman
trans-	across	transmit
un-	not; opposite of	unusual
under-	under; too little	underestimate

Table 4-2   Common Suffixes to Remember

Suffix	Definition	Example
-able, -ible	is; can be	affordable, sensible
-al, -ial	having characteristics of	universal, facial
-ed	past tense verbs; adjectives	the dog walked, buttered toast
-en	made of	golden
-er, -or	one who; person connected with	teacher, professor
-er	more	taller
-est	the most	tallest
-ful	full of	helpful
-ic	having characteristics of	poetic
-ing	verb forms; present participles	sleeping
-ion, -tion, -ation, -ition	act; process	submission, motion, relation, edition
-ity, -ty	state of	activity, society
-ive, -ative, -itive	adjective form of noun	active, comparative, sensitive
-less	without	hopeless
-ly	how something is	lovely
-ment	state of being; act of	contentment
-ness	state of; condition of	openness
-ous, -eous, -ious	having qualities of	riotous, courageous, gracious

Suffix	Definition	Example
-s, -es	more than one	trains, trenches
-y	characterised by	gloomy

Looking at Patterns and Rules

Making the effort to know about key repeated patterns or spelling rules can really help your spelling. The trouble with English, of course, is that every rule has an exception that you have to remember. *C'est la vie*, as the French say, shrugging their shoulders philosophically.

Here are some of the major rules worth knowing and examples of words employing them:

- **You use 'I' before 'E' except after 'C':** Spell BELIEVE with 'IE' but RECEIVE with an 'EI'; RELIEF has an 'IE' but CONCEIT uses 'EI' (as in 'I'm relieved I dumped my conceited oaf of a boyfriend').

- **You usually double the final consonant before adding an ending for a word composed of or ending with a consonant-vowel-consonant combination:** For example, FINAL → FINALLY, RUB → RUBBING, DIG → DIGGING.

- **You remove the 'e' before adding an ending where a verb ends with an 'e':** For example, FIRE → FIRING, ARRANGE → ARRANGING, SETTLE → SETTLING.

- **You change the 'y' to an 'i' before adding the suffix where a word ends with a 'y' and you're adding an 'es' or an 'ed' ending:** For example, SATISFY → SATISFIED, MULTIPLY → MULTIPLIES, CLARIFY → CLARIFIED.

- **You require only one letter to spell a short vowel sound:** For example, BAT, HOP, CAP, AND.

- **You add a second vowel to make a long vowel sound:** Next to the first vowel (for example, COAT, RAIN, DUE) or separated from the first vowel by a consonant (for example, GRADE, SURE, WIFE).

- **You use a short-sounding first vowel when two consonants are between vowels:** For example, DINNER, MANNER, RUNNING.

✔ **You can make the 'K' sound in four ways:**

- '**C**': CAT, VICTIM, PUBLIC
- '**CC**': SOCCER, OCCUPY, ACCURATE
- '**K**': KEEN, SKIN, KEEP
- '**CK**' **(usually follows a short vowel sound):** RACK, PICK, STOCKING

✔ **You can make the 'J' sound in three ways:**

- '**J**': Normally followed by 'A', 'O' or 'U' (for example, JAM, JOB, JUG)
- '**G**': Can be used when followed by 'E', 'I' or 'Y' (for example, GENTLY, AGITATE, EGYPTIAN)
- '**DGE**' **after a short vowel sound:** For example, EDGE, JUDGE, BRIDGE

✔ **You can make the 'CH' sound in two ways:**

- '**CH**': For example, WHICH, SUCH, TOUCH
- '**TCH**': For example, WITCH, CATCH, KITCHEN

✔ **You always follow the letter 'Q' with 'U':** For example, ENQUIRE, QUESTION, ACQUIRE

✔ **Using 'le':**

- **If the word uses a short vowel sound, use two consonants before the 'LE':** For example, TICKLE, HANDLE, BOTTLE
- **If the word uses a long vowel sound, use a single consonant before the 'LE':** For example, BUGLE, ABLE, NEEDLE

✔ **You never double the following letters:** 'V', 'J', 'K', 'W' and 'X'

✔ **Only a very few words imported into English end with 'V':** You always use 'VE' to make a final 'V' sound (for example, LOVE, BRAVE, BELIEVE)

✔ **You can make the 'SH' sound before a suffix in three ways:**

- '**TI**': For example, CAUTIOUS, PARTIAL, PATIENT
- '**CI**': For example, DELICIOUS, SPACIOUS, MUSICIAN
- '**SI**': For example, TENSION, EXPULSION, PENSION

✔ **When you use the letter 'S' between vowels, the result is a 'Z' sound:** For example, MUSIC, TEASE, RESERVE

✔ **You can make a hissy 'S' sound in two ways:**

– **'SS':** For example, MASSIVE, TRUSS, CONFESS

– **'CE':** For example, OFFICE, NOTICE, REJOICE

✔ **You usually use a single 'S' when making a plural with an 'S' sound:** For example, LEAD → LEADS, HAT → HATS, TIE → TIES. Sometimes an obvious extra syllable is in such words, which means that you need to add 'ES' (for example, BOX → BOXES, TWITCH → TWITCHES, LOSS → LOSSES)

Considering Other Spelling Approaches

In this section, we take a look at three other techniques for getting your spelling shipshape.

Minding mnemonic strategies

When using the *mnemonic* technique you apply a new word to each letter of the words you want to spell to create a memorable phrase.

Mnemonics isn't recommended for all words – in most cases it's got to be easier to learn and apply the spelling rules or just memorise the spellings of words by rote.

But for those particularly tricky words that you just can't seem to remember, mnemonics can be useful. They're often most effective when they're amusing. So, perhaps you remember how to spell the word BECAUSE more easily by memorising the following:

Bare **E**lephants **C**an **A**lways **U**ndertake **S**omersault **E**asier.

Or maybe DEODORANT is a problem for you (not that we're implying anything). In which case, try:

Desmond's **E**xotic **O**dour **D**ampened **O**rdinary **R**omance **A**nd **N**ookie **T**oo!

We advise using this strategy sparingly, but it can certainly help on the odd occasion. If you have any words that you know are particular personal trouble spots, try a mnemonic; and if you can't remember how to spell MNEMONIC, try:

> **M**any **N**ude **E**xpeditions **M**ade **O**llie **N**otorious **I**n **C**hichester!

Heeding homophones

Homophones are pairs or groups of words that sound the same but are spelt differently. Obviously, getting these words right is important because otherwise they can expose you. To do so, you have to know not only how the word is spelt, but also what it means. The context in which the word appears is really important.

We can't offer you a magic solution to sorting out any homophones that are troubling you. The only way is to get to know them and practise. See Table 4-3 for some examples of common homophones to remember.

Table 4-3	Common Homophones to Remember		
aisle/isle	for/fore/four	one/won	sole/soul
bare/bear	hair/hare	pair/pear	some/sum
be/bee	heal/heel	peace/piece	son/sun
brake/break	hear/here	plain/plane	stare/stair
buy/by/bye	him/hymn	poor/pour	stationary/ stationery
cell/sell	hole/whole	pray/prey	steal/steel
cent/scent	hour/our	principal/ principle	suite/sweet
cereal/serial	idle/idol	profit/prophet	tail/tale
coarse/course	in/inn	real/reel	their/there/ they're
complement/ compliment	knight/night	right/rite	toe/tow
dam/damn	knot/not	root/route	to/too/ two
dear/deer	know/no	sail/sale	waist/waste

die/dye	made/maid	sea/see	wait/weight
eye/I	mail/male	seam/seem	way/weigh
fair/fare	meat/meet	sew/so	weak/week
fir /fur	morning/ mourning	shore/sure	where/ were/ wear/we're

To test yourself, take the groups of homophones in the table and construct a sentence using each one. For example:

- ✔ It's over *there*.
- ✔ They've lost *their* football.
- ✔ *They're* very low on petrol.

Now jot down some examples of other groups of homophones of your own.

Knuckling down to remember words

When push comes to shove (and shove to manly slaps), the fact is that certain words don't have convenient short cuts; you just need to remember them.

For instance, you have to memorise spelling patterns such as words beginning with 'KN' and 'PN'. Otherwise you may forever confuse heavily armed medieval warriors (KNIGHTS) with the hours of darkness (NIGHTS) and never come to grips with your PNEUMATIC tyres or your PNEUMOTHORAX! Similarly, mix up 'BT' words and you can muddle up your DOUBTS and your DEBTS.

Having a Go: Practice Tests

The spelling section of the Key Skills test is a listening test. You're given a set of sentences, each with a missing word, and you have to listen to a word that completes the sentence and write in the correct spelling of that missing word.

Here are some important details:

> ✔ Time for the test is limited, and so think about how long you have to spend on each answer.
>
> ✔ You can change your answers at any stage while you're still in the spelling section of the test.
>
> ✔ After you move on from the spelling section, you can't make any further changes.

For the purposes of the practice tests that follow, you can either ask a friend to read out each sentence to you or, even better, visit www.dummies.com/go/teachersskillstests to access audio versions of the questions. All the answers can be found at the end of the chapter.

Test A

1. Roger answered the teacher's question _____.

2. Good subject _____ is required in order to teach.

3. He completed the task _____.

4. _____ the photocopier was not working.

5. The headteacher outlined _____ regarding school trips.

6. Teachers are expected always to arrive for work _____.

7. The _____ cupboard was in the departmental office.

8. The boy tried to _____ his failure to hand in his homework.

9. Reports must always be checked for _____.

10. _____ practical clothing should be worn.

Test B

1. The school provided an _____ environment.

2. There was a prize for pupils who _____ enough merit marks.

3. Her attitude to work was not _____.

4. After their PE lesson, the pupils were _____.

5. He found the exercise book _____ a pile of folders.

6. The pupil was _____ when questioned.

7. _____ behaviour will not be tolerated.

8. The teacher tested the class _____.

9. She asked _____ to go to the toilet.

10. Mary admitted she was _____.

Test C

1. He _____ the query on to his line manager.

2. She clearly explained the _____ of his choice.

3. It is _____ that the visit will be next month.

4. The outcome of the examination was _____.

5. The lesson _____ practical activities.

6. Sadly, Peter was _____ whether he could do it.

7. Michelle _____ the package she was expecting.

8. A cool breeze came _____ the open window.

9. Pupils _____ the poem to memory.

10. She was fine _____ for a slight headache.

Test D

1. The new course was an _____ opportunity.

2. The English teacher loved to _____ Shakespeare.

3. It was a _____ lesson.

4. The pupils _____ a model bridge.

5. _____ was banned in the school grounds.

6. There is a _____ between attendance and performance.

7. James's careless _____ caused an accident.

8. Two _____ by four gives eight.

9. Harriet disliked _____ behaviour.

10. The thought of the test made Timothy _____.

Test E

1. The smallest sound was _____ in the silent exam hall.

2. The _____ put away his guitar.

3. All pupils had to select their GCSE _____.

4. Silence fell as the teacher _____ the room.

5. They joined the _____ in the dining room.

6. She _____ to give her demonstration.

7. The children asked for an _____ of the rule.

8. The staff _____ about the best way forward.

9. She _____ her bag, looking for her keys.

10. The students were enjoying their _____.

Test F

1. The boy demonstrated _____ ability at rugby.

2. She made the final _____ for her lesson the next day.

3. _____ is a very important characteristic.

4. The children attempted to _____ their form tutor about what had happened.

5. The girl waited in _____ for her parents.

6. It is important to _____ all assessments accurately.

7. He spoke to the child's mother on the _____.

8. She took up a _____ teaching position at the school.

9. Every Thursday after school there was a _____ of the full staff.

10. The Maths department _____ to purchase a class set of calculators.

Checking out the Practice Test Answers

Here are the answers to the preceding section's questions. But don't peek before you've had a go at the questions!

Test A

1. INCORRECTLY: Best remembered by taking the root word CORRECT and then adding the affixes to create the adverb (flip to the earlier 'Getting to the roots' section).

2. KNOWLEDGE: Remember the silent 'K' in the root word KNOW and then add the suffix LEDGE to form the noun.

3. EFFECTIVELY: Build from the root word EFFECT. Note that in 'IVELY' endings the first vowel (the 'I' in this case) remains short.

4. UNFORTUNATELY: Build from the root word FORTUNE. As is often the case with words ending with an 'E', you drop the 'E' before adding the suffix.

5. PROCEDURES: The tricky part here is remembering that the hissing 'S' sound is made by the letter 'C', as in related words such as PROCESS and PROCEED.

6. PUNCTUALLY: Remember that you double the final single consonant of the root word PUNCTUAL before adding the 'Y' to create the adverb.

7. STATIONERY: An example of a homophone (check out the earlier section 'Heeding homophones'), and so you have to commit this one to memory. The word means office supplies (paper, pens, hole punches and so on) and is easily remembered by the fact that PAPER also ends with 'ER', whereas STATIONARY (meaning to stand still) ends with 'AR', like CAR.

8. JUSTIFY: As with most words ending with an 'I' sound, remember that this ends with a 'Y'.

9. ACCURACY: Start with the root word ACCURATE and then create the noun by removing the 'TE' and adding the 'CY' ending. Other similar examples include PREGNANT → PREGNANCY, CURRENT → CURRENCY, ADVOCATE → ADVOCACY.

10. APPROPRIATE: The heart of this word is built around the root word PROPER. Sounding out the syllables AP-PROP-RI-ATE may also be a useful strategy.

Test B

1. INCLUSIVE: When you hear this word, sounding out the component parts is easy: IN-CLU-SIVE.

2. ACCUMULATED: Contains several tricky parts; remember the initial 'ACC' and then the repeated letter 'U'. Perhaps the meaning of the word (to build up) helps you to recall these parts.

3. ACCEPTABLE: Unlike in the previous word, the double 'C' makes a hissing sound. Think of this in two parts: 'AC' with a hard 'C' making a 'K' sound, followed by the soft 'CE' combination.

4. EXHAUSTED: Best committed to memory because of its silent 'H'.

5. BENEATH: Again, a good one to memorise because of the 'EA' combination. Other examples occur in LEAP, HEAP, BEACH and so on.

6. DEFENSIVE: Begin with the root word DEFEND so that sounding out the word is straightforward (see the earlier 'Getting to the roots' section).

7. DISRUPTIVE: Simple phonics (check out 'Sounding off! Finding out about phonics' earlier in this chapter) works here, sounding out the component parts of the word: DIS-RUP-TIVE.

8. PERIODICALLY: As a wannabe teacher you need to become familiar with the word PERIOD (meaning lesson) and then simply add the suffix 'ICALLY'.

9. PERMISSION: The root word is PERMIT. Words following the same pattern are COMMIT → COMMISSION, OMIT → OMISSION, EMIT → EMISSION and so on.

10. GUILTY: Memorise this word because of its tricky 'GU' opening. Other words using the same pattern are GUARD, GUARDIAN and so on.

Test C

1. REFERRED: Follows the normal rule of doubling the final consonant when a word ends with the consonant-vowel-consonant sequence (read the earlier section 'Looking at Patterns and Rules' for details).

2. CONSEQUENCES: Best remembered by starting with the root word SEQUENCE and then adding the prefix (see the earlier 'Getting to the roots' section). Remember that, with consequences, one thing leads to another and in this word you have the repeated letter 'E'.

3. PROBABLE: Obviously this word is very similar to PROBABLY. Remembering the two together is a good idea, recalling that a single 'E' at the end of words is silent.

4. DOUBTFUL: One to remember because of its silent 'B'. Try remembering that DUBIOUS is part of the same word family.

5. INCORPORATED: Straightforward here. The root word CORPORATE is easily sounded out (COR-POR-ATE) before adding the affixes.

6. UNCERTAIN: Start with the root word CERTAIN, recalling that the 'CE' combination makes a soft 'C' sound, and then add the prefix.

7. RECEIVED: Remember the important spelling rule: 'I' before 'E' except after 'C'.

8. THROUGH: An example of a homophone (see the earlier section 'Heeding homophones') and so best learnt by heart. The alternative spelling THREW is the past tense of the verb to throw.

9. COMMITTED: Following the pattern of most words ending consonant-vowel-consonant, you double the final 'T' of COMMIT before adding the suffix.

10. EXCEPT: Remember the body of similar words (EXCEED, EXCITE) to form the opening of the word, and the rest of the word is a simple phonic representation (see the earlier section 'Sounding off! Finding out about phonics').

Test D

1. EXCITING: Remember the body of similar words (EXCEED, EXCEPT) to form the opening of the word and then follow the rule of removing the final 'E' before adding the suffix.

2. QUOTE: 'Q' is always followed by 'U'.

3. MEMORABLE: Sounding this word out into syllables helps: ME-MOR-ABLE.

4. CONSTRUCTED: A straightforward example of forming the past tense by adding the suffix 'ED'.

5. SLEDGING: As is normal with root words ending with an 'E', you remove the 'E' before adding the suffix (see the earlier 'Getting to the roots' section).

6. CORRELATION: As in the previous example, you remove the final 'E' from the root word CORRELATE before adding the suffix to create a noun.

7. BEHAVIOUR: Best memorised. The root word BEHAVE loses its final 'E' before adding the 'IOUR' suffix. Another example is SAVE → SAVIOUR.

8. MULTIPLIED: Apply the rule regarding root words ending with a 'Y', where you change the 'Y' to an 'I' before adding an 'ED' or 'ES' suffix.

9. INCONSIDERATE: Start with the root word CONSIDER (see the earlier 'Getting to the roots' section) then simply add the simple prefix IN and suffix ATE.

10. ANXIOUS: Just remember this one. The 'ANX' is a simple phonetic representation (see the earlier section 'Sounding off! Finding out about phonics') of the word sound.

Test E

1. AUDIBLE: Easily constructed by sounding the word out: AU-DI-BLE.

2. MUSICIAN: Although several alternatives exist for making the 'SH' sound, you can work this one out easily by taking the root word MUSIC (see the earlier 'Getting to the roots' section).

3. OPTIONS: Here's another 'SH' word. Again the root word OPT seals the deal.

4. ENTERED: An exception to the normal rule of doubling the final consonant when a word ends consonant-vowel-consonant (see the earlier section 'Looking at Patterns and Rules'). Remember this one.

5. QUEUE: Best remembered. Recall the rule that 'Q' is always followed by a 'U' and then think that queues are long to help recall the repetition of 'UEUE' at the end of the word.

6. PROCEEDED: Straightforward. Just add the 'ED' ending to make the past tense form.

7. EXPLANATION: Obviously emerges from the root word EXPLAIN, but sound it out so that you remember to omit the 'I': EX-PLA-NA-TION.

8. CONFERRED: Follows the normal rule of doubling the final consonant when a word ends consonant-vowel-consonant.

9. PATTED: To retain the short vowel sound in PAT you have to double the 'T' before adding the 'ED' suffix to create the past tense verb.

10. CONVERSATION: Beginning with the root word CONVERSE, you follow the normal rule of removing the final 'E' before adding the suffix to create the noun.

Test F

1. EXCEPTIONAL: Recall the body of similar words (such as EXCEED, EXCITE) to form the opening of the word; the rest of the word is a simple phonic representation concluding with the common suffix 'AL'.

2. ARRANGEMENTS: Building on the common root word ARRANGE, remember that to retain the long 'A' sound, you have to retain the letter 'E' before adding the concluding 'MENTS'.

3. RELIABILITY: Your starting point here is RELIABLE.

Listening carefully is important in constructing the end of the word – sound out I-L-I-TY.

4. DECEIVE: The rule to remember here is 'I' before 'E' except after 'C'.

5. RECEPTION: The hissy 'S' is made by the letter 'C' here, but the rest is straightforward to sound out before adding the common 'TION' suffix to make the noun.

6. RECORD: Again, this one is pretty easy to sound out, just remember that in English the hard 'K' sound is often made using the letter 'C'.

7. TELEPHONE: The tricky part of this word is the central 'F' sound, which is often constructed in English by 'PH'.

8. PERMANENT: Most of this word is simple enough to build up by breaking the sounds down, but concentrate on the tricky opening where the long vowel sound is made by the letter 'E'; worth learning this one.

9. MEETING: The long 'E' sound is constructed here using 'EE', but otherwise this word is simple.

10. DECIDED: You make the central hissy 'S' sound using the letter 'C'.

Chapter 5

Punching above Your Weight at Punctuation

*L*ike everyone else, when you use language you divide your thoughts up into units of meaning. The smallest such unit is a word, but you don't get very far communicating with single words (and you can end up sounding like a robot barking out orders). In order to convey more complicated meanings, you combine words into other units of meaning – such as clauses, phrases and sentences.

We discuss more about using these items in Chapter 6, but here we talk about how you indicate, separate and combine units of varying size with punctuation marks to make clear sense. If you're unclear on sentence and phrase construction, we suggest that you read Chapter 6 first to make sure that you're clear about it. Otherwise, you may come a bit unstuck when correcting the passages in the later 'Having a Go: Practice Tests' section.

In this chapter, we talk you through the importance of punctuation and all the marks you need to understand, from capital letters to start a sentence, via commas, to full stops to complete your thought. We also cover more subtle punctuation marks and their specific uses and give you a chance to practise your new-found skills with some error-filled passages to correct.

Discovering the Need for Pace

When you speak, you use your voice, variations in the pace at which you speak and your body language in all kinds of ways to convey meaning:

- ✔ You make natural divisions between the different units of meaning.

- ✔ You pause to show that you've ended one sentence and are beginning another or to show that you're 'changing direction' within a sentence or providing additional information.

- ✔ You change the intonation of your voice to emphasise certain words.

- ✔ You raise the inflection of your voice at the end of a sentence to indicate that you're asking a question.

- ✔ You lower the inflection of your voice to indicate that you're making a statement.

- ✔ You use your hands, face and bodily gestures to convey meaning.

Just think about the many, many meanings your nearest and dearest can get out of a simple statement like, 'So there you are, darling.' Especially when you supply a range of facial expressions and/or hand gestures!

When you're writing, you still want to convey the same variety of meanings:

- ✔ Where gaps and pauses occur in language.

- ✔ Where one sentence ends and another begins.

- ✔ How ideas connect to one another or are separated from each other.

That's where punctuation comes in.

 Punctuation is a set of markers you use to show connection and separation within what you write. The marks are part of a signposting system that helps readers find their way through your writing and – all being well! – to understand exactly what you mean.

Looking at Beginnings: Capital Letters

We don't like to be controversial for the sake of it, and so we start by looking at beginnings. (We once began at the end of a task and worked backwards, but we simply met ourselves starting out. It was quite a shock – we looked so innocent.)

As we discuss in this section, you use capital letters on only three occasions: when beginning sentences, for names of people, places and so on (which are called proper nouns) and for the sentence-within-a-sentence inside speech marks.

Kicking off sentences

A sentence always begins with a capital letter; the rule is as simple as that. So, the following sentence is incorrect:

> we walked to the shops.

You need to write:

> We walked to the shops.

The great news is that no exceptions apply to this rule. Whenever you start a new sentence, you need to use a capital lettter.

Starting proper nouns

Normal nouns don't require capital letters, but proper nouns do. A *proper noun* is one that refers to specific:

- ✔ **Events:** For example, Speech Day, Education Conference, Radio 1 Roadshow
- ✔ **Occasions:** For example, Christmas Day, Diwali, Bank Holiday
- ✔ **People:** For example, Mary, the Prime Minister, William Shakespeare

- **Places:** For example, London, Wembley Stadium, the National Theatre
- **Publications, theatre productions, films and so on:** For example, *A Christmas Carol, Chitty Chitty Bang Bang, The King's Speech*

The pronoun 'I' is also always given a capital letter, because it refers specifically to the writer.

Opening a sentence in speech marks

When you open speech marks within a sentence you're effectively starting a sentence-within-a-sentence. The beginning of this sentence-within-a-sentence, therefore, needs to begin with a capital letter:

> Marjorie said, 'The best way to get to Birmingham is to take the fast train from Euston.'

Here you see that the spoken words form a sentence in their own right, and so the first word of that sentence – 'the' – has to be capitalised, even though it sits within a larger sentence starting with the word 'Marjorie'.

Here's another way to write that sentence:

> 'The best way to get to Birmingham,' Marjorie said, 'is to take the fast train from Euston.'

Here the same rule applies. The first word of the spoken sentence needs a capital letter. Even though the speech is divided by the clause 'Marjorie said', which is inserted in the middle, the speech sentence functions on its own. The beginning of the second half of the speech sentence doesn't need a capital letter, because it isn't the start of a new sentence.

Pausing for Breath: Commas

Everyone needs to take a break now and then, and you don't want your readers to get breathless. Therefore, you use commas to separate words, phrases and certain clauses.

Working with commas

In this section, we run through four uses for commas.

Separating adjectives

One common use of commas is to separate adjectives:

> The angry, churning, raging sea swamped the boat.

Here the three adjectives all tell you something different about the sea. No matter how long the sequence of adjectives, you must separate them all with commas, even if you use only two (for example, 'the steaming, bubbling water').

Separating words in a list

You also put commas to work in lists:

> Jacob bought rice, chicken, curry paste, naan bread, popadoms and a selection of chutneys to make his evening meal.

This list is a variety of items or ingredients Jacob is using for his meal. You don't need to use a comma between the final two items in the list ('popadoms' and 'a selection of chutneys'), because the word 'and' already serves to separate them.

Never say never, though. You can add a comma between the final two items of a list if you want to: it's called the *Oxford* comma. But we're straying onto areas of writing style here.

If a list like this one has only two items, you don't use a comma. If Jacob is buying only two items, he'd be buying 'rice and chicken', not 'rice, chicken'.

For when to use semi-colons in lists, check out the later section 'Summing up semi-colons'.

Separating introductory words

When sentences begin with an introductory word, such as 'yes', 'no', 'well, 'oh' or okay', you separate the word from the rest of the sentence with a comma:

> Yes, I know that the game kicks off at eight.

> No, I wasn't sure whether you'd be in.

> Well, it's not really as simple as that.

Separating speech markers

Speech markers, which are words such as 'however', 'therefore' and 'perhaps', are often separated off using commas:

> It is, therefore, wrong to steal from shops.

> He was, however, still quite cheerful.

> It was, perhaps, because of his helmet that he survived.

In all these examples, when you read the sentences the commas appear as short pauses.

Considering commas in subordinate clauses

What do you call Santa's little helpers? Subordinate clauses (boom, boom!).

Subordinate clauses – which we discuss more in Chapter 6 – are effectively additional information within a sentence. They can't function on their own as a sentence, but add information for the reader. Therefore, you need to separate them off from the rest of the sentence, most commonly with commas. (Sometimes you can also use dashes or brackets, as we describe in the later section 'Perusing parentheses'.)

Here's a basic sentence that stands alone:

> Petra went skiing with her boyfriend.

Suppose, however, that Petra was always afraid of winter sports and you want to include this information using the subordinate clause (literally, the inferior or less important clause) 'who had always been nervous of winter sports'. As you can see, these words can't stand on their own: in order to have meaning they depend upon the main sentence. But you can insert these words in the main sentence as follows:

> Petra, who had always been nervous of winter sports, went skiing with her boyfriend.

This phrase contains additional, dependent information, and so the subordinate clause has to be separated off from the main sentence using commas. With some slight variation, you can add the same information at the beginning or end of the sentence, again separating it with a comma:

> Although she had always been nervous of winter sports, Petra went skiing with her boyfriend.

> Petra went skiing with her boyfriend, even though she had always been nervous of winter sports.

You never use commas to separate two complete sentences.

Finishing off with Separators

The punctuation marks we cover in this section are called *separators*. You use them to show where one sentence ends and – by logical extension – where the next sentence begins.

The most common separator is the full stop. Question marks and exclamation marks are variations on the full stop. They still serve the function of showing where one sentence ends and the next begins, but also give some extra information.

Asking questions

A question mark ('?') indicates – go on, see whether you can guess – that the sentence is asking a question. It usually requires some kind of personal response from the reader:

> Did you get that?

> Do you see what we're on about?

We hope that your response to these questions is 'yes'.

Conveying emphasis

You employ an exclamation mark ('!') to indicate that a sentence is spoken with emphasis. Here are some instances and examples:

> ✓ **As a warning:** 'Look out!'
>
> ✓ **To convey emotion:** 'I'm so mad with you!'
>
> ✓ **To give an insight into tone of voice:** 'I said be quiet!' (angry) or 'You're crazy!' (possibly humorous).

Speaking Up

You use speech marks and quotation marks to identify words spoken by (with speech marks) or written by (with quotation marks) another person and reproduced within writing. Speech and quotations are identified with the same punctuation marks, called *speech marks*. These marks can be single speech marks (') or double speech marks ("").

Seeing precisely what's said: Speech marks

You employ speech marks to surround the actual words a person speaks. Imagine that the following is part of a short dialogue between Peter and his friend George:

> 'I'm going to the cinema tonight,' said Peter.
>
> 'What are you going to see?' asked George.
>
> 'The new James Bond film,' Peter replied.
>
> 'I've been meaning to see that,' said George. 'Can I come along too?'

As you can see, the exact words Peter and George speak (and only the words they speak) are enclosed within speech marks. All other words that help readers understand what's going on (for example, 'said Peter' and 'asked George') aren't in speech marks because they aren't words spoken by the characters.

Indicating written quotes: Quotation marks

You use quotation marks to surround words that you're quoting from another source within your own writing. This material may be from a book, a newspaper, a pamphlet, a policy document and so on. For example:

> George Bernard Shaw, in his 1903 play *Man and Superman*, quips, 'He who can, does. He who cannot, teaches.'

Or:

> The school's Behaviour policy states, 'All teachers must report any incidents of physical violence, no matter what the cause.'
>
> In these examples you're reproducing the exact words of the written source and so you have to place them in quotation marks.

Pondering Other Punctuation Marks

In this section, we gather together some more important punctuation marks that you need to know about in order to write clearly. We cover apostrophes, parenthesis, hyphens, colons and semi-colons.

Approaching apostrophes

You use apostrophes in your writing for two reasons: to show contraction and to show possession.

Contraction

Contraction, of course, just means making something shorter or smaller. In terms of punctuation, it applies when individual letters or sections of words have been removed:

- ✔ cannot → can't
- ✔ of the clock → o'clock

✔ he will → he'll

✔ she would → she'd

✔ I have → I've

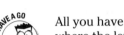

All you have to do is insert the apostrophe into the word where the letters have been missed out. Try the following ones on for size:

should not → _____

have not → _____

you are → _____

Possession

You bring out apostrophes to show when something belongs to something or somebody else. All you need to know is what's owned (usually an object or a person, but sometimes a point of view or a concept) and who owns it. So far, so good, we hear you cry: easy!

Many people try to make this usage complicated when, in fact, it's very simple. Just think about whether or not the 'owning' word ends or doesn't end with an 's'.

Words not ending in an 's'

Where the 'owning' word doesn't end in an 's', all you need to do to show possession is to add an apostrophe followed by an 's'. You don't have to worry about whether the owning word is singular or plural, that's the simple rule.

So, if Peter owns a pen, you say that it's (notice the contraction of 'it is' → 'it's', by the way) Peter's pen. If Mary has a motorbike, it's Mary's motorbike.

The same is true for the word 'children', even though it's a plural noun. Toys belonging to these children are the children's toys.

Words ending in an 's'

Where the 'owning' word does end in an 's', all you need to do to show possession is add an apostrophe after that 's'. Again, don't bother about whether the owning word is singular or plural.

So, if James has a jumper, it's James' jumper.

If some bishops own some Bibles, they're the bishops' Bibles. And that well-known tale *A Christmas Carol* by Charles Dickens is Charles Dickens' *A Christmas Carol*.

Sometimes people tell you that you have to think about whether the 'owning' word is singular or plural. Beware of this big red herring! This idea comes from the fact that plural nouns in English tend to end with an 's', but then so do quite a few singular words (especially names); plus quite a few plural nouns also don't end with an 's' (for example, children, cattle, fish).

Whether the 'owning' word is singular or plural doesn't matter. All that matters is whether or not it ends with an 's'.

Common mistakes with apostrophes

Using the possessive apostrophe is something that many people get wrong, and so we take a quick look here at the most common errors.

Grocers' apostrophes

No doubt you're familiar with the famous grocer's apostrophe, as it's called, because it's so often misused on signs outside grocery stores:

apple's   **pear's**   **potatoe's**

This error arises from a confusion between making a singular noun plural (by adding 's' or 'es') and showing possession by adding an apostrophe followed by 's'.

Possessive pronouns

Although a little counterintuitive, you never use an apostrophe with a possessive pronoun. So you write:

- ✔ his/hers/its *not* hi's or his'/her's or hers'/it's or its'
- ✔ yours *not* your's
- ✔ ours *not* our's
- ✔ theirs *not* their's

You've got to love English, haven't you? What a crazy language!

Carrying out joined-up thinking: Hyphens

Hyphens join two or more words together into a new compound word. So, you can join together the words 'well' and 'adjusted' with a hyphen to create a new adjective 'well-adjusted'. Or you can take three words 'mother', 'in' and 'law' and combine them using hyphens to create a new noun (or nightmare, depending on your perspective) 'mother-in-law'.

You also require hyphens when combining written-out numbers. So if you're required to write out numericals such as 74 and 49, you do so as 'seventy-four' and 'forty-nine'.

Perusing parentheses

A *parenthesis* (the plural is *parentheses*) is a word or phrase inserted into a sentence that would function perfectly well grammatically without the added digression, interlude or figure of speech.

You turn to a parenthesis when inserting an aside or interruption into your writing. Brackets, dashes and commas are the most common way of indicating one.

Subordinate clauses, ones separated off from the main sentence by commas, are a kind of parenthesis. Did you notice that we just used one? (Turn to the earlier section 'Considering commas in subordinate clauses' for more.) Plus, we include an example of a parenthesis in brackets in the preceding section – the joke about delightful mothers-in-law – on hyphens. That bit in dashes in the last sentence is another example. They're everywhere!

Whether you use commas, dashes or brackets, these parenthetical marks always need to come in pairs. What you start, you have to finish! So, if ever you're using – or looking for – a parenthesis, you need to have two commas, dashes or brackets.

Coping with colons

These colons have nothing to do with your digestive tract. Like semi-colons in the next section, they're an important way of displaying to a reader how ideas within your writing connect. Colons (and semi-colons) separate information but at the same time demonstrate differing degrees of connection between the information that comes before them and the information that follows them.

In general, you use colons for two purposes:

✔ To introduce lists

✔ To join explanations

Introducing lists

You don't always need a colon when you're introducing a list into a sentence; it depends on *how* you introduce it. The colon, however, can alert a reader to the fact that the list relates directly to what's gone before.

Here's an example of a list without a colon:

> Andrew's favourite authors were Charles Dickens, Henry James, T.S. Eliot and Peter Ackroyd.

The list needs no introductory colon, because it flows naturally within the main body of the sentence.

Here's an example of a list with a colon:

> Andrew had several favourite authors: Charles Dickens, Henry James, T.S. Eliot and Peter Ackroyd.

You need a colon here, because 'Andrew had several favourite authors' is a sentence in its own right and the following list goes on to give directly related, but separate, information.

Joining explanations

Sometimes colons are used to join two sentences (or a sentence and a sentence fragment) together where the second sentence (or fragment) offers a direct explanation of (or a direct logical connection to) the first. Here are a couple of examples:

> Hannah hates going to the zoo: she has a terrible phobia of snakes.

The second part (which could be a sentence on its own) provides a direct explanation for why Hannah doesn't like going to the zoo.

Here's another:

> There was only one place he wanted to go for his holiday: New York.

The sentence fragment 'New York' provides the explanation for the first sentence about the man's holiday.

Summing up semi-colons

You'll be relieved to know that semi-colons aren't what you're left with after a gastric band is fitted.

You use semi-colons in two contexts:

- ✔ To connect one complete sentence to another without using joining words (called *conjunctions* – as we describe in Chapter 6)
- ✔ To separate items in a list

Connecting sentences

When you join sentences with a semi-colon, they must have a logical connection to each other. Consider the following sentences:

- ✔ Sally lost her purse.
- ✔ She couldn't buy David's birthday present.

A clear connection exists between the two sentences and so you can use a semi-colon to join them directly to each other:

> Sally lost her purse; she couldn't buy David's birthday present.

Now look at two more sentences:

- ✔ William hates asparagus.
- ✔ He wears purple trousers.

No logical connection exists between these sentences, and so you can't join them to each other using a semi-colon. Of course, you can place them next to each other as separate sentences telling readers two different things about William.

Separating items in a list

You normally use commas to separate items in a list (as we discuss in the earlier section 'Working with commas'), but sometimes semi-colons are appropriate:

- ✔ When commas appear within items in the list, thus leading to excessive numbers of commas and confusion in the list (for example, 'several people were present: Bob, the builder; Sam, the fireman; Roger, the lodger').

- ✔ When the list is composed of longer sections of text (for example, 'going to the doctor is best if: a high temperature persists for more than 24 hours; swelling occurs around the mouth; the patient is unresponsive').

Having a Go: Practice Tests

In the tests that follow, we present you with a short passage that's punctuated incorrectly. Your task is to identify the deliberate mistakes and correct them. In each of the following passages you're looking to make ten corrections.

The Key Skills tests ask you to deal with only one kind of punctuation – omissions. In other words:

- ✔ They never ask you to take away punctuation marks or capital letters that *shouldn't* be present.

- ✔ They ask you only to insert punctuation marks or capital letters that *should* be present.

Nice and straightforward, we think.

Passage A

In the Classroom: Lessons and Learning

Earthly paradise school has three classroom rules which apply in all lessons. they are displayed in all classrooms and teaching spaces and they are printed in the front of the school diary. The rules are:

- Follow the teacher's instructions
- Arrive on time to lessons with the right equipment, including a bag books, diary and pen
- Be respectful and courteous at all times. Dont behave in any way which might offend others or prevent them from teaching or learning

Students who follow these rules consistently will be rewarded Students who do not will be followed up by their teachers. Subject areas use a variety of rewards and sanctions detention is a widely used sanction. (Parents/carers will be notified 24 hours in advance if a detention of more than 20 minutes is given. Parents/carers will be informed if there is no improvement in their childs behaviour because these students will be affecting both their own learning and that of others. They will also be contravening a teacher's right to teach.

Passage B

Unstructured observation of lessons can be a waste of time. It can also become boring very quickly. often there is so much general activity that it is difficult to notice anything in particular. There is always the problem of selecting relevant incidents. There is also a problem with interpretation making sense of what is taking place.

When observing experienced teachers it is often difficult to see what they are doing in order to manage the classroom with seemingly effortless skill They often seem to do little by way of obvious organisation yet everything seems to run like clockwork. Pupils seem to know what they should and shouldnt do at each point in the lesson when to listen to the teacher; how to tackle their work where to find resources how to move around the classroom without causing disruption; what to do at the end of a lesson. This is because what you see is the result of teachers working hard with pupils over a period of time to establish a set of rules and routines. By the time you see them teaching a class, teachers management techniques are often no more than prompting signals (such as a change of voice or eye contact) to pupils, or quiet reminders to individuals.

Passage C

Behind the door of number 46, alfred Bookman led the way down the brightly-lit hallway to the front door of the house. Behind him came a noisy and good-humoured group. Young and old alike, they were filled with the good spirits of a good day, helped along by a few glasses of good red wine festive fare and the hope of better to come on this Christmas Eve night. The actors – for that is who they were had done their work for the day, bringing a Victorian family Christmas to life at the Dickens House museum. Their footsteps and voices echoed merrily from the wooden floor to the high ceiling, as rich and bright as the thick red tinsel and baubles that festooned the staircase stretching up behind them.

Alfred did not share the high spirits of the others. In a moody silence he stalked ahead, threw back the bolts and opened the front door in spite of a stream of freezing air that suddenly flowed into the house, Alfred stood staring up and down the street, blocking the way.

Come on, Alfie' called out James Marley, one of the young men in a mock serious tone. 'Hurry up, and get out of the way. Were all back here tomorrow, and I'm dying for a drink.'

Passage D

There are a number of planned developments in the 14–19 curriculum. These come in the wake of the report of The working Group on 14–19 Reform (2004), chaired by Mike Tomlinson and indicate a new and broadening gamut of issues emerging within the field of A level teaching. These issues will inevitably have an impact on the nature of university teaching and secondary-higher education transition.

Statements by Ruth Kelly, the Secretary of State for Education, and the recent White Paper (DfES, 2005) indicate a political drive for further change and on-going development in this field including the potential for much greater flexibility in terms of the role and timing of assessment. The White Paper recognises the need to address issues of progression and assessment within A level qualifications, including the possibility, as initially recommended by Tomlinsons Working Group, of completing formal assessments at appropriate rather than at fixed points. also mooted is the possibility of a long, project-style assessment designed to reflect the demands of higher education and the workplace. This may be subject based, to reflect particular academic content skills based, to encourage the development of suitable abilities as learners; more broadly based to assess wider perspectives. Also suggested is the 'drawing down' of university modules for the most able students If initiated, these changes will have significant impact on the range of student experience at A level, an experience which is currently criticised for its narrowness of vision and its targeted focus on Assessment Objectives.

Passage E

it is a truth universally acknowledged, that a single man in possession of a good fortune, must be in want of a wife.

However little known the feelings or views of such a man may be on his first entering a neighbourhood this truth is so well fixed in the minds of the surrounding families that he is considered the rightful property of some one or other of their daughters.

'My dear Mr. Bennet' said his lady to him one day, 'have you heard that Netherfield park is let at last?'

Mr. Bennet replied that he had not.

'But it is,' returned she; 'for Mrs. Long has just been here, and she told me all about it.'

Mr. Bennet made no answer.

'Do you not want to know who has taken it' cried his wife impatiently.

'You want to tell me, and I have no objection to hearing it.'

This was invitation enough.

'Why my dear, you must know, Mrs. Long says that Netherfield is taken by a young man of large fortune from the north of England that he came down on Monday in a chaise and four to see the place, and was so much delighted with it, that he agreed with Mr. Morris immediately; that he is to take possession before michaelmas, and some of his servants are to be in the house by the end of next week.'

'What is his name?

'Bingley.'

Passage F

Please note that as part of the initial three weeks of the course you are required to undertake a weeks observation in primary school and to undertake a number of related activities The dates for this week's observation are Monday 20th – friday 24th September inclusive. You are expected to arrange this week's observation for yourself to confirm with me the details of your placement before the beginning of the course in September and to supply a letter confirming attendance after the week has been completed. This observation may be undertaken in any maintained primary school. The purpose of this week is to explore pupils educational experience at Key Stage 2 and key stage 3 to determine its potential impact on their transition to secondary school and to provide an important foundation for your work as a secondary teacher. There will be a particular focus on the teaching of English and literacy, which will underpin your consideration of English at secondary level.

A formal letter of introduction from the university to help with your approaches to primary schools is enclosed. If you have any further queries about this please do not hesitate to contact me.

Passage G

Writing up a Science Experiment

Aim: This is the reason for doing the experiment. It must state what is under investigation or what you hope to find out. For example To investigate how the reaction between zinc and hydrochloric acid depends on the temperature.

Hypothesis: this is the idea behind your plan which leads you to believe the experiment can be successful. It may also contain a prediction of the final answer supported by a reason). For example: I think that the reaction will go faster because the particles will be moving faster with more heat giving them a greater chance to collide and react.

method: This is what was actually done or is going to be done. It may need a diagram, which should always be labelled. It should be drawn in two dimensions and fully assembled, to ensure readers understanding.

The method should be reproducible (it should be written so that anyone else could repeat the experiment exactly).

Results: There are two aspects to the results:

- ✔ Data recording: all readings and measurements taken in the course of the experiment should be recorded. Results should be presented in such a way as to be easily read and understood; this may be in the form of a table.

- ✔ Data processing: results should also be 'treated' in this section – any calculations, graphs, etc. must be clearly explained and set out.

Conclusions: Results should be explained here and the aim answered. You must state what you found out in the investigation and look for general principles and patterns.

Evaluation: This is where you critically appraise the experiment (was the experiment satisfactory to explore the stated aim or were there weaknesses Could the experiment be improved? Where did errors come in?

Checking out the Practice Test Answers

Here we supply the corrected passages from the preceding section, with the required changes shown in bold and placed within square parentheses.

Passage A

In the Classroom: Lessons and Learning

Earthly Paradise School [**Paradise and School need capital letters, because they're both proper nouns**] has three classroom rules which apply in all lessons. They [**a capital T is required because this is the beginning of a sentence**] are displayed in all classrooms and teaching spaces and they are printed in the front of the school diary. The rules are: [**a colon is required here to introduce the following list**]

- ✔ Follow the teacher's instructions

- ✔ Arrive on time to lessons with the right equipment, including a bag, [**a comma is required here to separate elements in a list**] books, diary and pen

- ✔ Be respectful and courteous at all times. Don't [**an apostrophe is needed to show the contraction of do not → don't**] behave in any way which might offend others or prevent them from teaching or learning

Students who follow these rules consistently will be rewarded. [**a full stop is needed to mark the end of the sentence**] Students who do not will be followed up by their teachers. Subject areas use a variety of rewards and sanctions; [**a semicolon is used here to connect the two sentences, which logically link to one another**] detention is a widely used sanction. (Parents/carers will be notified 24 hours in advance if a detention of more than 20 minutes is given.) [**closing bracket is needed to complete the parenthesis**] Parents/carers will be informed if there is no improvement in their child's [**a possessive apostrophe is needed to indicate the behaviour of the child**] behaviour because these students will be affecting both their own learning and that of others. They will also be contravening a teacher's right to teach.

Passage B

Unstructured observation of lessons can be a waste of time. It can also become boring very quickly. Often [**a capital O is needed because this is the start of a new sentence**] there is so much general activity that it is difficult to notice anything in particular. There is always the problem of selecting relevant incidents. There is also a problem with interpretation: [**a colon is needed to demonstrate the strong logical connection between the first sentence and the following sentence fragment**] making sense of what is taking place.

When observing experienced teachers, [**the comma is required to separate the subordinate clause from the main clause**] it is often difficult to see what they are doing in order to manage the classroom with seemingly effortless skill. [**a full stop is needed to mark the end of the sentence**] They often seem to do little by way of obvious organisation, [**a comma is needed here in order to introduce the connective 'yet' which joins the two sentences**] yet everything seems to run like clockwork. Pupils seem to know what they should and shouldn't [**an apostrophe is needed to show that should not has been shortened to shouldn't**] do at each point in the lesson: [**a colon is needed here to introduce the following list, which connects logically to what has gone before**] when to listen to the teacher; how to tackle their work; [**semi-colon required to separate items in the list**] where to find resources; [**semi-colon required to separate items in the list**] how to move around the classroom without causing disruption; what to do at the end of a lesson. This is because what you see is the result of teachers working hard with pupils over a period of time to establish a set of rules and routines. By the time you see them teaching a class, teachers' [**an apostrophe is required here to demonstrate that the management techniques belong to the teachers, and as the root word is teachers, the apostrophe must come after the final 's'**] management techniques are often no more than prompting signals (such as a change of voice or eye contact) to pupils, or quiet reminders to individuals.

Passage C

Behind the door of number 46, Alfred [**a capital letter is required because Alfred is a proper noun**] Bookman led the way down the brightly-lit hallway to the front door of the house. Behind him came a noisy and good-humoured group. Young and old alike, they were filled with the good spirits of a good day, helped along by a few glasses of good red wine, [**a comma is needed because this is part of a list**] festive fare and the hope of better to come on this Christmas Eve night. The actors – for that is who they were – [**a second dash is**

needed to close the parenthesis] had done their work for the day, bringing a Victorian family Christmas to life at the Dickens House Museum **[museum, as part of a proper noun, requires a capital letter]**. Their footsteps and voices echoed merrily from the wooden floor to the high ceiling, as rich and bright as the thick red tinsel and baubles that festooned the staircase stretching up behind them.

Alfred did not share the high spirits of the others. In a moody silence he stalked ahead, threw back the bolts and opened the front door. **[a full stop is needed to mark the end of the sentence]** In **[a capital I is needed because this is the start of a new sentence]** spite of a stream of freezing air that suddenly flowed into the house, Alfred stood staring up and down the street, blocking the way.

'Come **[opening speech marks are required for the words James speaks]** on, Alfie,' **[a comma is needed before the final speech mark to divide the speech from the rest of the sentence]** called out James Marley, one of the young men, **[a second comma is needed in order to separate the subordinate clause from the main sentence]** in a mock serious tone. 'Hurry up, and get out of the way. We're **[an apostrophe is needed to show the contraction of we are → we're]** all back here tomorrow, and I'm dying for a drink.'

Passage D

There are a number of planned developments in the 14–19 curriculum. These come in the wake of the report of The Working **[working, as part of a proper noun, needs a capital letter]** Group on 14–19 Reform (2004), chaired by Mike Tomlinson, **[a second comma is needed to separate the subordinate clause from the main sentence]** and indicate a new and broadening gamut of issues emerging within the field of A level teaching. These issues will inevitably have an impact on the nature of university teaching and secondary-higher education transition. **[a full stop is required to mark the end of the sentence]**

Statements by Ruth Kelly, the Secretary of State for Education, and the recent White Paper (DfES, 2005) indicate a political drive for further change and on-going development in this field, **[a comma is required to separate the subordinate clause from the rest of the sentence]** including the potential for much greater flexibility in terms of the role and timing of assessment. The White Paper recognises the need to address issues of progression and assessment within A level qualifications, including the possibility, as initially recommended by Tomlinson's [**a possessive apostrophe is needed to show that this is the working group of Mike Tomlinson**] Working Group, of completing formal assessments at appropriate rather than at fixed points. Also mooted is the possibility of a long, project-style assessment designed to reflect the demands of higher education and the workplace. This may be: [**a colon is needed as an introduction to the following list**] subject based, to reflect particular academic content; [**a semi-colon is required to separate items within a list where commas appear within the items in the list**] skills based, to encourage the development of suitable abilities as learners; more broadly based, [**a comma is needed to separate information within the list item**] to assess wider perspectives. Also [**a capital A is required because this is the beginning of a sentence**] suggested is the 'drawing down' of university modules for the most able students. [**a full stop is needed to mark the end of the sentence**] If initiated, these changes will have significant impact on the range of student experience at A level, an experience which is currently criticised for its narrowness of vision and its targeted focus on Assessment Objectives.

Passage E

It [**a capital I is needed to begin the sentence**] is a truth universally acknowledged, that a single man in possession of a good fortune, must be in want of a wife.

However little known the feelings or views of such a man may be on his first entering a neighbourhood, [**a comma is required to introduce the subordinate clause**] this truth is so well fixed in the minds of the surrounding families, [**a comma is required to mark the end of the subordinate clause**] that he is considered the rightful property of some one or other of their daughters.

'My dear Mr. Bennet,' [**a comma is needed to separate the speech from the rest of the sentence**] said his lady to him one day, 'have you heard that Netherfield Park [**a capital letter is needed for the proper noun**] is let at last?'

Mr. Bennet replied that he had not.

'But it is,' returned she; 'for Mrs. Long has just been here, and she told me all about it.'

Mr. Bennet made no answer.

'Do you not want to know who has taken it?' **[a question mark is required because Mrs Bennet is asking a question]** cried his wife impatiently.

'You want to tell me, and I have no objection to hearing it.'

This was invitation enough.

'Why, **[a comma is required to separate the personal address from the rest of the sentence]** my dear, you must know, Mrs. Long says that Netherfield is taken by a young man of large fortune from the north of England; **[semi-colon used to demonstrate the connection of sentences]** that he came down on Monday in a chaise and four to see the place, and was so much delighted with it, that he agreed with Mr. Morris immediately; that he is to take possession before Michaelmas **[as a proper noun, Michaelmas requires a capital letter]**, and some of his servants are to be in the house by the end of next week.'

'What is his name?' **[closing speech marks needed]**

'Bingley.'

Passage F

Please note that as part of the initial three weeks of the course you are required to undertake a week's **[possessive apostrophe needed to relate observation to week]** observation in primary school and to undertake a number of related activities. **[concluding full stop needed for this sentence]** The dates for this week's observation are Monday 20th – Friday **[capital F needed for the proper noun Friday]** 24th September inclusive. You are expected to arrange this week's observation for yourself, **[comma needed to separate items in a list]** to confirm with me the details of your placement before the beginning of the course in September, **[comma needed to separate items in a list]** and to supply a letter confirming attendance after the week has been completed.

This observation may be undertaken in any maintained primary school. The purpose of this week is to explore pupils' **[the educational experience belongs to the pupils, so a possessive apostrophe is needed after the word pupils]** educational experience at Key Stage 2 and Key Stage **[both Key and Stage require capitals, because they are proper nouns]** 3; **[semi-colon is needed to demonstrate connection between the two sentences]** to determine its potential impact on their transition to secondary school and to provide an important foundation for your work as a secondary teacher. There will be a particular focus on the teaching of English and literacy, which will underpin your consideration of English at Secondary level.

A formal letter of introduction from the university to help with your approaches to primary schools is enclosed. If you have any further queries about this, **[comma is used to separate the subordinate clause from the main clause]** please do not hesitate to contact me.

Passage G

Writing up a Science Experiment

Aim: This is the reason for doing the experiment. It must state what is under investigation or what you hope to find out. For example: **[colon is used to connect to and introduce the next sentence]** To investigate how the reaction between zinc and hydrochloric acid depends on the temperature.

Hypothesis: This **[capital T needed, because this is a new sentence connected to the previous sentence fragment by a colon]** is the idea behind your plan which leads you to believe the experiment can be successful. It may also contain a prediction of the final answer (supported **[opening bracket required for the parenthesis]** by a reason). For example: I think that the reaction will go faster because the particles will be moving faster with more heat, **[comma needed to indicate beginning of subordinate clause]** giving them a greater chance to collide and react.

Method: **[capital M needed because this is the beginning of a new sentence]** This is what was actually done or is going to be done. It may need a diagram, which should always be labelled. It should be drawn in two dimensions and fully assembled, to ensure readers' **[possessive apostrophe needed to indicate the understanding of the readers]** understanding.

The method should be reproducible (it should be written so that anyone else could repeat the experiment exactly).

Results: There are two aspects to the results: **[colon needed to introduce the list]**

- ✔ Data recording: all readings and measurements taken in the course of the experiment should be recorded. Results should be presented in such a way as to be easily read and understood; this may be in the form of a table.

- ✔ Data processing: results should also be 'treated' in this section – any calculations, graphs, etc. – **[a hyphen is required to finish the parenthesis]** must be clearly explained and set out.

Conclusions: Results should be explained here and the aim answered. You must state what you found out in the investigation and look for general principles and patterns.

Evaluation: This is where you critically appraise the experiment (was the experiment satisfactory to explore the stated aim or were there weaknesses? **[question sentence, and so a question mark is needed]** Could the experiment be improved? Where did errors come in?) **[closing bracket to complete parenthesis required]**

Chapter 6

Getting to Grips with Grammar

*T*he notion of proper grammar is something that politicians (and others who want to carp about the poor state of literacy) use to beat people over the head with. They perpetuate two central myths:

✔ That a 'golden age' existed when everybody, regardless of age, gender, ethnicity, sexual orientation, creed or colour, wrote and spoke to grammatical perfection. *They didn't!*

✔ That some form of fixed grammar exists and that grammar is a unified and unchanging thing. *Not true!*

But the fact that contemporary language is constantly changing and developing, and inevitably grammar with it, doesn't mean that you don't need to understand and use correctly certain important elements of language. In order to see how people work with language in conventional and less conventional ways (especially when writing), you have to possess a clear understanding of grammar. Don't let this thought fill you with despair, though. Please remove from your face any expressions of panic, horror and pain, and make sure that you bear no resemblance to the proverbial rabbit in the headlights. Honestly, there's no need, because in this chapter we break down what you need to know about English grammar quite straightforwardly. We describe Standard English, all the different parts of speech (including the tricky ones) and how to build your sentences.

Introducing Standard English

This chapter describes the issues as they relate to Standard English – not because it's a superior version of English but because it's the agreed, shared medium of English that best ensures effective communication.

Standard English – sometimes known as Received Pronunciation (or RP) – concerns what you say or write: in other words, it's about the shared version of English that people understand across the English-speaking world.

To be absolutely clear: Standard English isn't to do with sounding posh or unposh (if that word existed!). Whether you come from Newcastle or New York, Oxford or Oklahoma, Dunstable or Delhi, Standard English isn't about your accent (how the words sound when you speak them).

Standard English is vitally important to ensure a shared medium of communication. If everyone agrees that when people say or write the word 'table' they're referring to an object made of some kind of hard material (usually wood, metal or plastic), with a smooth flat surface and a number of legs (usually three or four), which is used for eating and drinking on, humans can communicate with each other. They have an agreement about how language functions. If, however, you insist on calling that object a flower, the result is confusion:

> *It was about six o'clock when Peter finally got home from work. He walked straight into the kitchen, picked up a plate, a knife and a fork, and then went into the dining room. He pulled out a chair and sat down. He was starving! He took two cartons of Chinese food from his bag and placed them on the flower next to his plate.*

Readers may or may not guess what you're talking about from the context, but by failing to live up to the contract of language, you create a problem in terms of communication.

The same applies if you use dialect – local words for particular objects (such as 'daps' for plimsolls or 'kine' for cows) – or slang – very informal language. Dialect and slang cause real problems if the person you're speaking to or writing for doesn't understand the same dialect or slang.

For the same reason, when you put words together into phrases, clauses and sentences you have to follow the rules of Standard English. This stricture isn't about being awkward for the sake of it: it's about effective communication and making sure that anyone hearing or reading your words can understand what you're on about.

Meeting the Different Parts of Speech

As soon as they read the term 'parts of speech', some people immediately think that the subject is about to get complicated. Not so!

Parts of speech are simply the types of words you have available when you speak and write. Each part of speech has a different function, as we explain in this section. Here goes!

Noticing nouns, proper nouns and pronouns

Nouns are *naming* words and they're the most important type of word in the language: that's a big claim, we know, but think about it. When children are learning a language, nouns are the first words they discover: 'Mummy', 'Daddy' and 'cake'. Similarly, when adults are working with a new language or going on holiday, nouns are also the first words they encounter. After all, who doesn't make sure that they know the local words for 'beer', 'wine' and 'restaurant' before they step onto the plane?

Nouns are the words that tie you to the world and allow you to talk about it. They're also the words that carry the most meaning.

Look at the following passage – the opening two paragraphs of Oscar Wilde's *The Picture of Dorian Gray*. We've taken out all the nouns. How easy is it to understand what's going on?

> *The _____ was filled with the rich _____ of _____, and when the light summer _____ stirred amidst the _____ of the _____, there came through the open _____ the heavy _____ of the _____, or the more delicate _____ of the pink-flowering _____.*
>
> *From the _____ of the _____ of Persian _____ on which _____ was lying, smoking, as was his custom, innumerable _____, _____ _____ _____ could just catch the _____ of the honey-sweet and honey-coloured _____ of a _____, whose tremulous _____ seemed hardly able to bear the _____ of a _____ so flamelike as _____; and now and then the fantastic _____ of _____ in _____ flitted across the long tussore-silk _____ that were stretched in front of the huge _____, producing a kind of momentary Japanese _____, and making _____ think of those pallid, jade-faced _____ of _____ who, through the _____ of an _____ that is necessarily immobile, seek to convey the _____ of _____ and _____. The sullen _____ of the _____ shouldering their way through the long unmown _____, or circling with monotonous insistence round the dusty gilt _____ of the straggling _____, seemed to make the _____ more oppressive. The dim _____ of _____ was like the bourdon _____ of a distant _____.*

Difficult, isn't it? You can take an educated guess at what may go in some of the gaps, but in other cases you haven't a clue.

Nouns are central to people's understanding of what you speak and write, and so pay careful attention to them.

The following sections describe the various types of nouns.

Concrete nouns

Concrete nouns name the following:

- ✔ **Objects:** For example, 'table', 'chair', 'desk', 'pencil'.
- ✔ **People:** For example, 'man', 'woman', 'doctor', 'child', 'shopkeeper'.
- ✔ **Places:** For example, 'church', 'bathroom', 'river', 'school', 'office'.

Abstract nouns

These nouns name things you can't see, hear, touch, taste or smell: for example, 'anger', 'sadness', 'amusement', 'depression', 'parenthood', 'belief', 'thoughtfulness' and so on.

Proper nouns

Proper nouns always begin with a capital letter and name the following specific things:

- ✔ **Events:** For example, 'Graduation Day', 'Teaching Conference', 'Olympic Games' and the ever-popular 'Nudge a Judge Day' (at Lincoln's Inn, London).

- ✔ **Occasions:** For example, religious ones such as 'Easter Sunday', 'Eid', 'Yom Kippur' and 'Wesak'; royal ones including 'Trooping the Colour' and 'State Opening of Parliament'; and public holidays such as 'May Day' and less public ones such as 'Howl at the Moon Day' (26 October, if you're interested).

- ✔ **People:** For example, 'John Milton', the 'Queen' and 'Bridget Jones'.

- ✔ **Places:** For example, 'Birmingham', 'Boring, Oregon', 'Regent's Park' and 'Shakespeare's Globe Theatre'.

- ✔ **Publications, theatre productions, films and so on:** For example, *Dombey and Son*, *Dinosaur Attack Magazine*, *Dirty Dancing* and *Die Hard*.

Pronouns

Pronouns stand in for nouns (for example, 'I', 'you', 'he'/'she'/'it', 'we', 'you', 'they') to avoid repetition. For example:

> *George went to the theatre with Suzanne. When **they** arrived, George took Suzanne to the bar and bought **her** a drink.*

In this example, 'they' in the second sentence stands in for George and Suzanne and 'her' stands in for Suzanne.

Pronouns also include associated words such as 'mine', 'yours', 'his', 'hers', 'its', 'ours', 'theirs', 'me', 'him', 'her' and so on. For example:

> *'This book is mine,' said Helen. 'That one is yours.'*

The word 'mine' stands in for Helen, and you understand this because Helen is speaking. The 'yours' refers to the book of the person to whom Helen is speaking.

Collective nouns

These words name groups or collections (for example, 'choir', 'team', 'regiment', 'class', 'jury', 'orchestra', 'band'). Although these nouns include more than one person or object, you treat them as singular nouns when writing, and so you write 'an orchestra' or 'the class'.

This aspect is important when making sure that the subject and the verb of a sentence agree – more about that in the later section 'Working with Sentences'.

Compound nouns

You make compound nouns by combining two or more nouns to create a new one (for example, 'brother-in-law', 'court-martial', 'maidservant').

Non-countable nouns

You won't be surprised to hear that non-countable nouns are ones that can't be numbered. For that reason, they don't have a plural form (for example, 'music', 'cotton', 'furniture', 'sand').

Verbal nouns (gerunds)

You form these nouns from verbs by adding the suffix 'ing' (for example, 'swimming', 'running', 'mowing', 'cutting', 'feeling' and so on).

Take care that you distinguish between gerunds and *present participles* (the -ing form) of the verb, which take exactly the same form. For example:

- ✔ **Swimming is my favourite sport.** Here, the word 'swimming' is a verbal noun.

- ✔ **Paul nearly drowned while he was swimming.** Here, 'swimming' is a verb.

The words are exactly the same but their function is different.

Look at the following sentences and identify which of the 'ing' words are verbs and which are nouns:

- ✔ The farmer was used to killing chickens.

- ✔ Frances loves running.

- ✔ Refereeing had always been Terence's dream.

> ✔ Skydiving is a dangerous activity.
>
> ✔ He was driving erratically.

Here are the answers:

> ✔ The farmer was used to killing chickens. (Verb)
>
> ✔ Frances loves running. (Gerund)
>
> ✔ Refereeing had always been Terence's dream. (Gerund)
>
> ✔ Skydiving is a dangerous activity. (Gerund)
>
> ✔ He was driving erratically. (Verb)

Visiting the venue of verbs

A simple definition of verbs is that they're *doing* words. In terms of carrying meaning, they're the second most important type of word (after nouns).

We now look at the same Oscar Wilde passage as we quote in the preceding section on nouns, but this time we remove the verbs:

The studio _____ _____ with the rich odour of roses, and when the light summer wind _____ amidst the trees of the garden, there _____ through the open door the heavy scent of the lilac, or the more delicate perfume of the pink-flowering thorn.

From the corner of the divan of Persian saddle-bags on which he _____ _____, _____, as _____ his custom, innumerable cigarettes, Lord Henry Wotton _____ just _____ the gleam of the honey-sweet and honey-coloured blossoms of a laburnum, whose tremulous branches _____ hardly _____ to _____ the burden of a beauty so flamelike as theirs; and now and then the fantastic shadows of birds in flight _____ across the long tussore-silk curtains that _____ _____ in front of the huge window, _____ a kind of momentary Japanese effect, and _____ him _____ those pallid, jade-faced painters of Tokyo who, through the medium of an art that _____ necessarily immobile, _____ _____ the sense of swiftness and motion. The sullen murmur of the bees _____ their way through the long unmown grass, or _____ with monotonous insistence round the dusty gilt horns of the straggling woodbine, _____ _____ the stillness more oppressive. The dim roar of London _____ like the bourdon note of a distant organ.

Although this passage is fairly hard to read, because the verbs carry quite a lot of information, when you look at the surrounding nouns and other information, you can more easily fit the verbs that make sense into the gaps.

In the following sections, we discuss what verbs tell you about.

Physical actions

These verbs tell you how people or things are moving, or what they're doing. For example:

> Ursula **purchases** a cup of coffee and a slice of cake.
>
> The boy **leaps** across the ditch.
>
> The footballer **passes** the ball to the centre forward, who **scores** a goal.

The words in bold type are all verbs and tell you what actions people are doing.

Mental actions

These verbs work in exactly the same way as physical actions, but show you what's going on inside a person's head. For example:

> The writer **selects** his words with care.
>
> Kylie **ponders** what to do next.
>
> The Prime Minister **considers** his options.

The verb 'to be'

'To be' is an essential verb. Instead of telling you about actions, it simply states that something exists, as follows:

> 'I **am**', 'you **are**', 'he/she/it **is**'
>
> 'I **was**', 'you **were**', 'he/she/it **was**'
>
> 'I **have been**', 'you **have been**', 'he/she/it **has been**'
>
> 'I **will be**', 'you **will be**', 'he/she/it **will be**'

You rarely use 'to be' on its own but usually in conjunction with other verbs; it helps them and for this reason is known as an *auxiliary verb*. For example:

I **am** walking.

She **was** playing.

They **had been** helping their mother.

We **will be** flying to Paris tomorrow.

In each of these examples, the verb 'to be' assists another verb to create meaning, by telling you when certain events happened or will happen.

The verb 'to have'

The verb 'to have' is also really important. It's more often used on its own than the verb 'to be' (for example: I have a cold; he has a BMW; she has a diamond necklace), but it is also used – like the verb 'to be' – as an *auxiliary verb*. For example:

I **have** eaten.

They **had** driven.

We **will have** finished.

It also often acts as an auxiliary verb to help out the other auxiliary verb 'to be'. For example:

I **have** been.

I **had** been.

I **will have** been.

Other important things to know about verbs

In this section, we gather together some of the other aspects of verbs and their uses that you need to know:

✔ **Infinitive:** The infinitive is the 'to . . . ' form of the verb. Every single verb has this form, for example 'to smoke', 'to forget', 'to shout', 'to outwit' and so on.

✔ **Verb tenses:** All verbs have three main tenses:

– **Present tense (for things that are happening now):** For example, 'I eat' (simple present), 'I am eating' (present continuous), 'I have eaten' (present perfect), 'I have been eating' (present perfect continuous).

– **Past tense (for things that have happened):** For example, 'I ate' (simple past), 'I was eating' (past continuous), 'I had eaten' (past perfect), 'I had been eating' (past perfect continuous).

– **Future tense (for things that are going to happen):** For example, 'I will eat' (simple future), 'I will be eating' (future continuous), 'I will have eaten' (future perfect), 'I will have been eating' (future perfect continuous).

Notice how these different verb forms work – there is a straightforward formula (yes, language has formulae as well as maths!) for each:

– The simple forms = subject + verb

– The continuous forms = subject + relevant form of the verb 'to be' + present participle of main verb

– The perfect forms = subject + relevant form of the verb 'to have' + past participle of main verb

– The perfect continuous forms = subject + relevant form of the verb 'to be' + the present participle

Try creating examples of each of these forms for yourself, using the verbs 'to write', 'to undo' and 'to steal'.

Here are the answers:

✔ **Present tense (simple present):** I write, I undo, I steal; **(present continuous):** I am writing, I am undoing, I am stealing; **(present perfect):** I have written, I have undone, I have stolen; **(present perfect continuous):** I have been writing, I have been undoing, I have been stealing.

✔ **Past tense (simple past):** I wrote, I undid, I stole; **(past continuous):** I was writing, I was undoing, I was stealing; **(past perfect):** I had written, I had undone, I had stolen; **(past perfect continuous):** I had been writing, I had been undoing, I had been stealing.

✔ **Future tense (simple future):** I will write, I will undo, I will steal; **(future continuous):** I will be writing, I will be undoing, I will be stealing; **(future perfect):** I will have written, I will have undone, I will have stolen; **(future perfect continuous):** I will have been writing, I will have been undoing, I will have been stealing.

✔ **Subjects:** Every verb has a subject: the person or the thing that's doing the verb. So, in the sentence 'David slept', 'David' is the subject. In the sentence 'We rowed', 'we' is the subject.

✔ **Objects:** Sometimes verbs also have what is called an object – the person or thing that the verb is done to or for. So, in the sentence 'Sarah ate a peach', the peach is what the eating is done to! There are the two types of objects:

   – **Direct objects:** The person or thing _to_ whom the verb is done. So, in the sentence 'Terry kissed Virginia', 'Virginia' is the direct object. In the sentence 'Roger caught the train', 'train' is the direct object.

   – **Indirect objects:** The person or thing _for_ whom the verb is done (as opposed to the person or thing _to_ whom the verb is done). So, in the sentence 'Elsie read her grandchildren a story', 'grandchildren' is the indirect object of the verb 'to read' (and 'story' is the direct object). In the sentence 'The teacher gave the class a punishment', 'the class' is the indirect object of the verb 'to give' ('punishment' is the direct object).

✔ **Transitive verbs:** Transitive verbs are verbs that can take a direct object. Whenever a verb can be done to something, then it is a transitive verb. So, in the sentence 'The boy kicked the football', 'kicked' is a transitive verb – the football is the direct object of the kicking. In the sentence 'The football broke the window', 'broke' is transitive – the breaking is done to the window.

✔ **Intransitive verbs:** Intransitive verbs can't have a direct object. Examples of intransitive verbs are 'to rain', 'to snow', 'to protest', 'to speak', 'to die'. You can speak, you can even speak loudly or provocatively, but you can't perform the action on anything. It may snow, it may even snow thickly, but it doesn't perform the action on anything. Try adding objects to some of these verbs and you'll see that it just doesn't work. For example:

   The old man died the leg.

   It snowed the girl.

   The politician spoke the building.

Be careful, though. Don't mistake intransitive verbs with the simple sentences like 'I make', 'The girl eats' or 'The car stalled'. These verbs are used without an object, but that doesn't mean that they can't take an object if you want them to. Intransitive verbs can't take an object, no matter what.

✔ **Active sentences:** In active sentences, the subject is the person or thing that does the verb. If you write 'Florence climbed Mount Everest', Florence does the climbing. In the sentence 'The dog ate the bone', the dog does the eating. It is often easiest and best to use active sentences, because they are the most direct way of communicating your meaning. Pretty much all the way through this book you'll find we've used active sentences, because we want you to access this information in the clearest and easiest way. Which of these sentences works more clearly and concisely?

The man hit the nail in using a hammer.

A hammer was used by the man to hit in the nail.

Both sentences convey the same information to the reader, but the first is more direct.

✔ **Passive sentences:** In passive sentences, all normal rules are reversed; the subject isn't the doer of the verb but has the verb done to it. So, if you write 'Mount Everest was climbed by Florence', Mount Everest is the subject, but Mount Everest isn't doing the climbing, Florence is. Similarly, in the sentence 'The bone was eaten by the dog', the subject (the bone) doesn't do the eating.

The word 'by' in each sentence indicates the person or thing that's the doer of the verb. This is helpful, because it helps you to understand the way the sentence works and the relationship between the different parts of the sentence. As we said, active sentences are a more direct way of conveying information, but passive sentences can be used to provide some interesting variation in your writing, and can help you choose which aspects of a sentence you want to emphasise. The greatest emphasis in a sentence is always on the subject, so passive sentences can be useful.

Messing with modifiers

Modifiers is the technical term for adjectives and adverbs – and adjectival and adverbial phrases. They're so called because they modify the effects of nouns and verbs: adjectives add to nouns; adverbs add to verbs.

Here we look once more at the passage from Oscar Wilde that we consider in the earlier sections 'Noticing nouns, proper nouns and pronouns' and 'Visiting the venue of verbs'. This time we remove all the modifiers:

> *The studio was filled with the _____ odour of roses, and when the _____ _____ wind stirred amidst the trees of the garden, there came through the _____ door the _____ scent of the lilac, or the _____ _____ perfume of the _____ thorn.*
>
> *From the corner of the divan of _____ saddle-bags on which he was lying, smoking, as was his custom, _____ cigarettes, Lord Henry Wotton could just catch the gleam of the _____ and _____ blossoms of a laburnum, whose _____ branches seemed _____ able to bear the burden of a beauty so _____ as theirs; and now and then the _____ shadows of birds _____ flitted across the _____ _____ curtains that were stretched in front of the _____ window, producing a kind of _____ _____ effect, and making him think of those _____, _____ painters of Tokyo who, through the medium of an art that is _____ immobile, seek to convey the sense of swiftness and motion. The _____ murmur of the bees shouldering their way through the _____ _____ grass, or circling with _____ insistence round the _____ _____ horns of the _____ woodbine, seemed to make the stillness more oppressive. The _____ roar of London was like the ____ note of a _____ organ.*

As you can see, modifiers add little in terms of understanding the core meaning. You can read this passage largely without a pause and still gain a clear sense of what it's about. What the passage lacks, however, is colour and tone in the writing. Even the great Oscar Wilde appears a little bland without the colour of the modifiers.

Taking care with modifiers

The use of adjectives and adverbs can lead to many interesting and varied effects in writing. But you do need to use modifiers in moderation, because adding too many makes your writing overly rich and indirect. At their worst, they can also lead to imprecise thought about language.

The novelist Stephen King, in particular, declares war on adverbs, which he sees as nothing more (on most occasions) than an excuse for not choosing the right verb. Consider how much more effective a passage is when you write 'he stammered' (rather than 'he said haltingly'), 'she whispered' (as opposed to 'she said quietly') and so on, saving a whole load of repeated 'saids'!

Adjectives

Adjectives modify (or add to) nouns and you often make them by adding endings to other words (nouns, verbs and even other adjectives). Usually you can tell an adjective by its ending. We show the main endings for adjectives in Table 6-1.

Table 6-1	Commonly Used Adjective Endings
Ending	*Examples*
'able'/'ible'	comfortable, portable, edible, flexible
'al'	comical, exceptional, tyrannical
'ful'	fearful, tuneful, grateful
'ic'	public, historic, gastric
'ive'	furtive, expressive, impressive
'less'	clueless, featureless, useless
'ous'/'ious'/'eous'	adventurous, insidious, aqueous
'y'	icy, oily, hardy

Sometimes when adding the endings in Table 6-1 you need to change the root word (see Table 6-2).

Table 6-2   Changes to Root Words When Adding Adjective Endings

Adjective Ending	Root Word	Change Needed	Adjective
'al'	nature	drop the 'e'	natural
'y'	ice	drop the 'e'	icy
'ful'	beauty	change the 'y' to an 'i'	beautiful
'ous'	mystery	change the 'y' to an 'i'	mysterious
'ic'	history	drop the 'y'	historic

Adverbs

Adverbs modify (or add to) verbs. You form them in several ways, but the best approach is always to begin with the related adjective. Table 6-3 shows the various methods.

Table 6-3   Creating Adverbs

Rule	Adjectives	Adverbs
In most cases, simply add 'ly' to the adjective	formal colourful cheap	formally colourfully cheaply
If the adjective ends with a 'y', remove the 'y' and add 'ily'	easy happy groggy	easily happily groggily
If the adjective ends with 'able', 'ible' or 'le', replace the 'e' with a 'y'	probable possible gentle	probably possibly gently
If the adjective ends in 'ic', add 'ally' Note this exception: 'public' to 'publicly'	generic caustic economic	generically caustically economically
In a few cases, the adjective and adverb are the same	early fast hard high late near straight wrong	early fast hard high late near straight wrong

Pondering prepositions

Prepositions are words that indicate where things are and they normally deal with time, place and direction:

- ✔ **Time:** These prepositions tell you *when* something has occurred:

  – Peter brushed his teeth **before** going to bed.

  – **While** queuing for the till, Katy realised that she'd forgotten her purse.

  – **After** a while you'll get used to it.

- ✔ **Place:** These prepositions tell you *where* something has occurred:

  – The dog lurked **beneath** the table.

  – It is on the shelf **above** you.

  – The butcher's shop is **beside** the bakery.

- ✔ **Direction:** These prepositions show you the way in which something is moving:

  – The train steamed **through** the tunnel.

  – The balloon floated **upwards**.

  – The girl fell **down**.

Considering conjunctions

Conjunctions are words or phrases that you use to join sentences and elements of sentences together. These words usually serve to demonstrate how the joined sentences or elements relate to each other. They come in three varieties, as we describe in this section.

Co-ordinating conjunctions

These conjunctions join sentence elements that are the same as each other. They can join words, phrases or clauses, but must always join like with like.

The co-ordinating conjunctions are 'and', 'but', 'for', 'so', 'nor', 'or' and 'yet'.

Here are some examples:

> bread **and** butter
>
> under the fence **or** over the wall
>
> He came **but** she left.

Subordinating conjunctions

This kind of conjunction joins clauses and shows how they relate to one another. For example:

> I will go to the cinema **after** I have eaten my lunch.

The dependent clause 'I have eaten my lunch' is connected to the main clause 'I will go to the cinema' by the subordinating conjunction 'after', which demonstrates how these two elements connect.

Here's another example:

> He drowned **because** he could not swim.

The subordinate clause 'he could not swim' is connected by the conjunction 'because' to the independent clause 'He drowned', demonstrating the logical connection between the two.

Many subordinating conjunctions exist, but here are the main ones: after, although, as, as if, as well as, as much as, as though, because, before, by the time that, even if, even though, in order that, if, in case, once, only if, provided that, since, so that, than, that, though, until, unless, when, whatever, wherever, where, while and so on.

Correlative conjunctions

These conjunctions serve the same purpose as subordinating conjunctions, but they come in pairs. For example:

> either . . . or
>
> neither . . . nor
>
> both . . . and

not only . . . but also

So you can write:

Meredith liked **neither** doughnuts **nor** cabbage.

Keith loved **both** cricket **and** rugby.

Clawing at clauses

Clauses are the smallest unit of language capable of expressing a complete thought. In other words, they must contain at least a subject and a verb. You can divide clauses into main clauses and subordinate clauses.

Main clauses

Main clauses are formed, at minimum, of a subject and a verb, but may include more. Here are some examples of clauses:

William slept (subject + verb)

William slept soundly (subject + verb + adverb)

William slept soundly on the sofa (subject + verb + adverb + preposition of place + direct object)

Main clauses are always capable of standing on their own. In other words, a main clause is always a complete sentence.

Subordinate clauses

Subordinate clauses always depend upon a main clause. Without being attached to a main clause, a subordinate clause doesn't make sense.

Like main clauses, subordinate clauses can be of varying lengths and complexity, but at a minimum they always include a subordinating conjunction, a subject and a verb. For example:

However he felt . . . (subordinating conjunction + subject + verb)

However he felt about Mary . . . (subordinating conjunction + subject + verb + direct object)

However he felt about the beautiful Mary . . . (subordinating conjunction + subject + verb + definite article + adjective + direct object)

As you can see, although each of these examples fulfils the basic requirement of a clause (that it has at least a subject and a verb), the subordinating conjunction shows that it can't stand alone – the reader doesn't have enough information for the text to make sense. In order to complete meaning, the subordinate clause must be attached to a main clause. So, you can complete any of the above examples with the addition of, say, 'Tom knew he had to leave'.

Fitting phrases into your writing

A *phrase* is a small group of words that forms a meaningful unit within a clause (see the preceding section for more on clauses). The following examples of the different types of phrases show them within full clauses. In each case we highlight the phrase in italic:

- ✔ **Noun phrase:** These are constructed around a single noun (check out the earlier section 'Noticing nouns, proper nouns and pronouns' if you need a reminder about nouns). For example:

  – *A vast tree* dominated the park. **[focus on 'tree']**

  – He was *listening to a symphony* about life and death. **[focus on 'symphony']**

- ✔ **Verb phrase:** These are the verbal part of a clause (we cover verbs earlier in the 'Visiting the venue of verbs' section). For example:

  – He *was running* for the bus. **[focus on 'running']**

  – I *am going* to the theatre tonight. **[focus on 'going']**

- ✔ **Adjectival phrase:** These are constructed around an adjective. For example:

  – Theo has a *very unusual* tattoo. **[focus on 'unusual']**

  – She was a *highly enthusiastic* rugby supporter. **[focus on 'enthusiastic']**

  We describe adjectives (and adverbs) in the earlier section 'Messing with modifiers'.

- ✔ **Adverbial phrase:** These are constructed around an adverb. For example:

  – The train was progressing *very slowly*. **[focus on 'slowly']**

– If the fire alarm rings make your way *as calmly as possible* to the fire exit. [**focus on 'calmly'**]

✔ **Prepositional phrase:** These are built on a preposition (see the earlier section 'Pondering prepositions'), which always comes at the beginning of the phrase. For example:

– John lived *in the middle of London.* [**focus on 'middle'**]

– The train track ran *beside the most beautiful bay.* [**focus on 'beside'**]

Working with Sentences

We find that the most useful ways to think about sentences are from the point of view of their structure and their purpose.

Viewing sentences by structure

Considering sentences by structure involves you looking at the component parts that go into making them up.

Simple sentences

These sentences consist of a single main clause (flip to the earlier section 'Clawing at clauses' to read about clauses). At their most straightforward, therefore, simple sentences consist solely of a subject and a verb, but they can incorporate more:

Oliver sat. (Subject + verb)

Oliver sat on the chair. (Subject + verb + prepositional phrase)

Oliver sat uncomfortably on the chair. (Subject + verb + adverb + prepositional phrase)

Compound sentences

Compound sentences consist of multiple main clauses that are joined together using conjunctions, punctuation or both:

Oliver sat while Fran made him a drink. (Main clause + conjunction + main clause)

Oliver sat; he was too tired to stand. (Main clause + punctuation + main clause)

Oliver sat; he was too tired to stand, but he knew he had to get up again soon. (Main clause + punctuation + main clause + conjunction + main clause)

Complex sentences

These sentences consist of at least one main clause and one subordinate clause:

Roger, who was an expert on the novels of Jane Austen, was invited to give a television interview. (Start of main clause + subordinate clause + conclusion of main clause)

The moral of the story, should you wish to know, is to treat others as you would like to be treated yourself. (Start of main clause + subordinate clause + conclusion of main clause)

Compound-complex (or complex-compound) sentences

These sentences consist of multiple main clauses and at least one subordinate clause:

Although I like to go shopping, I couldn't go yesterday, and I prefer to go with friends. (Subordinate clause + main clause + second main clause)

We decided that the programme was on too late, but our children, who really wanted to see it, persuaded us to change our minds. (Main clause + beginning of second main clause + subordinate clause + conclusion of second main clause)

Complex to the max

Complex sentences can be truly, deeply complex. If you want to have a go at deciphering it, here's a complex sentence from the master of complex sentences – Henry James:

'The fact to be in possession of was, therefore, that his old friend, the youngest of several daughters of a poor country parson, had, at the age of twenty, on taking service for the first time in the schoolroom, come up to London, in trepidation, to answer in person an advertisement that had already placed her in brief correspondence with the advertiser.'

Looking at sentences by purpose

When classifying sentences according to their purposes, you can do so in four ways.

Statement sentences

These sentences make simple declarations or statements. For example:

> I think U2 is the greatest rock band of all time.

> I want to know how that works.

> Justine bought a hair-clip.

Interrogative sentences

These sentences ask questions.

They often use question words ('how', 'where', 'who', 'when', 'why', 'what') and always invert the subject and verb (such as 'are you' rather than 'you are'). For example:

> What are you talking about?

> Are you happy?

> How, under those circumstances, can we possibly go on holiday?

Exclamatory sentences

These sentences are generally a more emphatic form of the statement sentence. For example:

> I never want to hear that again!

> That is a really bad idea.

> No, you can't go to the pub.

Imperative sentences

These sentences give orders. For example:

> Turn left at the church, and then go straight ahead for 100 metres.

> Hurry up, Jane.

> Read as far as page 127.

Having a Go: Practice Tests

The grammar part of the Professional Skills Tests takes the form of a multiple-choice paper in three sections. Each section is in the form of a passage with blanks. You have to fill in these blanks by selecting the correct answer from a set of four possible options.

Specific instructions are provided at the start of each section of this part of the test, along with a sentence giving some context details about the passage you're working on.

The guidance given on the tests indicates that this section of the Literacy test is devised to test your ability to recognise where writing does and doesn't meet the conventions of written Standard English. In each case you have to complete the passage with selections from multiple-choice options, only one of which is correct. You have to read carefully to ensure that you make the correct choice.

In every case your answer needs to fulfil the following criteria:

- ✔ Comply with the rules of written Standard English.
- ✔ Make good sense within the context of the passage.
- ✔ Reflect the style and tone of the passage.
- ✔ Express meaning accurately, clearly and concisely.

Test A

This extract is from a letter to the parents of a child who has been awarded a school prize.

Dear Mr and Mrs Binns

We are delighted to inform you that your daughter Sarah has been awarded the Frances Dadds Cup in recognition of her work in the local community.

_____

_____.

   A) At Townville High School we value the work our pupils do in the local community, which we value highly.

   B) At Townville High School such work is highly valued.

C) At Townville High School it is very valuable to do such work.

D) At Townville High School our pupils are valued in this work.

Sarah was part of a team of Year 8 pupils

_____.

A) who has participated on a weekly basis in a community action programme.

B) which has participated on a weekly basis in a community action programme.

C) who have participated on a weekly basis in a community action programme.

D) which have participated on a weekly basis in a community action programme.

Sarah worked with dedication throughout the year, and showed commitment even when personal difficulties _____ prevented her.

A) could of

B) would have

C) could have

D) would of

There _____ from the staff in supporting this award.

A) was unanimous

B) are unanimity

C) are unanimous

D) was unanimity

Test B

This extract is from a school newsletter informing pupils of forthcoming school trips in which they may want to participate.

This term _____ a wide variety of trips taking place.

    A) there are

    B) there is

    C) there was

    D) there were

Make sure you read the following information carefully _____.

    A) as not all of these trips are open to pupils from all year groups.

    B) as not all of these trips is open to pupils from all year groups.

    C) as pupils from all year groups are not open to all trips.

    D) as not all year groups are open to pupils' trips.

Some of these trips will require a financial contribution.

    A) If so, make sure your parents/carers are asked before you apply.

    B) If so, make sure before you ask your parents/carers to apply.

    C) If so, make sure you ask your parents/carers before you apply.

    D) If so, ask your parents/carers to apply.

No applications to take part in any trips will be accepted without _____.

    A) the consent from your parents/carers.

    B) the consent of your parents/carers.

    C) the consent by your parents/carers.

    D) the consent with your parents/carers.

Checking out the Practice Test Answers

Here we identify the correct answers to the tests in the preceding section, with explanations as to why they're right. We also provide guidance on why the other options aren't appropriate.

Test A

This extract is from a letter to the parents of a child who has been awarded a school prize.

Dear Mr and Mrs Binns

We are delighted to inform you that your daughter Sarah has been awarded the Frances Dadds Cup in recognition of her work in the local community.

_____

_____.

Correct answer: B) At Townville High School such work is highly valued. **This sentence is unambiguous. It clearly states the value the school places upon the community action work its pupils engage in.**

A) At Townville High School we value the work our pupils do in the local community, which we value highly. **This answer can't be correct owing to the awkward repetition of the subordinate clause 'which we value highly'. The value of the pupils' work has already been established earlier in the sentence, and so this clause is redundant.**

C) At Townville High School it is very valuable to do such work. **This sentence creates ambiguity, because it implies that this kind of community action is valuable in the context of the school but may not be considered valuable elsewhere. It also implies that the value of the work depends in some way upon the school.**

D) At Townville High School our pupils are valued in this work. **This sentence doesn't make sense. The passive form of the verb 'are valued' doesn't fit with the active**

> **intention of the sentence, which is to express the value the school places on pupils' community action work.**

Sarah was part of a team of Year 8 pupils

_____.

Correct answer: B) which has participated on a weekly basis in a community action programme. **This must be the correct answer, because the subject of the sentence is 'a team of Year 8 pupils'. The word 'team' is a collective noun and therefore functions as a singular noun. For this reason it requires the singular form of the verb 'has'. It's also an impersonal noun, and therefore 'which' rather than 'who' is the appropriate word choice.**

> A) who has participated on a weekly basis in a community action programme. **The use of the word 'who' is inappropriate in relation to the collective noun 'team'.**

> C) who have participated on a weekly basis in a community action programme. **Two errors exist in this answer. First, the use of the word 'who' is inappropriate in relation to the collective noun 'team'; second, the 'have' form of the verb is plural in this context and can't, therefore, be used with the collective noun 'team'.**

> D) which have participated on a weekly basis in a community action programme. **In this answer, although the use of 'which' to refer to the 'team' is correct, the plural form of the verb 'have' is incorrect.**

Sarah worked with dedication throughout the year, and showed commitment even when personal difficulties _____ prevented her.

Correct answer: C) could have. In English, modal verbs such as 'could have' (or the contracted version 'could've') are often incorrectly written using their phonetic equivalent 'could of'.

> A) could of. **This phrase must be written 'could have'.**

> B) would have. **Here the verb 'would' is incorrectly used.**

> D) would of. **Here are two errors: the verb 'would' is incorrectly used and 'of' is written instead of 'have'.**

There _____ from the staff in supporting this award.

Correct answer: D) was unanimity. This answer is correct because in order to make the clause make sense, a main verb and a subject are necessary. The subject of the sentence is 'unanimity' – an abstract noun. Then, because this is a singular noun, a singular form of the verb 'was' is required.

A) was unanimous. **Although the singular verb form is correct, unanimous is an adjective and can't, therefore, serve as the subject of the sentence.**

B) are unanimity. **In this case, the subject noun 'unanimity' is correct, but the plural form of the verb 'are' is incorrect.**

C) are unanimous. **In this answer, the errors in A) and B) are combined.**

Test B

This extract is from a school newsletter informing pupils of forthcoming school trips in which they may want to participate.

This term _____ a wide variety of trips taking place.

Correct answer: B) there is. The subject of the sentence 'variety of trips' is a collective singular noun, and so requires the singular form of the verb.

A) there are. **As the subject of the sentence is singular, the plural form of the verb ('are') can't be used.**

C) there was. **Although the singular form of the verb is correct, the contextualising information makes clear that this newsletter is about trips that are yet to take place. The past tense form of the verb is, therefore, incorrect.**

D) there were. **The plural form of the verb is incorrect, as explained in relation to answer A). As in the previous answer, the contextualising information makes clear that**

this newsletter is about trips that are yet to take place. The past tense form of the verb is, therefore, incorrect.

Make sure you read the following information carefully _____.

Correct answer: A) as not all of these trips are open to pupils from all year groups. **This is the correct answer because it accurately conveys that some trips are open only to particular year groups.**

B) as not all of these trips is open to pupils from all year groups. **This cannot be correct, because the singular form of the verb 'is' does not agree with the plural noun 'trips'.**

C) as pupils from all year groups are not open to all trips. **This is incorrect because the emphasis is wrongly placed. Trips can be open to pupils, but pupils cannot be open to trips.**

D) as not all year groups are open to pupils' trips. **This is incorrect, as it implies that there are year groups that are not eligible to attend any trips.**

Some of these trips will require a financial contribution. _____.

Correct answer: C) If so, make sure you ask your parents/carers before you apply. **The active form of the verb works best in this case and the sentence accurately captures the requirement to gain parents'/carers' permission.**

A) If so, make sure your parents/carers are asked before you apply. **The use of the passive form of the verb ('are asked') creates a difficulty here. This sentence is unclear about who's to ask the parents/carers before applying.**

B) If so, make sure before you ask your parents/carers to apply. **Here the sense of the sentence is wrong. This sentence implies that the reason why the pupil or their parents/carers would apply for these trips is because they require a financial contribution.**

D) If so, ask your parents/carers to apply. **Here, again, the sense of the sentence is wrong. This sentence implies that if the trip doesn't require a financial contribution, pupils may apply without consulting their parents/carers.**

No applications to take part in any trips will be accepted without

_____.

Correct answer: B) the consent of your parents/carers. **This sentence demonstrates possession. The consent required to attend the trips belongs to the parents/carers. Therefore, it must be 'the consent of your parents/carers'.**

A) the consent from your parents/carers.

C) the consent by your parents/carers.

D) the consent with your parents/carers.

You can't use 'from', 'by' or 'with' to express possession, and so these words can't be the correct answer.

Chapter 7

Considering the Comprehension Test

*T*he comprehension section of the Skills Test is all about your ability to read accurately and to respond to your reading. To pass the test (and of course to work effectively as a teacher) you need to be proficient in reading quickly and accurately and inferring meaning, so that you can make secure judgements about the meaning of written text.

In this chapter, we present a process for productive reading of the test passages, and describe the types of texts and questions that you're going to encounter. After all, forewarned is forearmed!

Meeting the Comprehension Test

To help you have the best chance of success in the comprehension section of the test, we identify three crucial aspects as follows:

> ✔ **A process for reading in the test:** When you go into the test with a clear idea of how to approach your reading, you're in a much calmer and clearer headspace, and that can only help you to respond accurately (see the later section 'Following a process for tackling the test' for

details). As someone planning a career in teaching, you'll soon appreciate the importance of understanding effective and efficient processes.

✔ **The types of text you're likely to encounter:** In the later section 'Getting an idea of the passages', we look at the types of material you face in the test. Doing so helps you to be confident of the kind of material you'll be dealing with.

✔ **The types of question in the test:** The comprehension section of the test has a much wider variety of question types than any other section of the Literacy or the Numeracy Key Skills Tests. Therefore, we look closely at these and what you have to do in each case in the later section 'Examining the questions'.

As we suggest in Chapter 3, whenever you're studying for the Literacy test keep a dictionary and a thesaurus handy: no shame exists in needing to check up on the meaning of a word. While you're working on practice materials you want to have all the support you need at hand rather than struggling to complete the materials because you don't know the meaning of one or two words.

In fact, after you successfully gain your Qualified Teacher Status and take up a post as a teacher, keep a dictionary and thesaurus as part of your basic teacher's equipment. Doing so helps you with those day-to-day language problems you need to sort out – and you're modelling good study practices to your pupils as well.

Comprehending comprehension

At its most basic level, *comprehension* is about understanding what you're reading. But always remember the different levels of meaning that go into building up your understanding.

This process happens at three general levels:

✔ **Word level:** The work you do as a reader to make sense of individual words. Refer to what we write about phonics in Chapter 4 – the way you make connections between letters and combinations of letters and sounds – and the different ways in which you come to an understanding of what particular words mean in context.

✔ **Sentence level:** The next level of meaning in a text comprises much of the material we look at in Chapter 5, about the role of punctuation, and in Chapter 6 about how clauses, phrases and whole sentences create meaning. Plus, don't forget about the four major word classes (nouns, verbs, adjectives and adverbs) and the different types of meaning they convey.

✔ **Text level:** The final level of meaning is about the ways in which a whole text works together to create meaning – the sum of the parts. It can cover anything from very short texts (for example, advertisements, notes and letters) through medium-sized texts (articles and reports) to lengthy, full-blown texts (such as biographies, novels and academic texts).

Seeing how you make sense of writing

The strategies you use for gaining meaning at each of the levels in the preceding section vary greatly. On the one hand, phonics is great if you're trying to work out what an individual word says and how it sounds, but it isn't much use if you're trying to understand the meaning of *Hamlet*. On the other hand, thinking about the relationship between the subject and the object is great if you want to get into the nitty-gritty of what a particular sentence means, but doesn't help if you need to know what one of the words in that sentence means.

Success in this element of the test is all about matching your strategies to the demands of the different types of questions you face – and some questions will focus in on each of the three levels of meaning.

Comprehension isn't about a single thing, but is about the way that a set of different things work together to help you make sense of what you're reading.

Just to illustrate the point, try reading this passage:

Cna yuo raed tihs? Eonverye who can raed tihs rsaie yuor hnad. I cdnuolt blveiee taht I cluod aulaclty uesdnatnrd waht I was rdanieg. The pweor of the hmuan mind si phonemneal. Aoccdrnig to a rsearech taem at Cmabrigde Uinervtisy, it dseno't mtaetr in waht oerdr the ltteres in a wrod aepapr, the olny iproamtnt tihng is taht the frsit and lsat lteter be in the rghit pclae. The rset can be a taotl mses and you can siltl raed it whotuit a pboerlm. Tihs is bcuseae the huamn mnid deos not raed ervey lteter by istlef, but the wrod as a wlohe.

Surprisingly, you can make sense of it despite all the errors! Here's another example to illustrate the range of strategies you use when making sense of reading. Fill in the missing words in the following sentences:

- ✔ The sun rises in the East and sets in the _____.

- ✔ This animal is a klinger. This is another klinger. There are two _____.

- ✔ The flag is red, black and y _____.

Now think about the different kinds of knowledge you employ to help you complete the blanks.

In the first sentence you no doubt used your knowledge of the world. You know the way that movement of the heavenly bodies works, and so your experience of life tells you what word most likely goes at the end of the sentence. On this basis you can predict that the missing word is West without needing the word to be present.

In the second case you use a different kind of knowledge: your understanding of how the English language functions. A common way of forming plurals in English is to add an 's' at the end of the word, and so when you combine the first klinger with the second klinger you come up with two 'klingers' (which isn't a sentence we ever thought we'd be writing!).

In the third case you probably used a combination of three kinds of knowledge to build meaning and to predict the word 'yellow':

- ✔ **Logical connection:** The word has to combine with the adjectives 'red' and 'black' and so you predict that the missing word is a colour adjective.

- ✔ **Knowledge of the world:** Many flags are tricolours, and so when you see that the sentence is about a flag, you again predict that the missing word is a colour.

- ✔ **Initial phonic information:** The word begins with a 'y', which limits the particular colour to yellow. Without this cue, you'd have guessed the missing word was a colour, but not which one.

As you can see, comprehending comprehension requires you to understand that you have many resources at your disposal to help make sense of what you read. So, don't be intimidated. You already bring a lot of existing skills to the table when it comes to comprehension.

Following a process for tackling the test

The passage that you need to respond to in the Skills Test is between 600 and 700 words long. To give you a rough idea of what that looks like, this chapter so far runs to approximately 1,400 words and so the passage you'll be working on is about half that length. As a result, you have to read reasonably quickly, especially because you have a sequence of questions to respond to afterwards.

Despite the pressure of time, make absolutely sure that you read the passage more than once. For that reason, we recommend that you use the following three-stage process in the test:

1. **Carry out a first reading.** Read through the passage relatively quickly and without stopping. Don't stop over individual words that you don't understand or sentences that don't seem immediately clear. Press on, and often the initial difficulty is overcome. Besides, some of the questions require you to deal with the text as a whole, and so getting a sense of how the whole text works is important.

   Your initial reading helps you to:

   • Achieve an understanding of the passage as a whole

   • Gain an overview of the full range of issues it covers

   • Understand how the parts of the text relate to the whole

Don't be tempted at this stage to look at the questions and start trying to answer them. To do so without having read the passage all the way through in one go can be disastrous, because information occurring later in the passage may significantly modify what occurs early on.

2. **Read the questions.** Try to find out what the testers want you to do with the passage. Read through the questions so that you know what you're looking for in your targeted reading (in step 3). For this step, you're just mentally recalling sections of the passage that relate to the questions.

As you read the questions, separate out in your mind the ones that deal with specific extracts of the text and those that deal with the passage as a whole. Which questions can you answer quickly and easily, and which are going to take you more time – possibly even require further readings of the text? You can then decide which questions give you access to the largest number of marks the most quickly.

Remember your strategy. You don't have to answer the questions in the order in which they appear in the test paper. Go for the ones you can do quickest and easiest first to get a few quick marks under your belt.

3. **Undertake a targeted reading.** Focus on the sections of the text, the ideas in the text and the topics that the questions address. This time, you don't need to read the whole passage. Just read the sections of the passage you need in order to answer the questions and then answer them as you go along.

Whatever you do, don't panic. Start with the questions you are sure of. Don't waste time struggling with hard questions first – that only makes you worry. A few solid marks in the bank makes you feel like you're making good progress and builds confidence. Your subconscious mind will be working away in the background on some of the more difficult ones, and so leave the hardest questions until last. You can always guess in the last few seconds if you need to.

Getting an idea of the passages

The guidance for the test states that the single, complex text of 600–700 words is to be demanding. As befits a test aimed at people planning to enter the teaching profession, the passages are on issues relating to general issues in education, and as such they're accessible to people training to teach at primary or secondary level and in any subject area. If you want to see the kind of thing you have to respond to, take a look at publications in the general educational press or documents relating to education published by government agencies.

Keep yourself abreast of this kind of material by reading regularly in the educational press. Serious dailies such as *The Times*, the *Telegraph* and the *Guardian* regularly carry features on education, and reading these increases your confidence in handling this kind of text. Don't forget *The Times Educational Supplement*, a specific education publication that comes out each Friday. The website of the Department for Education (www.education.gov.uk) is also a useful source of information.

Read all these resources regularly, because if you're used to handling such materials, your confidence for the test is much greater.

Examining the questions

The comprehension test requires you to demonstrate a variety of skills:

- ✔ To identify the most important points of texts
- ✔ To infer and deduce meaning
- ✔ To distinguish facts from opinions
- ✔ To decide relative importance
- ✔ To present material from the original in different forms
- ✔ To retrieve information accurately
- ✔ To synthesise material from across the text
- ✔ To provide evidence to support or deny particular points of view

You may not be required to do all these things, but you'll certainly have to do a selection of them. Each correct response is awarded one mark.

In order to check out your ability to use the comprehension skills listed above, you can be asked a wide variety of types of question. In fact, the guidance identifies nine different kinds of question. These are in no particular order, so here goes. Take a deep breath!

✔ **Categorising statements:** Key categories are identified and you have to 'drag and drop' the provided statements into appropriate categories:

- There may be more statements than category options.

- An identified statement fits into only one of the category options.

- Multiple statements may fit into some of the category options.

- Some category options may not be appropriate for any of the statements.

✔ **Completing bullet-point lists:** You're supplied with a list of statements or points. You're also given the function of the bullet-point list you have to construct and the number of points you need to include. From this list of available options you're asked to:

- Select the most appropriate sentences or points for inclusion.

- Use them to construct your bullet-point list. This tests, in other words, your ability to identify the salient points from the passage relating to a particular topic. Remember that the statements on the list may be of different kinds:

  – Some are inappropriate for inclusion.

  – Some are appropriate for inclusion, but not as important as others.

- Your job is to create the best and most meaningful bullet-point list that you can.

✔ **Sequencing information:** You're provided with a list of statements and asked to place these statements in the order in which they should appear. This kind of question tests:

- Your logic as a reader.

- Your ability to sequence written material for meaning.

✔ **Presenting main points:** Some questions ask you to draw from a set of provided statements and construct the list that most accurately reflects the content of the text:

- You don't need to use all the statements.

- Some of the statements may be completely inappropriate.

- Other statements may be partially accurate but not fully reflect the meaning of the passage.

- Some of the statements may present popular opinions that relate to, but aren't contained in, the passage.

✔ **Matching summaries to text:** This type of question is based on summarising the meaning of sections of the text or the text as a whole. You have to make your selection from a set of options and identify the option that most closely reflects the meaning of the original text.

✔ **Identifying meanings of words and phrases:** Instead of concentrating on meaning at the sentence or text level, this type of question works at word and phrase levels. A word or short phrase from the original text is identified. Your role is to select from multiple-choice options the alternative word or phrase that most closely reflects the meaning of the word or phrase from the original text.

✔ **Evaluating statements about the text:** Some questions ask you to consider a range of statements and evaluate how far they're true in relation to the source text, or the extent to which the source text supports them as a point of view. You can be asked to rank these statements or place them in specified categories (for example, 'completely true', 'true to a point', 'untrue').

✔ **Selecting headings/sub-headings:** You're asked to select from a set of options the most suitable headings and/or sub-headings for organising the material of the source text.

✔ **Considering audience/readership:** You can be asked to establish a rank order for how important and/or useful the text would be to specified groups of readers.

Having a Go: Practice Tests

The comprehension part of the Professional Skills Tests comprises a single complex passage of between 600 and 700 words in length. It is followed by a sequence of questions asking you to respond to the meaning of the text.

Each question is worth a single mark.

Understood?

Test A

Passage

Well-trained teaching assistants are a key resource in many schools and are used very effectively. But without the proper training and supervision, teaching assistants could be doing more harm than good.

There has been a huge expansion of support staff in schools since 2005. But a new government-funded study suggests that pupils who receive help from teaching assistants are making less progress than classmates of similar ability.

Many teaching assistants are a key resource in schools. They relieve teacher workloads and can help improve class behaviour. Most are employed with specific responsibilities to work with individual children with special educational needs, providing much-needed extra support. Others are given more general classroom responsibilities.

Moreover, teaching assistants are not just part of the staff, but are part of a team. The assistance they give teachers and pupils leads to reduced teacher workloads and greater job satisfaction.

So why does a new report from the Institute of Education show that primary and secondary pupils supported by teaching assistants make less progress on average than those of similar ability, social class and gender who do not receive such assistance? In fact, the study shows the more support they receive, the fewer gains they make, which is an incredible claim.

The problem is that support staff tend to look after the pupils most in need, reducing their contact with the qualified teacher. Lead researcher of the report, Professor Peter Blatchford, said the results could not be explained by the lower attainment, special educational needs, family backgrounds or behavioural problems of those pupils who had help from teaching assistants because those factors had been accounted for. Equally, the lack of progress is not something that we can blame on the teaching assistants themselves. The problem is the way in which support staff are deployed and the way in which they are managed.

The main explanation seems to be that support staff are normally assigned to the pupils who require the most help – those with special educational needs or those with the lowest attainment. But the researchers found that the more time pupils spend with TAs, the less time they spend being taught by the teacher. As a result, pupils with the most need can become separated from the teacher and the curriculum.

Support staff also tend to have less training and a lower level of education than teachers. About two-thirds of the support staff in the study had not been educated beyond GCSE level. In effect, it's the equivalent of foisting bad teachers on poorly performing pupils, with an inevitable outcome.

Conversely, there is clear evidence that there is a positive effect on pupils' progress where teaching assistants are effectively trained to deliver specific support programmes, alongside well-planned lessons.

Ultimately, schools need to be clear on the fact that teaching assistants are not substitutes for teachers, but what they can do, given the right training and support, is help children with special needs to get the most out of school.

While teaching assistants are extremely dedicated – many work extra hours without pay – their routine deployment to pupils most in need seems to be the heart of the problem. This is not the fault of support staff. Policymakers and school staff need to rethink the way teaching assistants are used in classrooms and prepared for the tasks that teachers give them to maximise their help to teachers and pupils. Otherwise, despite the best intentions of government to get excellent teachers into schools through tough new recruitment policies, training and huge cash injections, it will all be undermined by the growing army of support assistants who end up at the sharp end of pupil contact.

Reproduced by permission of Imaginative Minds

Questions

1. Select four options from the list below to complete the bulleted list. The last bullet point has been completed for you. (In the actual Key Skills test you have to click on your choices one at a time and drag them to the bullet points.)

   ❑ teaching assistants are not good value for money

   ❑ pupils with teaching assistants receive less teacher support

   ❑ teaching assistants are involved in lesson planning

   ❑ pupils do not enjoy having teaching assistants

   ❑ many teachers do not use teaching assistants effectively

   ❑ lots of teaching assistants are very dedicated

   ❑ teaching assistants are more effective in the afternoon

   ❑ more effective training would make teaching assistants more effective

   ❑ teaching assistants usually work with pupils most requiring help

   ❑ most teaching assistants are designated to specific pupils

   The research report suggests that:

   ❑

   ❑

   ❑

   ❑

   ❑ schools need to reconsider their policies regarding use of teaching assistants

2. Read the statements below and decide whether:

   ✔ The statement is **supported** by the text (**S**).

   ✔ The statement is **implied** by the text or is implicitly supported by the text (**I**).

✔ The text provides **no evidence** or information concerning the statement (**NE**).

✔ The statement is **implicitly contradicted** or implicitly refuted by the text (**IC**).

✔ The statement is **contradicted** by the text (**C**).

❑ Pupils would be better off without teaching assistants.

❑ Pupils perform better with than without the support of a teaching assistant.

❑ Teachers give equal input to all pupils.

❑ Older pupils make more effective use of teaching assistants.

❑ Schools should consider using teaching assistants to fulfil the role of teachers.

❑ Teaching assistants are often valued staff members.

3. Select the best heading for the article. (In the actual Key Skills test you have to drag a tick into the box corresponding to your selection.)

❑ Teaching assistants are a waste of money

❑ Schools need to think again about teaching assistants

❑ Pupils learn better with teaching assistants

❑ Teaching assistants divide pupils and teachers

4. From the list below select three points that accurately convey information about teaching assistants provided in the text. (In the actual Key Skills test you have to drag a tick to indicate the appropriate statements.)

❑ Teaching assistants tend to be less well-qualified than teachers.

❑ Teaching assistants should not be involved in planning lessons.

❑ Teaching assistants' work is most effective in specifically targeted programmes.

❑ Teaching assistants do not like working in a general capacity.

❑ Teaching assistants work with all pupils with special educational needs.

❑ Teaching assistants should not be seen as substitutes for teachers.

5. From the list below select the two options closest in meaning to the following phrase as it appears in the context of the passage you have read. (In the actual Key Skills test you have to drag a tick into the boxes corresponding to your selections.)

There is a positive effect on pupils' progress where teaching assistants are effectively trained to deliver specific support programmes.

❑ Giving teaching assistants specific roles is likely to improve their effectiveness.

❑ Pupils' learning is better when teaching assistants are better trained.

❑ Teaching assistants' work is most effective when targeting specific interventions.

❑ Pupils do not generally progress with teaching assistants.

❑ Specific support programmes have the greatest impact on pupil learning.

Test B

Passage

Boys' underachievement in reading is among the top concerns of many schools. In preparation for the Commission's work, the National Literacy Trust undertook a survey of 226 schools in the UK, in which 76% of respondents said boys in their school did not do as well in reading as girls.

In evidence to the Commission, Emily Tudor, Deputy Headteacher at St Paul's Academy in Greenwich, described the challenge her school had faced:

> *10 years ago in a school made up predominantly of boys, the Year 11 lower ability English exam took place in a separate room to the higher ability. It was a painful scene. There were the empty seats of the boys who did not bother to turn up, and then there was that moment when they would start to put their pens down 25 minutes into a two-hour exam.*

Many respondents to the survey told similar stories. In response to these challenges 82% said they had strategies in place to support boys' reading. Boys do not represent a single homogenous underperforming group with a single and distinct identity. Schools are frequently identifying other factors (particularly ethnicity and social class) which influence boys' attitudes and achievement in literacy.

It is a frequent assumption that predominantly female staff at school benefits girls. While some studies have found a small benefit for boys of male teachers for maths, and for girls of female teachers for English, others have failed to find such a link. It appears that the research evidence does not back up this assumption about the impact of a feminised school workforce on pupil attainment.

However, there is some evidence that teachers award higher marks to pupils from their own gender. With women making up 85–90% of teachers in primary schools, this could be significant for boys' achievement.

In the National Literacy Trust's survey, some practitioners felt quite strongly that the issue is not about female teachers per se, but the lack of male staff in primary schools to model positive reading behaviour and attitudes. This can mean reading is perceived as a female pastime, and therefore girls are more comfortable with being good at reading and enjoying reading.

Many teachers mentioned boys' responses to curriculum topics as a factor in their underachievement. When asked what would make the most difference in raising boys' reading levels, one said, 'Freedom in the curriculum for children to pursue more child-led interests which would necessitate independent reading and encourage them to read more and more widely'.

Giving evidence to the Commission, writer and former Children's Laureate Michael Rosen argued that the current curriculum encourages closed questioning about texts, which displays a lack of interest in what the child really thinks about a piece of writing. This, he felt, is particularly off-putting for boys who, according to stereotype, are less keen than girls to please the teacher by answering correctly, and so switch off from the process. He suggested boys may be encouraged by more open-ended questioning in relation to texts, or resisting asking questions altogether in favour of open-ended talk, as this is shown to have an effect on willingness to read.

Phil Jarrett, National Adviser for English at Ofsted, argued that boys need to feel that the English curriculum matters, and 'that English as a subject is active, practical and productive. Therefore, work in English needs to engage with the world outside school, involving real audiences and real contexts for reading.' Making imaginative use of technology could also help boys to connect with the curriculum and motivate them to read for enjoyment.

Questions

1. Select from the list below the three headings that would be most appropriate to insert into the passage to organise its material. (In the actual Key Skills test you have to drag ticks into the boxes corresponding to your selections.)

   ❑ Boys' reading is a top concern for many schools

   ❑ Boys read as well as girls

   ❑ Teaching – a feminised workforce?

   ❑ Freedom to read

   ❑ Facts not fiction

   ❑ Gendered responses to the curriculum and assessment

2. Re-read Michael Rosen's views about boys' reading from the passage. Select three phrases from the list below that complete the following statement:

   Rosen believes that . . .

   ❑ closed questioning encourages better reading.

   ❑ children must be free to explore what they think about texts.

   ❑ girls are less keen than boys to please their teachers.

   ❑ teachers often switch off from the reading process.

   ❑ open discussion is more effective for boys than questioning.

   ❑ teachers are not interested in what children think about reading.

   ❑ talking about reading increases willingness to read.

3. From the list below select the three points that most accurately summarise the content of the report:

❏ Boys and girls respond differently to reading.

❏ Teachers need to reconsider their approaches to discussing reading.

❏ Most people believe that gender bias has an impact upon assessment.

❏ Most schools have strategies in place to support boys to develop as readers.

❏ Boys are convinced that English is a practical and productive subject that links to the world outside the classroom.

❏ Pupil voice can play an important part in helping teachers shape useful reading experiences.

4. The following list identifies potential audiences for the article. Some of these audiences would find the article more useful than others. Which group would find it most useful and which the least useful? (In the actual Key Skills test you're asked to drag an 'M' into the box next to the most likely audience and an 'L' into the box next to the least likely audience.)

❏ Individuals interested in becoming teachers.

❏ Parents of boys.

❏ Teachers in girls' schools.

❏ Headteachers of large secondary schools.

❏ English teachers (primary and secondary).

5. Read the statements below and, based on the evidence provided by the passage, decide which refer to: Boys (B); Girls (G); Both (Bo). (In the actual Key Skills test you have to drag the letters into the boxes corresponding to your selections.)

❏ Are frequently more motivated to please their teachers.

❏ Tend to respond less well to the limited choices available in the current curriculum.

❏ Benefit from more open opportunities to discuss personal responses to texts.

Checking out the Practice Test Answers

Here we provide answers to the questions in the preceding section, with brief explanations as to why they're right.

Test A

1. Select four options from the list below to complete the bulleted list. The last bullet point has been completed for you. (In the actual Key Skills test you have to click on your choices one at a time and drag them to the bullet points.)

   The research report suggests that:

   ❑ **pupils with teaching assistants receive less teacher support**

   This is explicitly stated in paragraph 6 and again in paragraph 7 of the text.

   ❑ **lots of teaching assistants are very dedicated**

   This is explicitly stated in the final paragraph of the article.

   ❑ **Teaching assistants usually work with pupils most requiring help**

   This is explicitly stated in paragraph 6 and again in paragraph 7 of the text.

   ❑ **most teaching assistants are designated to specific pupils**

   This is found in paragraph 3.

   ❑ schools need to reconsider their policies regarding use of teaching assistants

   This is stated in paragraph 11.

2. Read the statements below and decide whether:

   ✔ The statement is **supported** by the text (**S**);

   ✔ The statement is **implied** by the text or is implicitly supported by the text (**I**);

   ✔ The text provides **no evidence** or information concerning the statement (**NE**);

✔ The statement is **implicitly contradicted** or implicitly refuted by the text (**IC**);

✔ The statement is **contradicted** by the text (**C**).

Pupils would be better off without teaching assistants. (IC)

This view is implicitly contradicted by the text. Although the text states that pupils with teaching assistants make less improvement than pupils of comparable ability who don't have such support, it is implied that both groups of pupils do make progress. You can't, therefore, say that pupils would be better off without teaching assistants.

Pupils perform better with than without the support of a teaching assistant. (C)

The text explicitly contradicts this view. Pupils without teaching assistants perform better than those with. Note that this is different to the statement above which doesn't deal with comparison between pupils and their respective academic performance.

Teachers give equal input to all pupils. (C)

The text contradicts this view. Paragraph 7 states that teachers spend more time with pupils who don't have teaching assistants than with those who have.

Older pupils make more effective use of teaching assistants. (NE)

Nothing in the text relates to pupils' age, and so you have no evidence to support or to refute this statement.

Schools should consider using teaching assistants to fulfil the role of teachers. (IC)

The article says nothing on this topic. It does, however, state that teaching assistants tend to be less well-qualified than teachers and makes clear that pupils who receive less of their teachers' attention do less well. You can, therefore, say that the article implicitly contradicts this view.

Teaching assistants are often valued staff members. (S)

The article clearly states in paragraphs 3 and 4 that teaching assistants are an important part of school staffing teams.

3. Select the best heading for the article. (In the actual Key Skills test you have to drag a tick into the box corresponding to your selection.)

Schools need to think again about teaching assistants.

This is the best heading for the article because it captures most accurately the spirit of the article, which doesn't say that schools shouldn't use teaching assistants, nor that they're bad value for money, but which suggests that schools rethink the ways in which and the purposes for which they deploy such staff.

4. From the list below select three points that accurately convey information about teaching assistants provided in the text. (In the actual Key Skills test you have to drag a tick to indicate the appropriate statements.)

Teaching assistants tend to be less well-qualified than teachers.

This is clearly stated in paragraph 8.

Teaching assistants' work is most effective in specifically targeted programmes.

This is clearly suggested at the end of paragraph 9.

Teaching assistants should not be seen as substitutes for teachers.

Paragraph 10 makes this explicit.

5. From the list below select the two options closest in meaning to the following phrase as it appears in the context of the passage you have read. (In the actual Key Skills test you have to drag a tick into the boxes corresponding to your selections.)

There is a positive effect on pupils' progress where teaching assistants are effectively trained to deliver specific support programmes.

Teaching assistants' work is most effective when targeting specific interventions.

Although this seems similar to the first option from the list, it more clearly encapsulates the emphasis upon specific learning interventions.

Specific support programmes have the greatest impact on pupil learning.

This accurately captures the original statement's focus upon pupils' learning and progress.

Test B

1. Select from the list below the three headings that would be most appropriate to insert into the passage to organise its material. (In the actual Key Skills test you have to drag ticks into the boxes corresponding to your selections.)

Boys' reading is a top concern for many schools

The general content of the article – and particularly the opening section – focuses on the issue of boys' reading and how different the experience of reading is for boys than for girls. The statistics presented demonstrate that this is a priority area for many schools as they work with their pupils. This is, therefore, a good heading to select for the early part of the article.

Teaching – a feminised workforce?

The information presented in the article highlights the large proportion of teachers (especially at primary level) that is female. The article goes on to question the potential significance of this when it comes to the experience of boys as readers, which makes this heading a good candidate for the central part of the text.

Gendered responses to the curriculum and assessment

The article goes on to suggest that the ways in which the assessment system (and teachers) require pupils to respond to their reading may benefit girls over boys, and so this is a good option to select for the latter part of the article.

2. Re-read Michael Rosen's views about boys' reading from the passage. Select three phrases from the list below that complete the following statement.

Rosen believes that . . .

Children must be free to explore what they think about texts.

The passage makes clear that Rosen believes teachers need to allow children more autonomy in setting their own agendas when it comes to reading.

Open discussion is more effective for boys than questioning.

Rosen clearly believes that the limited and often 'closed' ways in which children are asked to respond to texts fails to capture their imaginations and fails to free them as readers. So he advocates more open approaches to talking about reading.

Talking about reading increases willingness to read.

He believes that creating classroom environments in which pupils feel free to talk in more unconstrained ways about their reading will have a positive impact on their desire to read more.

3. From the list below select the three points that most accurately summarise the content of the report:

Teachers need to reconsider their approaches to discussing reading.

Paragraph 9 makes clear that if teachers are to create conditions more favourable to the development of positive and excited readers – especially boys – it is important to rethink the ways in which reading is approached and the ways in which talk about reading is managed in the classroom.

Most schools have strategies in place to support boys to develop as readers.

In paragraph 4 of the text it is clear that the development of strategies to address the issue of boys' reading is a priority for the vast majority of schools. What is not clear is whether these strategies are actually effective and having any impact.

Pupil voice can play an important part in helping teachers shape useful reading experiences.

Paragraph 8 of the text suggests that teachers should listen much more closely to what pupils have to say about their own reading – both what they would like to be reading and the ways in which they would like to approach reading.

4. The following list identifies potential audiences for the article. Some of these audiences would find the article more useful than others. Which group would find it most useful and which the least useful? (In the actual Key Skills test you're asked to drag an 'M' into the box next to the most likely audience and an 'L' into the box next to the least likely audience.)

All the groups identified may well have some interest in the article, because it touches on their work or parental roles in a variety of ways. However, the following represents the most likely option:

Teachers in girls' schools. (L)

Although teachers of girls may well find the material in this article of professional interest – and it does have specific things to say about the way that boys and girls read and could benefit from being taught differently – teachers in girls' schools are the least likely target audience for this article, given its headline focus on boys.

English teachers (primary and secondary). (M)

This article focuses heavily on the teaching of reading, and so the most likely audience for it is teachers of English, the people who most frequently deal with this issue.

Questions such as this one may well reflect to some extent personal interpretations. Reading isn't a precise science, and nor is comprehension, and so you may feel that several reasonably arguable responses exist. If this is the case, you need to think about the answers that best fit the brief of the question on such occasions.

5. Read the statements below and, based on the evidence provided by the passage, decide which refer to: Boys (B); Girls (G); Both (Bo). (In the actual Key Skills test you have to drag the letters into the boxes corresponding to your selections.)

Are frequently more motivated to please their teachers. (G)

Paragraph 9 tells you this.

Tend to respond less well to the limited choices available in the current curriculum. (B)

See paragraph 8 of the text.

Benefit from more open opportunities to discuss personal responses to texts. (Bo)

Whereas girls tend to be more compliant and to work with the system, Michael Rosen's view makes clear that more open opportunities to discuss reading benefit all pupils.

Part III
Numeracy Skills

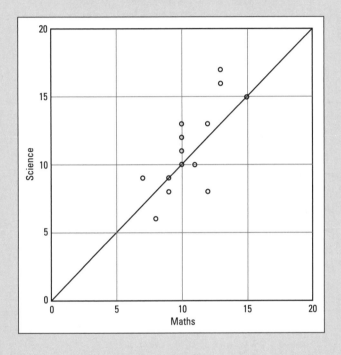

Go to www.dummies.com/go/teachers
professionalskillstests for free audio
practice tests.

In this part . . .

🗸 Make sense of mental arithmetic and pass this section with flying colours.

🗸 Work out word questions with no worries!

🗸 Go to town with tables and graphs and sweep the statistics section.

🗸 Check how well you're doing with on-screen practice questions.

Chapter 8

Making Sense of Mental Maths

*T*he mental arithmetic test has gained an unfair reputation as 'the hard bit' of the Skills Tests; although you may need to do a bit of study and practice before you can rock it, compared to what you'll be doing when you're on a teacher training course it's hardly climbing Everest. The test is demanding, certainly, and you do need to think quickly, but as long as you keep your wits about you, you can do well on the test.

Here are the key facts about the mental arithmetic test:

✔ You have to answer 12 questions.

✔ You hear each question through headphones, twice.

✔ You then have about 18 seconds of silence to work the answer out.

✔ You have access to a small whiteboard and pen and so don't need to do everything in your head.

✔ You can't go back and change your answer: when your time on a question is up, that's it.

The good news is that the questions are much less involved than the on-screen questions (see Chapter 9) and sometimes you'll even be able to write down an answer straight away.

In this chapter, we describe the test processes, focus on fractions and the like, and present you with some real-life mental arithmetic to try out for yourself.

Blitzing through the Basic Arithmetic Processes

To succeed in the mental arithmetic section, you need pretty solid basic maths skills. You can do reasonably well if you know how to add up and take away, as well as divide and multiply big numbers by small numbers; if you find these things difficult, check out *Basic Maths For Dummies* by Colin Beveridge (Wiley), which goes into them in much more detail (a completely impartial suggestion, of course). To do *really* well on the test, you need to be able to multiply and divide with bigger (or more complicated) numbers too.

In this section, we take you through these processes, and give you an overview of all-important decimals.

Dealing with decimals

Before you do anything else, repeat this mantra: 'there's nothing magical about decimal points'. All they do is tell you where the whole number ends and the decimal part starts – just like when you see a price such as £19.99, the dot (the decimal point) marks the end of the whole number of pounds and the start of the pence – the bits of money that are smaller than pounds.

The main trick to have under your belt for the decimal questions in the mental arithmetic section is being able to multiply and divide by them.

Here's a recipe for multiplying decimals:

1. **See whether your first number has a decimal point.** If it does, count how many digits it is from the end of the number and write it down. I put a circle around this number so I don't mix it up with anything else.

2. **See whether your second number has a decimal point.** If it does, count how many digits it is from the end of the number and write it down, also in a circle.

3. **Multiply the first and second (uncircled) numbers together, ignoring the decimal points.**

4. **Add up your circled answers from steps 1 and 2, and then put a decimal point that many spaces from the end of the number you got in step 3.** If your number isn't long enough to go back that many spaces, put zeros on the front of it until it is!

So, to multiply 1.2 by 0.007, you write down '1' in a circle (because the dot in 1.2 is one digit from the end) and '3', also in a circle, because the dot in 0.007 is three digits from the end. Then you multiply 12 by 7 to get 84. Now, because you've got a total of four in the circles, you want to move the decimal point back four spaces, but you've only got two spaces to work with. It's easily fixed: you turn 84 into 00084. Now you can move the decimal point four spaces back from the end of the number to get 0.0084.

Also do a quick check to say 'I'm expecting a small number, and so that's plausible'. If you end up with 840,000, you should be suspicious.

Dividing by decimals isn't any harder than multiplying, but it is different:

1. **Find the decimal point in the *second* number and count how many digits it is from the end.**

2. **Move the decimal point in *both* numbers that many spaces to the right (if you go off the end of the number, fill in any gaps with a zero).**

3. **Do the division and get the answer!**

Therefore, to work out 345 ÷ 0.05, you move the decimal point in both numbers two places to the right, filling in the gaps in the first number with two zeros to get 34,500: 34,500 ÷ 5 = 6,900.

As a rule of thumb, dividing by something smaller than 1 makes your number bigger, while dividing by something larger than 1 makes it smaller. This means you can check your answer makes some sense!

Dividing confidently

Division is one skill that most candidates need to brush up on for the mental arithmetic section. We don't know whether it's just because most people rarely have a real need to divide things by hand (if we didn't use division all the time as tutors, we'd be reaching for the calculator too), but we've never met a student yet who said 'division? Bring it on!'.

In this section, we give you two methods for dividing:

> ✔ **Cancelling method:** This doesn't always get you to the final answer, but often makes the sum simpler. Making sums simpler is always a good thing, right?

> ✔ **Traditional long division:** We explain this in a way that helps you remember why it works (and how to do it). Ready?

Dividing by cancelling

Dividing by cancelling is a great way to make an ugly division sum – such as 840 ÷ 240 – into a much easier one. The principle of cancelling down is the same as the one we discuss later on with fractions (see 'Simplifying fractions') – in fact, division sums and fractions are really the same thing. But don't tell anyone, it's a secret.

Here's how dividing by cancelling works:

1. **Find a number (a *common factor*) by which you can divide both the first and second number (good ones to try are 10, 2, 5 and 3, in roughly that order).**

2. **Divide both of the numbers in the sum by your common factor.**

3. **Keep doing so until you can't see any more numbers to divide by – and then do the long division (check out the next section).**

For instance, for 840 ÷ 240 you can see that they're both multiples of 10, and so you cancel the sum down to 84 ÷ 24. Then you notice that both numbers are even, and so 2 is a common factor: divide both numbers by 2 to get 42 ÷ 12. They're still both even and so you can cancel to 21 ÷ 6. Both of these numbers are in the three times table, and so you can divide both by 3 to get 7 ÷ 2 – which is much easier to work out than 840 ÷ 240!

The final answer to 840 ÷ 240 is the same as 7 ÷ 2, which is 3.5.

Doing long division

Sometimes spotting a common factor (as we describe in the preceding section) is difficult, or perhaps the cancelling way of simplifying takes a bit longer than you like. In that case, you need to do *long division,* which is far less terrifying than you may think!

 All you need to do is split each digit into several piles, put the leftovers into the next pile and repeat the process – just as if you're splitting money up between people.

Imagine that you want to divide £174 between three people. You begin with one £100 note, seven £10 notes and four £1 coins (maths world doesn't have any fivers or twenties, just powers of ten).

You want to divide the £100 note up, but you don't want to tear it! You can, however, turn it into ten £10 notes and add those to the pile of £10s. Therefore, to the original seven you add the extra ten, giving you seventeen £10 notes.

If you split those seventeen notes up between three people, each person gets five £10 notes (3 × 5 = 15) with two £10 notes left over. You can change those into 20 £1 coins and add them to the pile – you now have twenty-four £1 coins. If you split those up between three people, everyone gets eight and nothing's left over. Each person has five £10 notes and eight £1 coins (174 ÷ 3 = 58). We lay this process out in Figure 8-1.

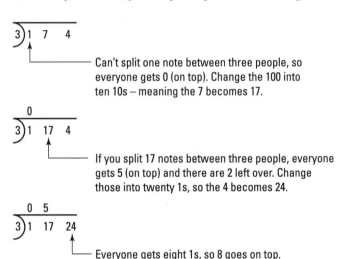

Figure 8-1: Long division process for 174 ÷ 3 = 58.

We now go into a bit more detail about how you work out the number of piles and amount of leftovers – and how you write out a long division sum!

Working out a times table

If you don't know the times table for the number you're dividing by, you need to work it out. Here's how you find the times table for, say, 13:

1. **Write the numbers 1 to 10 in a list, one below the other. Then write a 'multiply' sign followed by the times table you're working out, followed by an equals sign, after each one. In this case, you'll have '1 × 13=', '2 × 13=' and so on.**

2. **Write the number you're interested in next to the '1 × 13'. In this case, you'd have '1 × 13 = 13'.**

3. **Add your number (13) to the last thing you wrote down and write it down below it.** You'd have 26 next to '2 × 13=', 39 next to the '3 × 13 =' and so on.

4. **As a check, you should have the original number with a '0' next to '10 × 13 ='.**

So, for 13 you have 13, 26, 39, 52, 65, 78, 91, 104, 117 and 130 – that's the 13 times table!

Handling piles and leftovers

Splitting notes into piles can be a little time-consuming, and so practising long division questions until you can do them quickly is well worthwhile – sadly, we know of no short cut.

We can give you a recipe, though! To find out how many piles and how many leftovers you have, here's what you do:

1. **Work out the times table for the number you're dividing by, if you haven't done so already.**

2. **Find the biggest number in the time table that's smaller than the number you began with.** So, if you're splitting 100 into 13 groups, the number you want is 91.

3. **Locate the number to the left of your answer in step 2, which is 7 in this example.** This is the number that everyone gets, and it goes 'above the line' when you write it out (see the next section).

4. **Work out the difference between your number (100) and the answer in step 2 (91) – in this case, it's 9.** This is the number of leftovers (or the *remainder*); you write this in front of the next number when you write it out.

That's it! 100 is 13 piles of 7 with 9 left over.

Writing it out

Now we go through a full-on long division sum. Flex your muscles, take a deep breath and follow along with 9,893 ÷ 13 in Figure 8-2:

1. **Draw a bus stop like the one in Figure 8-2.** Swap the order of the numbers so that the thing you're dividing goes underneath and the thing you're dividing by goes in front.

2. **Look at the first digit and figure out how much each person gets and how many are left over if you divide by the number in front.** Here, you're splitting 9 between 13 people; everyone gets nothing and 9 are left over.

3. **Write the number everyone gets above the digit and the leftovers directly in front of the next digit.** In Figure 8-2, you see the 0 above the first 9, and the 8 next to it has now become 98.

4. **Repeat steps 2 and 3 for each number until you get to the end!**

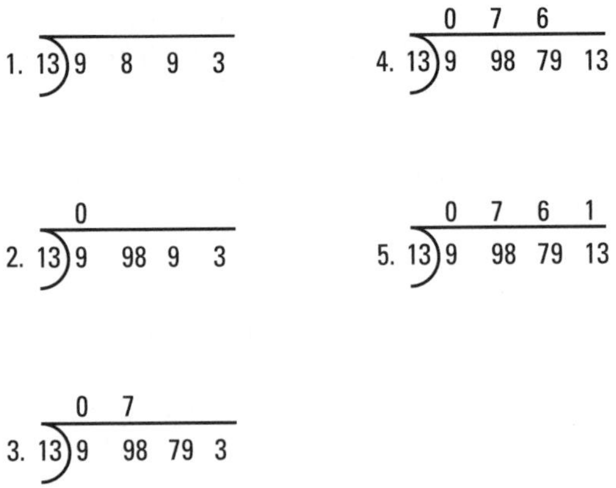

```
                                    0   7   6
1. 13)9  8  9  3            4. 13)9  98  79  13


         0                          0   7   6   1
2. 13)9  98  9  3           5. 13)9  98  79  13


     0   7
3. 13)9  98  79  3
```

Figure 8-2: Long division example for 9,893 ÷ 13.

So, to split up 98, everyone gets 7 (13 × 7 = 91) with 7 left over; you now have 07 above the bus stop and the second 9 becomes 79.

To split up 79, everyone gets 6 (13 × 6 = 78) and one left over; you have 076 above the bus stop and the three at the end becomes 13.

To split up 13, everyone gets 1; you have 0761 above the line and 9,893 ÷ 13 = 761!

 Give yourself plenty of space between the digits under the bus stop! If you're not careful, you can end up running out of room to write your numbers, and when it's hard to read the numbers you've written, it's hard to do sums with them!

Multiplying longhand

As well as dividing with confidence, you need to be able to multiply to do well in your mental arithmetic test. In this section, we show you how to do so – with any size of number!

Here's the recipe (check out Figure 8-3 to see what's going on). We're multiplying 27 by 314 as an example:

1. **Split each number up into hundreds, tens and units.** 27 = 20 + 7; 314 = 300 + 10 + 4.

2. **Draw out a grid with each of the split parts of the first number in the columns and all the split bits of the second number in the rows.** For this example, you have two columns and three rows, as in the left-hand side of Figure 8-3.

3. **Work out, in each cell of the grid, the number at the top of the column multiplied by the number at the left-hand end.** For instance, the bottom-right cell would be 7 × 4 = 28. The middle of Figure 8-3 shows all the answers for this one.

4. **Add up all the numbers inside the grid.** That's 27 × 314 = 6,000 + 2,100 + 200 + 70 + 80 + 28 = 8,478.

 This method works, no matter how long the numbers are (and even with decimals) – but obviously the more complicated the numbers, the more places you can go wrong.

	300	10	4
20			
7			

	300	10	4	
20	6000	200	80	6000
7	2100	70	28	2100
				200
				70
				80
				28
				8478

Figure 8-3: Multiplying 314 by 27 with the grid.

Working with Parts of the Whole

When you have the tools of basic arithmetic under your belt (as we discuss in the earlier section 'Blitzing through the Basic Arithmetic Processes'), the rest of the mental arithmetic section is all about applying them!

In this section, we describe the ways in which you may need to work with 'parts of the whole' – numbers that aren't whole numbers, such as fractions, percentages and proportions.

Finding fractions of a number

The process for discovering a fraction of a number is really straightforward. Imagine that you need to find 3/4 of 264:

1. **Divide the number by the bottom of the fraction:**
   264 ÷ 4 = 66.

2. **Multiply the answer by the top of the fraction:**
   66 × 3 = 198.

If you like, you can remember the mnemonic "Bus stop the bottom, times by the top." We know maths teachers who would *hate* that, which is all the more reason to remember it.

You can multiply by the top first and then divide if you prefer, but doing the division first makes for smaller numbers to work with!

Simplifying fractions

In pretty much every 'parts of the whole' question, you end up *simplifying,* or *cancelling down,* a fraction. For example, remember that 3/6 is the same thing as 1/2? Well, that's an example of cancelling down – giving a fraction that has the same value, but with the smallest possible whole numbers.

Simplifying fractions makes use of the very important rule that whenever you multiply the top and bottom of a fraction by the same number, you end up with a fraction with the same value – that is, 1/4 has the same value as 25/100 (multiplying the top and bottom by 25). The rule works the other way, too: if you divide top and bottom by the same thing, you get a fraction with the same value: 50/100 = 1/2 (if you divide both numbers by 50).

Here's how you simplify a fraction, in detail:

1. **See whether the top or bottom number is a whole number – and if it isn't, multiply it by something until it is.**

   If the number after the decimal point ends in five, double both numbers; otherwise, try multiplying both by 10.

2. **Find a number by which you can divide evenly both the top and the bottom.**

3. **Divide the top and bottom by the number you picked in step 2.**

4. **Repeat steps 2 and 3 until you have no more numbers to divide by (except for 1, which never helps).**

The fraction you end up with is your simplified fraction!

For example, what's 2.4/5 in its simplest form? First, you need to get rid of the decimal, and so you multiply top and bottom by 10. Now you have 24/50. You can divide both of those numbers by 2 to get 12/25. No number (apart from 1) goes into both 12 and 25, and so that's your simplified fraction.

Performing perfectly with percentages

You're pretty much guaranteed to see at least one percentages question in the mental arithmetic section – and most likely in the on-screen tests, too. (In Chapter 9 we provide a different method for dealing with percentages that's more suited to calculator work; if you're happy with the arithmetic, it may well work for you.)

Comparing fractions and percentages

The idea of a *percentage* is to describe the proportion of interesting things in a group as 'so many in 100' so that you can make a fair comparison.

For example, if Matt scores 83 per cent of his penalties and Nick scores 34 penalties out of 40, which of the two is the better shot? Here's how you work out Nick's percentage:

1. **Write the information as a fraction: in this case 34/40.**

2. **Cancel it down to its simplest form: 17/20.**

3. **Divide 100 by the bottom number: in this case, 100 ÷ 20 = 5.**

4. **Multiply top and bottom by this number: 85/100.**

5. **'Over 100' is the same as per cent and so Nick is the better shot.**

 The percentages you have to deal with in the mental arithmetic section are much less involved than the on-screen ones, and generally involve 'nice' numbers. We don't mean that they say complimentary things about your hair, but that they divide evenly into 100.

Watch out for these two things:

> ✔ **Read the question carefully!** Sometimes the test setters try to sneak one past you by saying something like 'what percentage of penalties did Nick *miss?*'. In that case, you just need to take your answer away from 100. (For this example, the answer would be 15 per cent.)

✔ **A few bottom numbers come up quite frequently.**
Memorise the numbers you multiply by in step 4 for
bottoms of 5 (multiply by 20), 8 (multiply by 12.5), 10
(multiply by 10), 20 (multiply by 5), 25 (multiply by 4)
and 50 (multiply by 2).

Percentage of a number

Here's a quickish way to find a percentage of any number,
especially because you usually see only multiples of 5 per
cent in the exam. Say that you want to find 35 per cent of 420:

1. **Split the percentage number up into tens and fives
   (here, you need three lots of 10 per cent and one lot
   of 5 per cent).**

2. **Find 10 per cent of the number by dividing it by 10:
   in this case, 42.**

Careful, this only works for 10 per cent – you don't get
5 per cent if you divide by 5! You can find 5 per cent
by finding 10 per cent and then dividing by 2. In this
example, that's 21.

3. **Multiply your 10 per cent answer by the number of
   10 per cents you need: 3 × 42 = 126.**

4. **Add on the 5 per cent if needed to find your answer:
   126 + 21 = 147.**

You can use a similar method when the setters are unusually
mean and ask for a percentage that's not a multiple of 5: you
can find 1 per cent by dividing your 10 per cent by 10, or even
0.5 per cent by halving your 1 per cent. You're unlikely to be
asked to do this, but it's worth knowing just in case!

Fractions into percentages

Converting fractions into percentages is much easier than
you may think – especially if you can divide! Here's how you
convert 7/8 into a decimal:

1. **Write down the top number, a dot and as many zeros
   as you think you need (three is plenty).**

2. **Divide the top number by the bottom number: you
   get 0.875 in this case.**

3. **Move the decimal point two places to the right to get
   your answer: 87.5 per cent.**

Percentages into fractions

Turning a percentage into a fraction is easy: you just write the number and then '/100': for example, 84 per cent is the same thing as 84/100.

Turning it into a fraction in its lowest form is just a case of cancelling the fraction down: 84/100 = 42/50 = 21/25.

If you're given something with a decimal point in it – such as 62.5 per cent – multiply the top and bottom by the same number (usually 2 or 10) to get rid of the decimal point before you start cancelling down: 62.5/100 = 125/200 = 25/40 = 5/8.

Fiddling with further fractions

If you're asked to find the fraction that one number makes of another, you need to cancel down your fractions. Here's all you do:

1. **Put the smaller number on top of the bigger number to make a fraction.**

2. **Multiply top and bottom by the same number (usually 2 or 10) until you get rid of any decimal points.**

3. **Cancel the fraction down (see the earlier section 'Simplifying fractions' for details) and when it's in its simplest form, you have your answer!**

For example, to find what fraction 4.8 is of 84, you would write down the fraction 4.8/84, multiply top and bottom by 10 to get 48/840, then simplify: divide both parts by two to get 24/420, by two again to get 12/210, and again for 6/105. You can't divide by two any more, but you can divide by 3 to get 2/35, so 4.8 is 2/35 of 84.

Playing with proportion

To find the proportion that one number makes of another requires that you're pretty confident with cancelling down fractions and decimal division, and so spend some time on those topics if you struggle with them (flip to the earlier sections 'Simplifying fractions' and 'Dealing with decimals', respectively).

The *proportion* one number is of another means exactly the same thing as the fraction one number makes of another – except that you normally express it as a decimal. Here's how you find the proportion that 68 is of 80:

1. **Write down the two numbers as a fraction: 68/80.**

2. **Cancel down as far as you can: 68/80 = 34/40 = 17/20.**

3. **Put a dot and as many zeros as you think you need after the top number (three is plenty) and divide by the bottom number: 17 ÷ 20 = 0.85.**

You have your answer!

Alternatively, you can convert the fraction into a percentage – 85 per cent here – and then move the dot back two places to get 0.85.

Answering Real-life Maths Problems

Most of the questions in the mental arithmetic and on-screen sections ask about things you can measure – most often money, time and distance, but occasionally also volumes and weights. Most of these things work exactly like normal numbers, and if you're comfortable with decimals (which we explain earlier in this chapter in 'Dealing with decimals'), you'll have no problems at all.

The one real-life thing that misbehaves slightly is time: because an hour contains 60 minutes rather than 100, you have to be a little careful when you work out time sums.

Making sense of money

No doubt you've worked with money before (it's surprisingly popular these days). You know that £1 has 100 pence and that you can add, subtract, multiply and divide money just like you can with normal, decimal numbers.

Where things get tricky in the mental arithmetic section is when you have to convert between currencies. Although you can do this in other ways, we recommend using the *Table of Joy*, which you can read more about in Chapter 9.

A typical question may go as follows: a teacher pays €240 in entry fees to take her school group into a museum in France. One pound is the same as €1.20. How much does she pay in pounds?

1. **Draw out a noughts-and-crosses style grid.** Leave plenty of space for labels at the top and on the left.

2. **Ignore the first column for the moment and label the next two columns 'pounds' and 'euros'.** Now leave the first row alone and label the next two rows 'rate' and 'money'. Figure 8-4 shows how it's done.

3. **Fill in the numbers you know.** Rate/pounds is 1 and rate/euros is 1.20, because one pound is the same as 1.2 euros. Money/euros is 240.

4. **Shade in the grid like a chessboard.** Find the two numbers on the same-coloured squares (1 and 240) and write them down with a multiplication sign between them; then write a divide sign followed by the other number. The result is $1 \times 240 \div 1.2$.

5. **Work out the sum!** This one's a little tricky, but you can turn it into $2{,}400 \div 12$, which is 200.

	£	€
Rate		
Money		

	£	€
Rate	1	1.20
Money		240

$$\frac{1 \times 240}{1.2} = \frac{2400}{12} = 200$$

Figure 8-4: Currency conversion with the Table of Joy.

When you divide by a decimal, a good idea is usually to multiply the top and the bottom by ten until you get whole numbers.

Currency conversion requires nothing more than that. The Table of Joy works every time, in either direction, and doesn't require a lot of thinking. The hardest thing about this particular sum is doing the division!

Taking care of time

The time questions you see in the mental arithmetic questions are a bit of a dark horse: they seem like they ought to be quite easy, but you can make errors in a lot of places – and the nature of a computerised test is that if you make a single mistake, you lose the mark.

Typical time questions involve working out how long a complicated series of events is going to take or when the events will finish.

Here's how you work out how long a series of events takes – for example, if a school has eight 40-minute classes per day and breaks of 25 minutes and 55 minutes:

1. **Work out any repeated times (for instance, 'eight 40-minute classes') by multiplying.** In this example, that would be 40 × 8 = 320 minutes.

2. **Add together all the sets of minutes you've worked out or been given.** For instance, here you add 320 + 55 + 25 = 400 minutes.

3. **Convert this number into hours and minutes by dividing by 60 (in this case, 6): the remainder (40) is the number of minutes.** Therefore, the school day lasts 6 hours and 40 minutes.

You may be given a complicated bunch of times, told when an event starts, and asked when the event finishes. In that case, all you need to do is add the time on to the start time you're given – for instance, assume that the school day we describe above starts at 8:55 a.m. By the way, you almost always need to use the 24-hour clock in your answers in the mental arithmetic test:

1. **Decide whether your start time is in the afternoon, and if it is, convert it into the 24-hour clock by adding 12 to the hours.** You don't need to do that for this one.

2. **Add the hours in the start time to the hours in the duration.** In this case, that's 8 + 6 = 14.

3. **Add the minutes in the start time to the minutes in the duration.** Here, that's 55 + 40 = 95.

4. **See whether your minutes number is 60 or more, and, if so, take 60 away from it and add 1 to the hours.** For this example, your hours are now 15 and your minutes 35.

5. **Take 24 off if your hours number is more than 24.** This is unlikely, but possible.

6. **Put a 0 in front of the number if either your hour number or minutes number is less than 10.** Here, the hours are still 15 and the minutes 35.

7. **Write down the hours and then the minutes.** The answer is that the school day ends at 15:35.

Working with weight and volume

As with money (see the earlier section 'Making sense of money'), the normal rules of arithmetic work exactly the same for weights (measured in grams or kilograms) and volumes (measured in millilitres or litres) as they do for normal numbers.

A *litre* is how much water you find in a medium-sized bottle; a litre contains 1,000 millilitres. As it happens, a litre of water weighs almost exactly 1 *kilogram;* a kilogram is also the same as 1,000 grams.

The most common question you see in mental arithmetic tests about weights or volumes involves planning some kind of experiment where you need a certain amount of chemicals for each experiment, a certain number of experiments per student and a certain number of students in a class. (Variations on this theme make up almost all the weights and volume questions in the Numeracy test.)

Here's how you do such a question. Imagine that you need 50 millilitres of vinegar for each experiment, each student is to do the experiment twice and 30 students are in the class. How many litres of vinegar do you need?

1. **Figure out how much of the material each student needs.** Multiply the number of experiments each student does (2) by the amount of vinegar (50 millilitres) to get 100 millilitres.

2. **Multiply this number by the number of students.** In this case, that's 100 × 30 = 3,000 millilitres.

3. **Make sure that you answer the question you're asked!** 3,000 millilitres is the same as 3 litres and so your answer needs to be 3.

Step 3 is where you can easily get caught out. Often the question asks how many bottles of a certain size the teacher needs, which involves dividing the amount you work out by the size of the bottles. Generally, you can't buy fractions of a bottle and so if you need 7.2 bottles, your answer is 8.

The basic idea is always the same: work out how much of the substance is needed and work from there to get the answer they're looking for. Make sure to give the answer in the units they ask for – millilitres, litres or bottles!

Converting distances

Converting between miles and kilometres comes up quite frequently in the mental arithmetic section. The test gives you sensible numbers to work with, and tells you to use the approximation that 5 miles is the same as 8 kilometres.

The conversion strategy is always the same: you multiply the distance you're given by one of the numbers (either 5 or 8) and divide by the other. The trick is to decide which one to use! Luckily, the number for kilometres is always higher than the one for miles, and so you need to multiply by the bigger number (8) to get kilometres.

Here's the recipe form:

1. **Multiply your distance by 8 to find kilometres; multiply by 5 if you want miles.**

2. **Divide by the other number: if you want kilometres, divide by 5; to get miles, divide by 8.**

That's it! If you have 72 kilometres to convert into miles, you multiply by 5 (to get 360) and divide by 8 (to get 45 miles).

Covering rates and speed

Your mental arithmetic section may include a question involving speed, distance and time. These ones can take a little bit of study to get used to how they work, but after you've done a few they start to drop into place – especially if you use a tool called the *formula triangle,* which is almost (but not quite) as useful as the Table of Joy (from the earlier section 'Making sense of money').

The formula triangle

The formula triangle is something you may have come across at school, probably in physics, but don't worry if not: after you read this section you'll know exactly how to use it! We show it in Figure 8-5.

$$S = D \div T \qquad D = S \times T$$
$$T = D \div S$$

Figure 8-5: The speed (S) distance (D) time (T) triangle.

We like to remember the order the letters go in from left to right as 'Sooty Doesn't Talk'. But if you make up your own mnemonic, you'll find it easier to remember: the ruder the better.

Here's how the triangle works: you cover up the letter you're trying to find (S for Speed, D for Distance or T for Time) and see what you're left with. If it's two things on the same row, you multiply the values; if not, you divide the top value by the bottom value.

For example, if you drive 400 miles at 50 miles per hour, how long does it take?

1. **Decide what you know and what you're looking for.** In this case, you know the distance (D) is 400 and the speed (S) is 50. You want the time.

2. **Cover up the thing you want to find – here, the T.** You're left with a D on top of an S.

3. **Divide the distance (400) by the speed (50) to get the time, which is 8.** The journey takes 8 hours.

Similarly, if you walk at four miles per hour for six hours, how far do you go?

1. **Decide what you know and what you're looking for.** You know the speed (S) is 4 and the time (T) is 6. You want the distance.

2. **Cover up the thing you want to find – the D.** You're left with an S next to a T.

3. **Multiply the S (which is 4 in this case) by the T (which is 6).** $4 \times 6 = 24$ and so you travel 24 miles.

What to watch out for

The people who set the exam can be crafty little beggars. Now and again they try to make it harder for you by giving you distances in the 'wrong' unit – for example, you may have a speed given in miles per hour and a distance in *kilometres*. Yelp! If they're mean enough to drop this bombshell, you have to convert the kilometres into miles first. Read the earlier 'Converting distances' section if that sounds tricky.

Similarly, the setters may give you a time in minutes rather than hours. If they do, shake your fist at them briefly and convert the time into hours – or, if you prefer, check out our guide to sneaky speeds and using the Table of Joy in Chapter 9. In all cases, you should get a nice round answer.

Other rates

You often see other rates given in the test – price per kilogram, for example, or miles per gallon.

The little word 'per' is a great big flashing signal that says 'you can use the formula triangle'. Place the rate (the number you're given) in the bottom left, the thing before the 'per' on top and the thing after the 'per' in the bottom right. Have a look at Figure 8-6 to see what we mean.

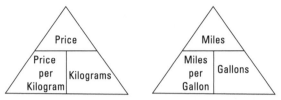

Figure 8-6: 'Per' units and the formula triangle.

You can use this formula to string together questions that seem a bit nasty, like this one:

> *A car has a fuel consumption of 9 miles per litre. Fuel costs £1.40 per litre. How far can the car travel on £70 of petrol?*

Here's how it works:

1. **Draw out the formula triangles for fuel consumption and fuel cost.**

2. **Circle the numbers you know.** In this case, you have the number of pounds (the top of the fuel cost triangle), the cost per litre (the left of the fuel cost triangle) and the consumption (the left of the fuel consumption triangle).

3. **Find a triangle where you know two numbers and work out the third.** Here, you can figure out the right side of the price triangle (how many litres) – it's 70 ÷ 1.4 = 700 ÷ 14 = 100 ÷ 2 = 50.

4. **Take the number you now know for the other triangle (the number of litres is on the right of the consumption triangle).** Work out how far you can travel by multiplying 50 by 9 = 450 miles.

Having a Go: Practice Tests

This section is your chance to put into practice everything we describe in this chapter! We provide five (count 'em!) mental arithmetic tests for you to try out.

You can use these questions as you like: you can get a friend to read them out to you to a strict schedule, as if you're in the test, work through them at your own pace with your book open in front of you or visit www.dummies.com/go/teachersskillstests and download the audio version. All the answers can be found at the end of the chapter.

Test A

In the mental arithmetic tests, you hear each question twice and then have 18 seconds to work out the answer. You don't get to skip back or enter an answer after your time is up.

Questions

1. A school has 150 Year 11 students and 93 of them are expected to go on to sixth form. What proportion of the students are not expected to go on to sixth form? Give your answer as a decimal.

2. A school books five 52-seater coaches for a trip. Eight classes of 28 students each, as well as eight teachers and six parents, are booked on the trip. How many more students can go on the trip?

3. A school recorded 80 unauthorised absences last year. That figure decreased by 15 per cent this year. How many unauthorised absences were there this year?

4. Three-eighths of a teacher's hard disk is full. What is three-eighths as a percentage?

5. A student plans a 64-kilometre bike ride for charity. Using the conversion that 5 miles is the same as 8 kilometres, how many miles is she going to ride?

6. A teacher takes four minutes to mark each homework assignment. He starts marking at 5:15 p.m. on Sunday and marks 24 assignments without stopping. What time does he finish? Use the 24-hour clock.

7. The school's Amnesty International group holds a cake sale to raise funds. It sells 20 rock cakes for 50p each and 12 slices of carrot cake for £1.50 each. It spent £5 on ingredients. How much profit does the group make on the sale?

8. Twelve students take part in a sponsored swim. They raise £1.50 for each length they swim. Each student swims 64 lengths. How much do they raise altogether?

9. Three-quarters of the 152 staff in a school attend the daily briefing. How many staff do not attend?

10. In a school year of 150 students, one morning 18 students are late. What percentage of the school year is this?

11. A student is 12 years and 6 months old. His reading age is 18 months ahead of his real age. What is his reading age in years?

12. What is $625 \div 0.01$?

Test B

You hear each question twice and then have 18 seconds to work out the answer. You can't skip back or enter an answer after your time is up.

Questions

1. What is $915 \div 0.001$?

2. A student is 8 years and 6 months old, and has a reading age of 9 years and 3 months. How many months is her reading age ahead of her actual age?

3. A headteacher arranges meetings to congratulate 51 students who have performed above expectations. Each meeting will take four minutes. What is the minimum number of 45-minute classes she needs to meet all the students?

4. The school minibus travels 8 miles on a litre of petrol. Its tank holds 55 litres of petrol. How far can the minibus travel on a full tank of petrol?

5. In a football squad of 15 players, 3 are specialist goalkeepers. What percentage of the squad does not specialise in goalkeeping?

6. In one sixth-form class, 70 per cent of the students have passed their driving test. In another, 18 out of 25 students have passed. What is the difference between the percentages of students who have passed their driving test?

7. A school pays a sixth-former £8 per hour to update the school's website. He works six hours per week for four weeks. How much does the school pay him altogether?

8. One hundred and fifty students pay £1.50 each for tickets to a school disco. The DJ costs the school £130. How much profit does the disco make?

9. An assembly hall has 15 rows, each with 20 seats. Year 11 consists of nine classes, each of which has 26 students. If all the students in Year 11 attend assembly, how many empty seats will there be?

10. One hundred and thirty five out of 250 students are girls. What proportion of the students are boys? Give your answer as a decimal.

11. A test contains 28 questions. The pass mark is 75 per cent. How many questions must students answer correctly to pass the test?

12. A school year contains 120 students. Five-eighths of the students study French as a foreign language. How many students study French as a foreign language?

Test C

You hear each question twice and then have 18 seconds to work out the answer. You can't skip back or enter an answer after your time is up.

Questions

1. In a class, three of the thirteen boys are left-handed. Five of the twelve girls are left-handed. What percentage of the class is left-handed?

2. Petrol costs £1.40 per litre. A minibus travels seven miles per litre of fuel. How much would it cost to travel 100 miles in the minibus?

3. What is $3.7 \div 0.01$?

4. The Year 6 intake from eight local primary schools is coming to visit for an open day. Each school is sending an average of 45 pupils. The teacher co-ordinating the visit decides to split the visitors into groups of 12 to do activities through the day. How many groups will there be?

5. Students studying Further Maths spend 4 of their 25 time-tabled lessons learning maths. What proportion of their time-table is not spent on maths? Give your answer as a decimal.

6. A student who has been diagnosed with dyslexia is allowed 20 per cent extra time in his English exam. The standard length of the exam is one hour and 30 minutes. How long is the exam for the student, in minutes?

7. A student scores 60 per cent in a mock exam and 54 out of 75 in a final exam. What is the difference between his percentage scores?

8. The school day starts at 8:45 a.m. There are five lessons of 50 minutes, plus a morning break of 15 minutes and a lunch break of 55 minutes. What time does the school day end? Give your answer using the 24-hour clock.

9. A teacher reckons she needs eight classes to teach the first topic in a language course, six classes to teach the second topic and twelve classes to teach the final topic. If she has three classes available per week, what is the minimum number of weeks she needs to teach the course?

10. A class raises £161.70 to split equally between seven charities. How much does each charity receive?

11. A science experiment requires 120 millilitres of distilled water. Each of the 15 students in a class is to perform the experiment four times. How many litres of water will be needed?

12. One hundred and sixteen students sign up for a sponsored charity walk. Three-quarters of them actually take part in the walk. How many students take part?

Test D

You hear each question twice and then have 18 seconds to work out the answer. You can't skip back or enter an answer after your time is up.

Questions

1. Thirty-five per cent of the students in a class wear glasses. There are 20 students in the class. How many students wear glasses?

2. A bus travels 24 miles on its journey to school, taking 45 minutes. What is its average speed in miles per hour?

3. A quarter of a class of 28 students take part in a conference. How many students don't take part in the conference?

4. A school organises a mini-rugby tournament. Six local schools send squads of 14 players, and four more schools send squads of 8 players. How many players are involved in the tournament?

5. What is 86.24×0.1?

6. The school librarian reports that the library loaned out 500 books in the previous half term, and 475 of them were returned on time. What proportion of the books were *not* returned on time? Give your answer as a decimal.

7. A teacher budgets for four exercise books per student each school year. She has three classes of 20 students and two classes of 25 students. How many exercise books will she need?

8. The head of Year 11 orders drinks and food for the end-of-year party. He orders five crates of cola (each of which costs £12), eight packets of hot-dog buns (each of which costs £3) and fifteen packets of hot dogs (each of which costs £4). How much does he spend altogether?

9. A teacher drives an average of 35 minutes each way to school and back, five days a week. How many hours does she spend driving in a six-week half-term?

10. As part of a blood-donation campaign, 12 students each donate 400 millilitres of blood. How many litres of blood do they donate altogether?

11. For a school trip to the USA, students are advised to take £120 in spending money. One pound is approximately $1.50. How many dollars should each student take?

12. Forty students went on a school skiing trip. Fourteen of them had been skiing before. What percentage of the students on the trip had been skiing before?

Test E

You hear each question twice and then have 18 seconds to work out the answer. You can't skip back or enter an answer after your time is up.

Questions

1. On a school trip, the rules require at least one adult for every eight students. If 96 students are booked on the trip, what is the smallest number of people that can go altogether?

2. What is 952×0.001?

3. A student is 15 years and 9 months old. He's going to take his Grade 8 music exam in eight months. How old will he be when he takes his Grade 8 music exam? Give your answer in years and months.

4. A hotel room for a teacher at a conference for three nights costs a total of €255. If one euro is worth 80 pence, how much does the hotel room cost in pounds per night?

5. At a parents' evening, a teacher arranges 27 appointments of five minutes each, with a quarter-hour break in the middle. If the parents' evening starts at 5:30 p.m., when should it finish? Give your answer using the 24-hour clock.

6. A teacher claims 40p per mile in travel expenses for trips to an examiners' meeting. She makes six trips, each of 15 miles. How much money does she claim? Give your answer in pounds.

7. What is 5/8 as a percentage?

8. In an exam, 36 out of 200 candidates are taking the Latin paper. What proportion of the candidates will not take the Latin paper? Give your answer as a decimal.

9. Twenty-five students sit a spelling test and six of them get full marks. What percentage of the students is this?

10. A school trip costs each student £120. Four-fifths of this was spent on accommodation. How much was spent on accommodation for each student? Give your answer in pounds.

11. Last year, a season ticket for the school bus cost £58. The bus company puts the prices up by 10 per cent. What does the season ticket cost this year? Give your answer in pounds and pence.

12. A class sells raffle tickets to raise money for charity. Each student sells, on average, 12 tickets for 50p each. There are 25 students in the class. How much money do they raise, in pounds?

Checking out the Practice Test Answers

The overall pass grade for the Numeracy test is 63 per cent – that is, 18 out of 28. If you do about as well on the two parts of the test, you want to be getting roughly 8 or 9 mental arithmetic questions right.

Test A

1. **0.38.** 57 students out of 150 are not expected to go on to sixth form. 57/150 is the same as 19/50, which is 38/100 or 0.38.

2. **22.** There are a total of 5 × 52 = 260 seats available. The eight classes have 8 × 28 = 224 students; plus 14 adults makes 238 seats taken up. Finally, 260 – 238 = 22 seats remaining.

3. **68.** To find 15 per cent of 80, you can say that 10 per cent of 80 is 8 and 5 per cent of 80 is 4, and so 15 per cent of 80 is 12. This year, there are 80 – 12 = 68 unauthorised absences.

4. **37.5.** 3/8 is the same as 75/200 or 37.5/100.

5. **40.** Multiply 64 by 5 (to get 320) and divide by 8 to get 40.

6. **18:51.** Altogether, he takes 4 × 24 = 96 minutes to do the marking. That's one hour and 36 minutes. Added to 5:15 p.m., that's 6:51 p.m., or 18:51.

7. **£23.** The rock cakes make (20 × 0.5) = £10. The carrot cakes make (12 × 1.5) = £18. The group takes in £28 and spent £5, making a profit of 28 – 5 = £23.

8. **£1,152.** Each student raises 64 × 1.5 = £96, and £96 × 12 = £1,152. (You can complete this question in several ways.)

9. **38.** The quick way is to see that a quarter of the staff *do* attend. That's 152 ÷ 4 = 38. Alternatively, you can work out 3/4 of 152 = 152 ÷ 4 × 3 = 114, and then do 152 – 114 = 38.

10. **12 per cent.** 18/150 is the same as 3/25, or 12/100.

11. **14 years.** Eighteen months is the same as one year and six months. In six months' time, the student will be exactly 13; in another year, he will be exactly 14.

12. **62,500.** You have to move the decimal point two places to the right from the end of 625 and fill the gap with zeros.

Test B

1. **915,000.** You have to move the decimal point three spaces to the right.

2. **9.** The easiest way to work out this question is to say 'in 6 months, she'll be 9 years old, and in another 3 months she'll be 9 years and 3 months. That's 9 months altogether.'

3. **5.** The interviews will take 51 × 4 = 204 minutes. Four 45-minute classes would be 180 minutes, and five classes 225, and so the head needs five classes.

4. **440 miles.** $8 \times 55 = 440$.

5. **80 per cent.** Twelve out of the 15 are not specialist goal-keepers. That's the same as 4/5, which is 80 per cent.

6. **2 per cent.** 18 out of 25 is the same as 72/100 or 72 per cent. $72 - 70 = 2$.

7. **£192.** He earns $8 \times 6 = £48$ per week. $£48 \times 4 = £192$.

8. **£95.** The total income is $150 \times 1.50 = £225$. The profit is $225 - 130 = £95$.

9. **66.** There are $15 \times 20 = 300$ seats in the hall. There are $9 \times 26 = 234$ students in the year. $300 - 234 = 66$ spare seats.

10. **0.46.** The number of boys is $250 - 135 = 115$. The fraction of boys is 115/250, or (if you divide top and bottom by 5) 23/50, which you can work out directly by long division; alternatively, you can say it's the same as 46/100. As a decimal, that's 0.46.

11. **21.** Seventy-five per cent is the same as three-quarters. One-quarter of 28 is 7, and so 3/4 is 21.

12. **75.** One-eighth of 120 is $120 \div 8 = 15$. Five-eighths is $15 \times 5 = 75$.

Test C

1. **32 per cent.** There are 8 left-handed students out of 25. To get from 25 to 100, you multiply both numbers by 4, to get 32/100.

2. **£20.** One litre costs £1.40 and takes the minibus 7 miles; so each mile costs 20p. $20p \times 100 = £20$.

3. **370.** You have to move the decimal point two places to the right.

4. **30.** There are $8 \times 45 = 360$ students visiting. $360 \div 12 = 30$.

5. **0.84.** The students spend 21 out of 25 lessons doing other things. You can do $21 \div 25$ directly using long division, or you can say 21/25 is the same as 42/50 or 84/100.

6. **108 minutes.** One hour and 30 minutes is 90 minutes; 20 per cent of 90 is 18 minutes (10 per cent is 9, so 20 per cent is 18), and so the total time is 90 + 18 = 108.

Common mistakes in Question 6 include not converting into minutes, and just giving the candidate's extra time rather than total time.

7. **12 percentage points.** 54 out of 75 is the same as 18 out of 25, or 72 per cent. The percentage point difference is 72 – 60 = 12.

8. **14:05.** The five lessons make 250 minutes, and the breaks make 70 minutes, for a total of 320 minutes. That's five hours and 20 minutes after 8:45 a.m. The school day ends at 2:05 p.m.

9. **9 weeks.** She needs a total of 8 + 6 + 12 = 26 classes. 26 ÷ 3 = 8 2/3, and so she needs 9 weeks altogether.

10. **£23.10.** 161.70 ÷ 7 = £23.10

11. **7.2 litres.** The experiment will be done 15 × 4 = 60 times, and 60 × 120 millilitres = 7,200 millilitres, which is 7.2 litres.

12. **87.** One-quarter of 116 is 116 ÷ 4 = 29, and three-quarters is 29 × 3 = 87.

Test D

1. **Seven.** Ten per cent of 20 is 2, and so 5 per cent is 1 and 30 per cent is 6: 6 + 1 = 7.

2. **32 miles per hour.** If a bus travels 24 miles in 45 minutes, it travels 8 miles in 15 minutes, or 32 miles in an hour. Alternatively, it travels 48 miles in an hour and a half, or 96 miles in three hours: 96 ÷ 3 = 32.

3. **21.** A quarter of 28 is 28 ÷ 4 = 7, and 28 – 7 = 21.

4. **116.** There are 6 × 14 = 84 players from the six large squads, and 4 × 8 = 32 from the smaller squads. That's a total of 84 + 32 = 116.

5. **8.624.** You have to move the decimal point one place to the left.

6. **0.05.** Twenty-five out of 500 books were not returned on time. You can work that out directly using long division, or you can say 25/500 = 5/100 = 0.05.

Notice that you don't need to go all the way down to 1/20 – you hit something that's easy to work out before you reach the simplest form of the fraction.

7. **440.** She has a total of (3 × 20) + (2 × 25) = 60 + 50 = 110 students, and 110 × 4 = 440.

8. **£144.** The cola costs 5 × 12 = 60. The buns cost 8 × 3 = 24. The hot dogs cost 15 × 4 = 60. He spends 60 + 60 + 24 = £144.

9. **35 hours.** She spends 35 × 2 = 70 minutes a day in the car, which is 70 × 5 = 350 minutes per week, or 350 × 6 = 2,100 minutes in a half term. 2,100 ÷ 60 = 210 ÷ 6 = 35 hours.

10. **4.8 litres.** 12 × 400 = 4,800 millilitres, which is 4.8 litres.

11. **$180.** The sum is 120 × 1.5 = 180.

12. **35 per cent.** 14/40 is the same as 7/20. To get from 20 to 100, you multiply top and bottom by 5, which gives 35/100.

Test E

1. **108.** At least 96 ÷ 8 = 12 adults needed; including the 96 students, that makes 108 people altogether.

A common mistake here is to forget to add the 96 students on – the question asks about the smallest number of people *altogether*.

2. **0.952.** You need to move the decimal point three places left from the end.

3. **16 years and 5 months.** In three months, he'll be 16 years old, with five of the eight months remaining.

4. **£68.** You can work out this question in several ways. We'd say that one night costs 255 ÷ 3 = €85, and €85 × 0.8 = 85 × 8 ÷ 10 = £68.

5. **20:00.** The appointments take 27 × 5 = 135 minutes, plus 15 minutes for coffee makes 150 minutes – or two and a half hours. Two and a half hours after 5:30 p.m. is 8 p.m.

6. **£36.** She travels a total of 6 × 15 = 90 miles: 90 × 0.4 = £36.

7. **62.5 per cent.** If you don't know this one by heart, you can work it out by doing 500 ÷ 8 = 250 ÷ 4 = 125 ÷ 2 = 62.5.

8. **0.82.** The number of candidates not taking Latin is 200 – 36 = 164. The fraction of candidates not taking Latin is 164/200, which is the same as 82/100, which is 0.82.

A common mistake on Question 8 is to give the answer 0.18 – the proportion of candidates who *are* taking Latin.

9. **24 per cent.** To get from 25 to 100, you multiply top and bottom by 4: 6/25 = 24/100.

10. **£96.** A fifth of 120 is 120 ÷ 5 = 24. Four-fifths is 24 × 4 = 96.

11. **£63.80.** 10 per cent of £58 is £5.80, and 58 + 5.80 = 63.80.

12. **£150.** Each student raises 12 × 50p = £6 × 25 = £150.

Chapter 9

Stepping up to the Screen: Arithmetic Review

*T*echnology is great and a real boon for exams. Whereas you used simply to worry with paper and pencil, now you can fret in front of a snazzy electronic screen! Mind you, some people are never content: we can imagine pupils in previous centuries complaining about the stress caused by those 'new-fangled writing slates'.

But whether you're happy with or harassed by computers, the fact is that you do see 16 of the 28 questions in your Numeracy test on a screen rather than hearing them through headphones. To cheer you up, here are a few things that make these questions easier than the mental arithmetic ones:

✔ **You get to use a calculator.** Though not a particularly great calculator, because it's part of the testing software rather than a proper, grown-up calculator, it's good enough for all the sums you need to do. It's very similar to the basic calculator that comes installed on your PC, or a simple desk calculator – but not a fancy scientific one.

✔ **You have more time for each question.** You're expected to answer 16 questions in 36 minutes, giving you a little more than two minutes for each question.

✔ **You get to manage your own time.** If you find a question easy, you can race through it in order to spend more time on harder questions.

✔ **You're allowed to skip questions.** You can return to them later if time allows.

The one downside of these extra advantages is that the questions in the on-screen section tend to be more involved than the mental arithmetic part.

In this chapter, we run you through the maths skills you need to succeed at many of the on-screen questions: dealing with 'parts of the whole' (a blanket term for percentages, ratios, fractions and the like), working with real-life maths, handling basic statistics (ranges and averages) and identifying patterns (trends).

For all you need to know about reading and doing sums with tables and graphs, check out Chapter 10. Plus, don't forget that Chapter 2 has details about the exact format of the on-screen questions.

Playing with Parts of the Whole: Percentages

Many of the questions in the on-screen section of the test involve *parts of the whole* – describing one number in terms of its relationship to another. For instance, if you talk about a '10 per cent increase' or 'half-price offer', you're using parts of the whole to describe a number.

You can describe numbers using parts of the whole in four main ways: using percentages, ratios, fractions and proportions. Nothing is different about ratios, fractions and proportions from the same topics in the mental arithmetic section, and so feel free to head to Chapter 8 to review them; percentages, on the other hand, get a little bit more involved in the on-screen section.

Juggling with the Table of Joy

Percentages become really straightforward when you use a tool called the *Table of Joy*. You can use this simple grid to figure out what you need to type into the calculator to work out a percentage, ratio, conversion, pie-chart angle or any one of a dozen other useful things.

Here's how it works using the example of converting 26.2 miles into kilometres using the conversion 5 miles = 8 kilometres. Follow along with Figure 9-1.

	Miles	Kilometres
Rate	5	8
Marathon	26.2	

a)

b)   26.2 × 8 ÷ 5 = 41.92

Figure 9-1: The Table of Joy (a), the table, and (b), the calculation.

1. **Draw a big noughts-and-crosses grid, leaving plenty of space for labels.**

2. **Label the last two cells in the top row with the units of the things you're working with: here, that's kilometres and miles.**

3. **Label the last two cells in the first column with the kinds of information you have: in this case, rate and marathon.**

4. **Fill in the numbers in the obvious places: 5 is miles/ rate, 8 is kilometres/conversion and 26.2 is miles/ marathon.**

5. **Shade the grid like a chessboard.**

6. **Find the two numbers on the same coloured squares (here, 8 and 26.2 are both on white squares) and write them down with a × sign between them.**

7. **Write down a ÷ sign and the other number: for this example, your sum reads 8 × 26.2 ÷ 5.**

8. **Type this all into the calculator and you get 41.92, which is the distance in kilometres.**

The great thing about the Table of Joy is that, although the labels may change, and the numbers certainly will, the method is always the same: put the numbers in the right cells, shade it in, write the sum and work it out. It's a handy little badger – so much so, that we use it in pretty much all of the maths-related chapters.

Putting percentages in their place

The word *per cent* simply means 'out of every hundred' – if you think about words such as 'century', 'centimetre' and even 'cent', you notice that they all mean something to do with 100!

The idea of using percentages is to show the size of something in comparison to the whole. If you're told that the price of a rail ticket just went up by a pound, you can't tell whether that's a lot compared to the original price. But if we tell you that the price went up by 10 per cent, you have a better idea of how big an increase it was.

In this section, we show you how to work out a percentage of a total, percentage increases and decreases and percentage point differences – which are deceptively easy, we promise!

Percentage of a total

By 'percentage of a total', we mean any question where you're interested in a certain part of a larger group, and have to work out one of the following:

- ✔ the size of the part;
- ✔ the size of the total; or
- ✔ the percentage of the larger group that the smaller group makes up.

The Table of Joy (from the preceding section) works brilliantly for all three types of question. Just remember that the number you start from – or the number in the whole group – is always 100 per cent.

For example, imagine that you have 150 students in a school year and the rugby squad consists of 21 students. What percentage of the students is in the squad? Figure 9-2 shows the steps to take, as follows:

1. **Draw out your Table of Joy noughts-and-crosses grid, leaving plenty of space for labels.**

2. **Label the two right-most columns as 'students' and 'per cent' and the two lowest rows as 'part' and 'whole'.**

3. **Put in the information you know: part/students is 21, whole/students is 150 and whole/per cent is 100, because it always is.**

4. **Shade the table like a chessboard and write down the Table of Joy sum: 100 × 21 ÷ 150.**

5. **Work out this calculation (using the calculator, if you like) – you get 14, and so 14 per cent of the year plays in the rugby squad.**

a)

	Students	Per cent
Whole	150	100
Part	21	

b) 100 × 21 ÷ 150 = 14

Figure 9-2: Solving percentage problems with the Table of Joy: (a) the table, and (b) the calculation.

Solving problems of the other two types works in exactly the same way. You draw the grid, put the numbers you know where they belong (and 100 in the whole/per cent square) and work out the sum. Simples!

Percentage increase and decrease

Things get a little trickier – though not much – when you come to percentage increase and decrease. For instance, if you're offered a 10 per cent discount on a £75 pair of trainers, how much do they cost?

The good news is you can still use the Table of Joy from the earlier section 'Juggling with the Table of Joy'. The bad news – and it's not all that bad – is that you have to be a bit more careful with your numbers.

The central idea is that if you decrease a price by 10 per cent, you're left with (100 – 10) = 90 per cent of the original price. If you increase something by, say, 15 per cent, you get (100 + 15) = 115 per cent. This is the number that goes into the 'after/per cent' square of the Table of Joy grid.

Similarly, if you're asked for the percentage increase or decrease between two prices, the change is the difference between your 'after/per cent' number and 100. Here's how you solve the example of the on-sale trainers:

1. **Draw out your Table of Joy grid, labelling the columns as 'pounds' and 'per cent' and the rows as 'before' and 'after'.**

2. **Fill in the numbers you know: before/per cent is always 100, before/price is 75 and after/per cent is (100 – 10) = 90.**

3. **Shade in the grid and write down the sum: 75 × 90 ÷ 100.**

4. **Work out the sum – the sale price of your rubber-soled running shoes is £67.50.**

If you're given something the other way round – for instance, you're told that 450 students in a school achieved A*–C grades in English last year and 504 did so this year – and you're asked to find the percentage increase, here's the method:

1. **Draw out your Table of Joy grid, labelling the columns as 'students' and 'per cent' and the rows as 'before' and 'after'.**

2. **Fill in the numbers you know: before/per cent is always 100, before/students is 450 and after/students is 504.**

3. **Shade in the grid and write down the sum: 504 × 100 ÷ 450.**

4. **Work out the sum – you get 112.**

5. **Find the difference between this answer and 100: here, it's 12 more, and so the number of good English grades increased by 12 per cent.**

Percentage point differences

Percentage point differences are deceptively easy – the only hard thing is noticing that they're the easy ones! All the term means is the difference between two percentages – so you simply work out the two percentages and take them away!

A typical question asks something like 'A student scored 16 out of 25 in one test and 21 out of 30 in another. What was his percentage point improvement?'

For the sake of good form, here's the recipe:

1. **Work out the first percentage: $16 \times 100 \div 25 =$ 64 per cent.**

2. **Work out the second percentage: $21 \times 100 \div 30 =$ 70 per cent.**

3. **Find the difference between the percentages: here, the second test is better by $70 - 64 = 6$ percentage points.**

Mastering Measures

Pretty much all the on-screen test has to do with 'real-life' maths, which involves counting and measuring real things rather than working with abstract numbers and solving for x. In this section, we take you through what you need to know about weights, measures and the like, in particular:

- ✔ Making sense of money
- ✔ Keeping track of time
- ✔ Working with weight and volume

Many of the techniques you need for this section build on what you required for the mental arithmetic test – so make sure that you're fully up to speed with the sections in Chapter 8 before you tackle these!

Calculating complicated money sums

Most of the money sums you encounter in the on-screen section of your Numeracy test are variations of the ones you see in the mental arithmetic section – except that, because you have use of a calculator and less time pressure, they're likely to be a bit more involved, and usually involve finding information from a table or graph. (If that's something you find difficult, don't panic: Chapter 10 explains everything you can possibly want to know about reading graphs and tables.)

The kinds of questions you can expect involve one of four things:

- ✔ Working out the total cost of something, usually a trip or a production.
- ✔ Finding the profit or loss for an event.
- ✔ Picking the best (that is, cheapest) option.
- ✔ Converting between two currencies.

Total cost

Finding the total cost of a bill or anything else is more fiddly than difficult, the kind of question where, if you get it wrong, the reason's more likely to be because of carelessness than not knowing what to do.

Here's how you tackle total cost questions:

1. **Read the question carefully to get an idea of what's happening.**

   Keep your eyes peeled for any mischief the question setters may be trying to get away with, such as mentioning discounts or late fees.

2. **Go through the question again, but this time write down what's being bought, how much of it, how much it costs per unit and how much it costs altogether (which is the last two things multiplied together).** Lay these numbers out in neat columns, because doing so is much easier than trying to piece together numbers from all over the page!

3. **Apply any discounts or fees that apply to each thing in turn.** Write these numbers in another column to the right.

4. **Add up the final column.** That's your total cost!

Profit and loss

Repeat after us: 'the hardest thing about profit and loss calculations is laying everything out neatly!' We know, we sound like we're nagging. But honestly, the more clearly you organise your work – especially with complicated sums like this sort – the less likely you are to get confused and make mistakes.

Here's how we recommend tackling a profit and loss type question:

1. **Read the question carefully to figure out what's going on and make a note of any information that looks important.**

2. **Create two columns: 'spending' and 'income'.**

3. **Read the question again, and for each bit of money that's spent or that comes in, work out how much it is and write it down (with a label) in the appropriate column.**

4. **Read the question again and make sure that you didn't miss anything.**

5. **Add up all the spending and write the total at the bottom.**

6. **Add up all the income and write the total at the bottom.**

7. **Find the difference between the spending and income: if spending is higher than income, the answer is your loss; if income is higher, the answer is your profit.**

Cheapest option

The tests contain two different kinds of 'cheapest option' questions: an easier one that's simply 'which of them costs less?', and a harder one that's 'which of these is better value?'.

The 'which costs less?' version is very straightforward: you just work out the cost of each thing and decide which costs the least.

The 'which is better value?' version is a bit harder, but not much: it just means 'which of these is cheaper *per unit*?'. That is to say, if you buy two apples for 80p, they're 40p per unit and better value than apples that are 45p each.

Here's how you work out the value per unit:

1. **Calculate the total cost.**

2. **Find out how many units you're buying – how many items, grams, litres or whatever you're working with.**

3. **Divide your answer from step 1 by the answer from step 2 to get your cost per unit.**

To find the best-value option, you simply find the option with the lowest cost per unit.

Currency conversion

The test may ask you to convert between two different currencies: for instance, to change £250 into euros if you know that the exchange rate is €1.20 to the pound.

To handle such questions, you sit down again at the Table of Joy (see the earlier section 'Juggling with the Table of Joy'):

1. **Set out your noughts-and-crosses grid with the headings 'pounds' and 'euros' in the columns and 'rate' and 'money' in the rows.**

2. **Fill in what you know: rate/pounds is 1, rate/euros is 1.20 and money/pounds is 250.**

3. **Shade in the grid like a chessboard and work out the Table of Joy sum on the calculator: 1.20 × 250 ÷ 1 = €300.**

Tackling time

You can find almost all the time sums that you need to be able to deal with in Chapter 8 on mental arithmetic – working out differences in time, start times and end times and speeds. We do cover a couple of extra bits and pieces here, though: reading timetables and working out more difficult speeds.

Timetables

If you've ever had the pleasure of travelling by bus or train, you've almost certainly seen a timetable like the one in Figure 9-3. These days, you can usually find all the information you want about travel times on the Internet or via an app, but you can still see the occasional big version if you look hard enough.

Sheffield	07:10	07:40	08:10	08:40	09:10	09:40
Stockport	08:10	08:40	09:10	09:40	10:10	10:40
Manchester	08:22	08:52	09:22	09:52	10:22	10:52

Figure 9-3: Example of a timetable.

In the test, you may need to find the last train that arrives before a particular time, the first train that leaves after a particular time or how long a journey takes.

Reading a timetable is easy enough. To find out when a bus or train is due at a particular stop, here's what you do:

1. **Find the stop – usually they're listed in the left-hand column (make sure that you're looking at the correct timetable, though: in real life you often have one timetable for each direction).**

2. **Read across the times until you reach the column corresponding to the bus or train you're looking for.**

3. **The number you see is the time, in the 24-hour format.**

Sneaky speeds

Chapter 8 covers most of what you need to know about speeds, but sometimes you get a really unpleasant question that involves times that aren't whole numbers of hours. Yuk.

The Table of Joy rides to the rescue here (check out 'Juggling with the Table of Joy' earlier in this chapter)! The method works with any speed/time/distance question, but here we just run through the most common type: a typical question such as 'An athlete runs 6 miles in one hour and 15 minutes. What was her average speed?'

1. **Draw out your Table of Joy grid and label the columns as 'miles' and '*minutes*': that's right, we said it, minutes.**

2. **Label your rows as 'journey' and 'per hour'.**

3. **Fill in the numbers you know: journey/miles is 6, journey/minutes is 75 and hour/minutes is 60, because an hour has 60 minutes.**

4. **Shade in the grid and work out the Table of Joy sum on the calculator – 6 × 60 ÷ 75 = 4.8 – to find the number of miles the athlete would run in an hour, or her speed in miles per hour.**

This technique works just as well for kilometres or whatever distance unit you're asked to use.

Working with weight, volume and distance

You don't need to know much about weight, volume and distance for the test apart from a few simple (and very similar) facts about the metric system (which we define in Chapter 8):

✔ One litre is the same as 1,000 millilitres.

✔ One kilogram is the same as 1,000 grams.

✔ One kilometre is the same as 1,000 metres.

✔ One metre is the same as 100 centimetres (note, a hundred not a thousand – remember how 'cent' words usually have something to do with the number 100).

You may also need to convert between different units in the test – again, this is a job for the Table of Joy (read the ever-useful earlier section 'Juggling with the Table of Joy' for details)! Unless it's one of the metric conversions above, you're given the conversion rate.

Say that you want to make a cake and the recipe calls for 16 ounces of flour and you know that an ounce is about 28 grams. You want to know how much that is in grams:

1. **Set out your Table of Joy grid and label the columns 'ounces' and 'grams' and the rows 'rate' and 'cake'.**

2. **Fill in the numbers you know: rate/ounces is 1, rate/ grams is 28 and cake/ounces is 16.**

3. **Shade in the grid like a chessboard and work out the Table of Joy sum on the calculator: 16 × 28 ÷ 1, which works out to 448 grams.**

Reeling in the Ranges (and Averages)

You don't need to know much about statistics to get through your Numeracy test – which is pretty good news, no matter how interesting we think statistics is! You do, however, need to know about finding three kinds of average (the mean, median and mode) and two measures of spread (the range and the interquartile range). In this section, we show you how.

Meeting the three averages

Three averages? That's right – in maths, you can use different kinds of average for different situations. In your Numeracy test, you need to know how to calculate three specific averages:

> ✓ **Mean:** The meanest thing the test setters can ask, it's the total value of the data, divided by how many observations there are.
>
> ✓ **Median:** The value of the observation in the middle.
>
> ✓ **Mode:** The most common observation.

The *mean* is the total divided by the count; the *median* is the middle number; and the *mode* is the most common.

Mean

The mean of a set of numbers is what you'd get if you shared their value out equally. To find the mean of a list of numbers, here's what you do:

1. **Add up all the numbers.**

2. **Divide by how many numbers were in the list.**

Don't worry if the result isn't a whole number!

If you have a table instead of a list of numbers, the process is a bit trickier – have a look at the table in Figure 9-4 and follow along:

1. **Find how many things are in each row, by multiplying the frequency (how many things are in the group) by the value. In the table, these numbers would be 0, 12, 8, 6 and 4.**

2. **Add up all these numbers and the result is your total. Here, it's 30.**

3. **Find how many things there are altogether, by adding up the frequency column. Here, it's 25.**

4. **Divide your answer from step 2 by your answer from step 3. In this example, the mean is 30 ÷ 25 = 1.2.**

Siblings	Frequency
0	6
1	12
2	4
3	2
4	1

Figure 9-4: Finding the mean, median and mode of a grouped frequency table.

Median

Finding the median – the middle number – of a list isn't too tricky. Here's what you do:

1. **Put the numbers in order – going up or going down, it doesn't matter.**

2. **Count how many numbers are in the list.**

3. **Add one to your number and divide by two – not getting a whole number is fine:**

   - If your answer to step 3 is a whole number, find that number in the list – so, if you have a list of nine numbers, you find the fifth element and that's the median.

   - If your answer to step 3 isn't a whole number, find the two numbers in the list either side of it – so, if you have 12 numbers, you get 6.5 and you look for the sixth and seventh numbers.

4. **Find the mean of these two numbers and that's your median.**

If you have a table, finding the median is slightly easier, because the numbers are already in order. Here's the recipe:

1. **Add up the frequency column to find out how many things exist. In Figure 9-4, for example, there are 25 things.**

2. **Add one to this number and then divide it by two. That gives you 13 here.**

3. **Work down the frequency column one row at a time, keeping a running total – so, in Figure 9-4, you'd have 6, 6+12=18, 18+4=22, 22+2=24, and 24+1=25.**

4. **Keep going until your running total reaches your answer from step 2 or higher, and at that point you've reached the median group: the value of that group is the median – in this example, it's 1.**

Mode

The mode (in some cases, also known as the *modal value* or the *modal group*) is the easiest of the three averages to find: it's just the value that shows up more than any other. Here's how you find the mode of a list of numbers:

1. **Put the numbers in order.**

2. **Count how often each number shows up: whichever one has the highest count is the mode.**

How easy is that! If you can believe it, the recipe is even simpler for a table: just find the group with the highest frequency and that's the modal group. If you're still looking at Figure 9-4, the mode of those data is 1.

Spreading the news of ranges and quartiles

An average on its own doesn't tell you very much about a set of data. For example, if you have a group of 100 average-sized people, that group may have the same mean height as a group of 60 jockeys and 40 basketball players. If you're talking casually, you can say that people in the first group are about 170 centimetres tall, give or take 5 centimetres, and people in the second group are 170 centimetres tall, give or take 50 centimetres. The question is, how do you make something as vague as 'give or take' into a statistic?

Two methods are available that you care about (the rest you probably don't):

✔ **Range:** Tells you the difference between the highest and lowest value.

> ✔ **Interquartile range:** A bit more involved but gives a slightly fairer picture (because it ignores the extremes).

Read on to find out more!

The range

Finding the range of a set of numbers could hardly be easier:

1. **Find the highest value.**

2. **Find the lowest value.**

3. **Find the difference between them and that's the range.**

Really . . . that's it!

The interquartile range

Quartiles are variations on the median (which we define earlier in 'Meeting the three averages'): in a sense, the upper quartile is 'a typical high value' and the median of the upper half, and the lower quartile is 'a typical low value' and the median of the lower half. They're not particularly interesting in their own right (as concerns the on-screen tests), but you use them to find the interquartile range.

Here's how to find a quartile:

1. **Put the list in order and count how many items it contains.**

2. **Add one to the number: for the lower quartile, find a quarter of this number; for the upper quartile, find three-quarters of it (don't worry if you don't get a whole number).**

   - If you have a whole number, you want that number item in the list. For instance, with seven items the lower quartile is the second item and the upper quartile is the sixth.

   - If you don't have a whole number, you want to find the mean of the numbers on either side of it. For instance, with a list of 50, you get 12.75 as the number for the lower quartile, and you'd find the mean of the 12th and 13th numbers. The upper quartile number is 38.25, and so you'd find the mean of the 38th and 39th numbers.

When you've found the quartiles, finding the interquartile range is just as simple as finding the range:

1. **Find the upper quartile.**

2. **Find the lower quartile.**

3. **Find the difference between them and that's the interquartile range.**

Tracking Trends

This section isn't about catwalk fashions or the latest Internet hot topics. *Trend* in this context is any kind of consistent pattern.

For example, what's the next item in this sequence: 2, 4, 6, 8, . . . ? (You got 10, right? Good. We'd also accept 'who do we appreciate'.) That sequence is an example of a trend and that's really all you need to do: spot the pattern and carry it on.

You may be asked in the test to decide whether a pattern has a consistent trend (something like 'true or false: school attendance improved each year?'). That can be a bit of a booby-trap question, because even if attendance dropped for just one year (or even stayed the same), the answer is false. It's only true if *every* year saw an increase.

Carrying on extrapolating

Extrapolating is a fancy word for 'carrying on the pattern'. In this kind of question, you're asked what you expect a value to be in (say) one year or two years, assuming that the current trend continues. That's exactly what you did in the 2, 4, 6, 8 example, but for completeness, here's the recipe:

1. **Write down the numbers in the sequence you're looking at.** This may involve reading them off a graph or a table.

2. **Spot the pattern by looking for the difference between the numbers.** In the 2, 4, 6, 8 example, the pattern is 'add two each time'.

3. **Carry the pattern on as long as you need to.** If asked for the next number, you answer 10; if asked for the number three years after the 8, you think: 10, 12, 14 and say 14.

The pattern can go down instead of up!

Minding the gap: Interpolating

Interpolating means 'filling in the gap' (and isn't a description of what the international police force does). For example, if you have a sequence such as 2, 5, . . . , 11, 14, what value is missing? You can spot the pattern easily – it goes up in threes, and so the missing number is 8.

Here's the recipe for this kind of question:

1. **Write down the numbers either side of the gap and work out the difference between them.** Here, you write down 5 and 11, and the difference is 6.

2. **Decide what fraction of the way between the numbers the thing you're looking for is.** For example, if there's one number missing, it's halfway between its neighbours. If there are two missing – which is very unlikely – the missing numbers are one third and two thirds of the way between the neighbours.

3. **Find this fraction of the gap.** Half of 6 is 3.

4. **Add this number on to the number before the gap.** 5 + 3 = 8, which is the answer.

Chapter 10

Getting on Top of On-Screen Tests with Tables and Graphs

In This Chapter

▶ Pulling up a chair to data tables

▶ Charting the course of simple graphs

▶ Conquering complex graphs

*T*ables and graphs crop up frequently in the daily duties of a teacher (as we explain in Chapter 2), and so unsurprisingly they feature prominently in the on-screen part of the Numeracy test. But never fear, because in this chapter we cover everything you need to know about handling test questions with these items.

Fortunately, you don't need to know about every last type of obscure graph (those that frequent the more outlandish joints on the outer fringes of the graph nightclub scene), only the following fairly straightforward ones: bar graphs, line graphs, pie charts and scatter graphs. In addition, you need to be able to handle box-and-whiskers plots and cumulative frequency graphs, and because these ones are a bit more involved they receive their own special section.

Although we discuss all the main types of graph you're likely to see on the test, the questioners are at liberty to throw in variations on any type and we can't possibly cover every eventuality. If you see a graph in the test that you don't recognise, don't panic – just use the principles you know from this chapter to figure out what's going on and take your best shot. Giving your best-guess answer is always better than no answer at all.

Dealing with Data Tables

Data-table questions are the most common kind you encounter in your Numeracy test. They vary from the pedestrian kind of question (such as 'how many people ride bikes to school on Tuesday?') to working out the proportion of students who get A*s in geography and Cs in history, which is a lot easier than it sounds.

When you've completed a few table questions, the hardest part can be paying attention to precisely what the testers are asking of you. Therefore, after you come to an answer, always go back and check that you've really answered the question they asked.

Reading about regular data tables

Figure 10-1 is a regular data table that shows the test scores of several students.

Class	Boys	Girls	Total
6A	13	13	26
6B	14	16	30
6C	12	15	27
6D	17	11	28

Figure 10-1: A run-of-the-mill data table.

To read a value from it – for instance, how many boys are in class 6D – here's what you do:

1. **Locate the column you're looking for (in this case, 'boys').**

2. **Find the row you're looking for ('6D').**

3. **Read across your row until you get to the column you want: the number in this cell is what you're after (17 boys in class 6D).**

Unfortunately, the chances of a Numeracy test asking you anything quite so straightforward are slim to none. You're much more likely to be asked to work out statistics from the table (such as the range and/or an average of one of the columns; see Chapter 9), or to perform sums on the data (for instance, finding the biggest difference between the columns).

In these cases, you simply find the appropriate numbers from the table, do the sum you're asked for and give the answer. For example, to discover the mean number of students in each class, you find the total number of students per class (26 + 30 + 27 + 28 = 111) and divide by the number of classes (111 ÷ 4 = 27.75). Look back to the 'Meeting the three averages' section of Chapter 9 if you're not sure what we mean by 'mean'.

Doubling up with two-way tables

A particular kind of table that crops up all the time is the two-way table (see Figure 10-2): it looks like a regular table, but has the totals at the end of each row and column. You may think that this makes things harder, but in fact having that information makes finding items such as averages a lot easier.

| | | Regular exercise | | |
		Yes	No	Total
Healthy breakfast	**Yes**	8	9	17
	No	8	5	13
Total		16	14	30

Figure 10-2: A two-way table.

However, the question you're most likely to see with two-way tables is a 'fill in the blanks' question – some of the cells will be empty and you have to fill them in, like the world's easiest Sudoku. Here's how:

1. **Find a row or column that has numbers in all but one of its cells.**

   • If it's missing its total, add up the numbers and fill in the blank.

   • If it's missing another number, add up all the numbers that aren't the total, take that away from the total and fill this number in the empty cell.

2. **Stop if you're finished; but if some cells are still empty, return to step 1 and do the same process again.**

Meeting table-element criteria

A common kind of table question involves finding all the elements in the table that meet certain criteria. For example, if a table shows the actual age and reading age of several students, you may be asked to select all the students whose reading age is six months or more ahead of their actual age.

You may also be asked to use a table – either a regular one or a two-way one – to find the proportion (or fraction, ratio or percentage) of observations that fit a particular criterion: such as 'what percentage of the students have a reading age higher than their actual age?' or 'what fraction of the boys achieve A grades or better in religious studies?'.

In each case, the procedure is the same:

1. **Find out the total number of observations.**

   Be careful – if you're given two conditions, as in the religious studies question, make sure that you get the right total. In that example, it's the total number of *boys,* not the total number of students.

2. **Find out how many observations fit all the criteria.**

3. **Work out the second number as a proportion (or whatever you're asked for) of the first.**

Sussing out Simple Graphs

You need to know about four kinds of graph that we'd call relatively straightforward in the on-screen section of your Numeracy test:

✔ **Bar graph:** The height of each bar shows you the value it represents.

✔ **Line graph:** How high the line is shows you the value it represents.

> ✔ **Pie chart:** The angle in the middle of the slice of pie shows you the proportion of the total it represents.
>
> ✔ **Scatter graph:** Each mark – usually a cross, a star or a square – gives you two pieces of information. The distance above the bottom axis tells you one value, and the distance across from the left-hand axis tells you the other.

In this section, we run through the sums you need to know for each of them.

Battling it out with bar graphs

A bar graph usually looks like the skyline of a built-up city: a series of skyscrapers of different heights.

Sometimes, you see bar graphs sideways on. Sideways bar graphs work just the same way as regular, upright bar graphs except that you may need to tilt your head 90 degrees to make the recipes work. Or you can just replace 'up' with 'across' and vice versa, but where's the fun in that?

You come across three kinds of bar graph in the tests:

> ✔ **Single-bar graph:** The simplest kind of bar graph, where each bar represents the value of a single category.
>
> ✔ **Multiple-bar graph:** Bars representing several different categories are shown side by side in several different groups.
>
> ✔ **Stacked-bar graph:** Values of several different categories show up one on top of the other.

In all three cases, the key thing about the bars is their height: the higher the bar, the higher the value it represents.

Single-bar graphs

A *single-bar graph* is one where you're keeping track of only one variable at different times or in different categories. It's probably the simplest graph you see in a Numeracy test and by far the easiest to read. Figure 10-3 shows an example.

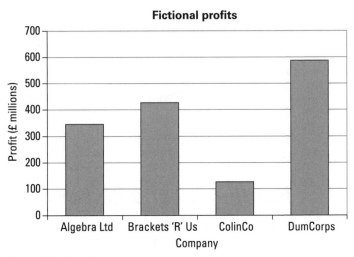

Figure 10-3: A single-bar graph.

To see what to do to read a single-bar graph, imagine that you want to know ColinCo's fictional profit:

1. **Work out which of the bars represents the category you're measuring.** Normally, you find this information at the bottom of the graph, but it can also be written on the graph itself, or in a key telling you which colour or pattern represents what. In Figure 10-3, ColinCo is the third bar along.

2. **Find the top of the bar.** Mentally draw a horizontal line to the axis.

3. **Read the value on this axis (making your best guess if the answer is between two marked numbers).** This is the value the bar represents (ColinCo's profit is about £120 million).

Multiple-bar graphs

A *multiple-bar graph* takes the idea of a single-bar graph a bit further – Figure 10-4 has an example. Here, you can see several different clusters of bars: each cluster is a single-bar graph (in this case, showing a single student's scores in a mock and a real exam) with five distinct clusters (one for each student).

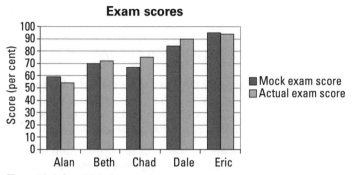

Figure 10-4: A multiple-bar graph.

To read a multiple-bar graph, you use exactly the same process as for single-bar graphs: you identify the correct bar (using the key and the labels on the axis) and read the value off as before. So, you can easily say that Beth scored 70 in her mock exam and 72 in the actual exam.

Stacked-bar graphs

Stacked-bar graphs are yet another variation on the single/ multiple-bar graphs theme. Personally, we think that stacked-bar graphs are a horrible kind of graph, much less easy to read than the other kinds, but some people – especially examiners – insist on using them. Figure 10-5 shows an example (using the same data as the earlier Figure 10-1).

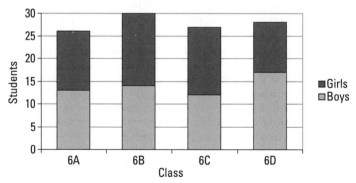

Figure 10-5: A stacked-bar graph.

The idea of stacked-bar graphs is that you get a sense of the relative sizes of the groups you're comparing, as well as the size of the total. Here's how you read this kind of beastie, for example to find the number of girls in class 6C:

1. **Identify the bar (or section of a bar) you're interested in.** Use the labels on the axis and the key – you're looking for the top part of the third bar if you want to know about the girls in 6C.

2. **Locate the value of the upper limit of the bar or bar section by reading across from the top to the vertical axis.** Here, that's 27.

3. **Find the value of the lower limit of the bar or bar section by reading across from the bottom to the vertical axis.** In this case, that's 12.

4. **Take your answer from step 3 away from your answer in step 2 to find the value of the bar or bar section.** The answer is that 15 girls are in class 6C.

Working with stacked-bar graphs is easy enough when you get the hang of it, but we don't recommend using them in real life!

Lining up and shooting down line graphs

Line graphs are probably the most common graph you see in real life. Whenever you're showing how a value changes over time – whether it's temperature, profits, weight or anything else – a line graph is the obvious and logical choice for showing it.

The main idea of a line graph is that you can read off the value of what you're measuring or counting at any time by seeing how high the line is at that point. You can also see when the measurement reached a certain value by finding the time when the line was the right height.

You get two types of line graph:

✔ **Single-line graph:** Has just one line to read.

✔ **Multiple-line graph:** Unsurprisingly, has several lines to choose from.

Single-line graphs

You don't have much to think about when you're reading a value from a single-line graph (see Figure 10-6)! The only tricky thing is deciding whether you need to find the value you're given on the horizontal axis (which is most of the time) or the vertical axis. About 90 per cent of the time, it's completely obvious because the value is only on one of the axes.

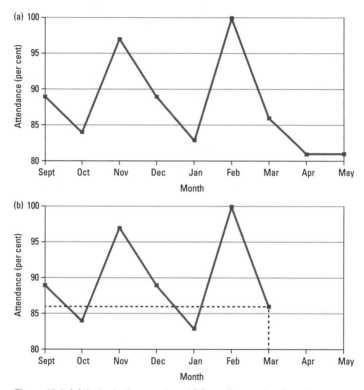

Figure 10-6: (a) A single-line graph and (b) reading a value from it.

When it's not quite so obvious, you need to match the kind of information you have with the labels on the axis.

Here's what you do to read a line graph – for example, to find the attendance for March:

1. **Find the value you're looking for on the correct axis (March is on the horizontal axis).**

2. **Place a ruler on the value you find, at right angles to the axis, and locate where the ruler crosses the line (if you're working from the vertical axis, it may cross in more than one place and you have to figure out the point you need for the question at hand).**

3. **Keep the ruler on the same point on the line and rotate it 90 degrees so that it's at right angles to the other axis.**

4. **Read off the value on this axis – that's your answer, which is 86 per cent in this case.**

 You can see line-graph questions asking for something such as 'the time when the temperature was 20 degrees and falling' – in which case, your ruler crosses the line in two places and you want the one where the line is sloping down and to the right – getting cooler as time increases.

Multiple-line graphs

As the name suggests, multiple-line graphs (see Figure 10-7) have several lines representing different things – possibly the temperature in several different cities through the day or truancy rates in several different schools over time.

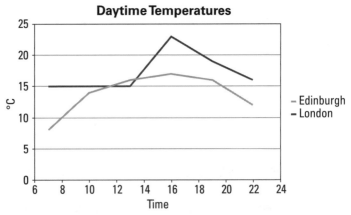

Figure 10-7: Multiple-line graphs.

They're just as easy to read as single-line graphs, with one slight added difficulty: you have to figure out which line to look at. You do so by picking the line with the correct colour or pattern from the legend, a box you normally find to the right of the graph.

Pigging out on pie charts

Pie charts are so-called because they look (but unfortunately don't smell) like a pie (check out Figure 10-8). Some well-meaning types call these circle graphs, but they're wrong and you can tell them we said so.

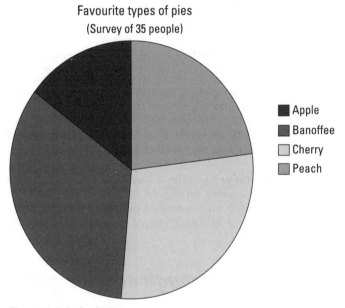

Favourite types of pies
(Survey of 35 people)

Apple
Banoffee
Cherry
Peach

Figure 10-8: A pie chart.

Pie charts differ from bar and line graphs in that the *size* (rather than the height) of the elements is what shows how important they are – the bigger the slice of pie, the higher the value of the thing it represents.

The key idea of pie charts is that each slice of the pie is a fraction of a whole circle – and the value it represents is the same fraction of the whole amount. For instance, if a slice represents 25 people out of 100, it shows up as a quarter of the circle.

Now, measuring an angle on a screen isn't at all easy, and so a limit applies to the kind of pie-chart question you can be asked on the test. Here are some typical examples:

- ✔ **Biggest or smallest grouping (which is the biggest or smallest slice?).** In Figure 10-8, the biggest is Banoffee and the smallest is Apple.

- ✔ **Whether a grouping is more or less than a quarter or a half of the total.** You can judge this by seeing whether the corresponding slice is bigger or smaller than a quarter or a half of a circle. Peach, for instance, is clearly less than a quarter in Figure 10-8, but Cherry is between a quarter and a half.

- ✔ **Comparing the relative sizes of slices.** Is one bigger than, smaller than or the same size as another?

- ✔ **Approximating the fraction of the circle taken up by a slice.** You might need to select the slice that corresponds to – say – about a fifth of the total (Peach, as it's slightly less than a quarter), or about 40% (Banoffee, as it's not much less than a half). .

Often, you're given the numbers or percentages that each slice represents, written on the graph or in the legend. In that case, testers can question you on anything that it's possible to ask about in a table (flip to the earlier section 'Dealing with Data Tables')!

Seeing through scatter graphs

You use a scatter graph (see an example in Figure 10-9) to compare observations of two different things at once. For example, you can use one to compare students' performance in a mock exam against their performance in real exams, or to compare the distance people have to travel to school against how long their journey takes.

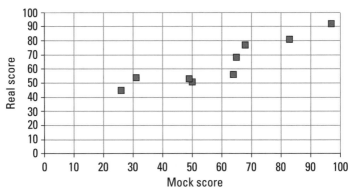

Figure 10-9: A scatter graph.

Each symbol on the graph (usually a square, a star or a cross) represents two measurements, one on each axis. Here's how you use them:

1. **Find the symbol you're interested in.**

2. **Read directly down from the symbol to the horizontal axis and find the value (that's the value of whatever the horizontal axis measures).**

3. **Read directly left from the symbol to the vertical axis and find the value (that's the value of whatever the vertical axis measures).**

So, the student who's farthest to the right in Figure 10-9 scored 97 in the mock exam and 92 in the actual exam.

If that was it for scatter graphs, they'd be absolutely no challenge! But you need to be aware of a few variations: scatter graphs with a line on and finding statistics (such as range or highest scores) from scatter graphs.

Using scatter graphs with a line

You see a line on a scatter graph for two reasons:

✔ When you're comparing two things that you'd reasonably expect to be about the same (such as a mock exam score and a real exam score, as you can see in Figure 10-10).

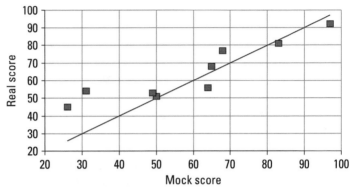

Figure 10-10: A scatter graph with a line.

✔ When a correlation, or relationship, exists between two measurements (for example, height and weight). In such cases, the graph may show the *line of best fit* – the value of one thing you'd expect to see for the other.

In either case, the test may set you two extra kinds of questions: one involving the number of observations above, below or on the line; and one involving the observations farthest from the line.

Number of observations

If you have a line on your scatter graph, it divides the graph into *three* parts:

✔ Observations with a higher value on the vertical axis than their horizontal score would suggest (above the line).

✔ Observations with a lower value on the vertical axis than their horizontal score would suggest (below the line).

✔ Observations with exactly the value on the vertical axis as their horizontal score would suggest (on the line).

For instance, the squares above the line in Figure 10-10 represent students whose real exam score was higher than their mock score and the squares below the line represent students with lower scores in their real exams than in their mocks. Any squares on the line would represent students who got the same mark in both exams.

A typical question asks 'how many' or 'what proportion of' the observations fall into one of the categories. Working out how many is easy – it's just a case of counting the crosses in the relevant part of the graph; working out the proportion (or percentage, or fraction) is only slightly harder.

Here's what you do to work out the fraction of students in Figure 10-10 who improved their scores between the mock and the final:

1. **Find how many students improved, by counting how many squares are above the line (their real scores are higher than their mock scores).** You find six such students.

2. **Discover the number of students altogether, by counting the total number of symbols.** You can see nine altogether.

3. **Work out the first number as a fraction of the other.** Six out of nine is 2/3.

Finding the proportion or percentage is exactly the same, but you replace 'fraction' with 'proportion' or 'percentage' as appropriate!

Farthest away

You may also be asked about the observation that's farthest away from the line. The testers can phrase this question in several ways, including:

- ✔ The student who showed the greatest improvement. . . .
- ✔ The observation with the greatest difference. . . .
- ✔ The observation farthest away from the expected. . . .

Watch out for a direction being implied. If the question says 'the greatest improvement', that means the farthest observation from the line *on the upper side*. If it says 'the greatest difference', it means the farthest observation from the line *on either side*. Here's how to find that observation:

1. **Decide whether you're looking for the farthest point above the line, below the line or in either direction.**

2. **Pick out the points that look as if they're farthest above or below the line (for the technical reason why, check out the nearby sidebar 'Looking up and**

down'), ignoring any that are clearly close to the line – don't go making extra work for yourself!

3. **Look at each of the possible points in turn and make a note of how far it is above or below the line.**

4. **Find the point that has the highest distance from the line, and use it to answer whichever question the test asks!**

For example, the student with the biggest improvement in score went from 31 in the mock to 54 in the final exam.

Finding statistics

Frequently, a scatter-graph question asks you to find a simple statistic based on the graph, typically the range or the median (which we define in Chapter 9). Here's how you find the range:

1. **Decide what you're finding the range of and look for the appropriate axis:** If you're looking at the vertical axis, find the values of highest and lowest observations (ignoring the horizontal axis completely). If you're looking at the horizontal axis, find the values of the left-most and right-most observations (ignoring the vertical axis completely).

   For example, if you're looking for the range of the actual exam scores in the earlier Figure 10-10, you pick the vertical axis.

2. **Find the difference between the two relevant values and this is your range.** In this example, the range in real scores is from 45 to 92, a range of 47; the range in mock scores is from 26 to 97, a range of 71.

Looking up and down

You always want to look at the *vertical* distance from the line in farthest-from-the-line scatter-graph questions, because graphs are almost always set up with the thing you're given (the *control* or *independent* variable) on the horizontal axis and the thing you're measuring (the *dependent* variable) on the vertical axis. The main cause – for example, actual age or height – goes on the bottom axis and the effect – reading age or weight – goes on the left.

You find the median in exactly the way you'd expect:

1. **Decide whether you're looking at the horizontal or the vertical axis.**

2. **Count up the number of observations altogether.**

3. **Add one to the count and halve the answer to work out which number observation is in the middle (for the nine students in Figure 10-10, you want the fifth student).**

4. **Find the lowest-valued observation (measured on the axis you want): that's number 1.**

5. **Find the next-lowest (number 2) and so on until you reach the number(s) you found in step 3.** If you had only one answer in step 3, the value of the observation you found in step 4 is the median. If you had two answers in step 3, find the mean of the two numbers you found in step 4 and this is the median.

The median score in the mock exam was 64, and the median score in the actual exam was 56.

In this example the same student had the median scores in both exams but that's not always the case.

Grafting Away at Complex Graphs

In this section, we discuss two less-than-simple graphs that crop up on the on-screen test:

- ✔ **Box-and-whiskers plot:** Shows the lowest and highest scores in a group, as well as three values in the middle (the lower quartile, the median and the upper quartile, which we discuss in Chapter 9 and the next section).

- ✔ **Cumulative frequency graph:** Height of the line shows how many items in a group have a score of less than a particular value.

Getting the better of box-and-whiskers plots

The box-and-whiskers plot (see Figure 10-11) is a completely different kind of graph to the ones we describe in the earlier section 'Sussing out Simple Graphs'. The idea is to show, at a glance, how a set of data is *distributed:* in other words, you get to see how widely spread out the data are, as well as where they're centred.

Box plot of football league points

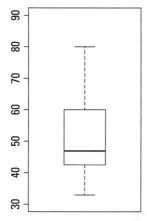

Figure 10-11: Box-and-whiskers plot.

This section assumes that the box-and-whiskers plot is upright, but the same techniques can be used for side-to-side box plots as well!

You can probably see from the example in Figure 10-11 where the name 'box and whiskers' comes from – the middle of the graph is a 'box' (with a line across it) and the ends are two 'whiskers', each with a line at the end.

Box-and-whiskers graphs tell you five pieces of information:

- ✔ **Lowest value:** The value at the end of the lower whisker. Looking at Figure 10-11, the team with the fewest points had 32 points.

- ✔ **Lower quartile:** The value 25 per cent of the observations are smaller than. For this example, it's about 42, and so a quarter of the teams had between 32 and 42 points. This value is at the lower end of the box.

- ✔ **Median:** The value 50 per cent of the observations were smaller than. Here, that's 47, and so half of the teams had between 32 and 47 points. This value is the line in the middle of the box.

- ✔ **Upper quartile:** The value 25 per cent of the observations were *larger* than. That's 60 here – a quarter of the teams had more than 60 points. This value is at the upper end of the box.

- ✔ **Highest value:** The value at the end of the highest whisker. In this graph, that's 80 points.

You can see that the graph divides everyone into four equal groups: the lower whisker contains a quarter of the observations; the bit of box below the line contains the next quarter; the bit of box above the line the third quarter; and the upper whisker the final quarter.

Knowing this information makes reading off any of the five values you need easy.

Working out ranges

In the test you may be asked to give the *range* – the difference between the highest and lowest value – or the *interquartile range* – the difference between the upper and lower quartile. Both of those numbers are easy.

To find the range:

1. **Find the highest value (the end of the upper whisker).**

2. **Find the lowest value (the end of the lower whisker).**

3. **Calculate the difference between them and that's the range (in Figure 10-11, the range is 80 – 32 = 48).**

You can also think about the range as the 'size' of the graph (between the ends of the whiskers).

The interquartile range is the size of the box:

1. **Locate the value of the upper quartile (the top of the box).**

2. **Find the value of the lower quartile (the bottom of the box).**

3. **Calculate the difference between them and this is the interquartile range (in Figure 10-11, the interquartile range is 60 – 42 = 18).**

Comparing distributions

Instead of seeing a single box-and-whiskers plot in a Numeracy test all on its little lonesome, you generally see several lined up for comparison.

Typically, the kinds of questions you come across involve:

✔ Reading a value from the correct graph.

✔ Answering true or false questions about these answers.

✔ Spotting a trend in a particular value.

Of these questions, only spotting a trend is at all tricky. But then you can refer to Chapter 9, which explains how to spot a trend from a set of given numbers.

Adding in cumulative frequency graphs

The cumulative frequency graph (see Figure 10-12) is probably the weirdest of the graph family. The word *cumulative* comes from the same root as *accumulate,* and has a similar meaning: it just means 'adding up as you go along'.

The value on the vertical axis of a cumulative frequency graph shows how many observations are smaller than the corresponding value on the horizontal axis. That sounds like gibberish and so here's an example: looking at the graph in Figure 10-12, you can see that 35 students (on the vertical axis) scored 57 points or fewer (on the horizontal axis).

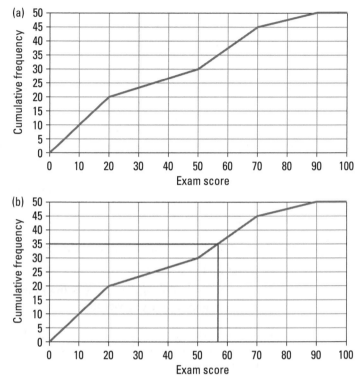

Figure 10-12: (a) A cumulative frequency graph, and (b) reading a value from it.

Reading off values

Test setters can ask you to read a cumulative frequency graph in two ways: finding a value that a certain number of observations are higher (or lower) than; or finding how many observations are higher (or lower) than a given value.

To find out the value a certain number of observations are lower than, here's what you do:

1. **Find the number you're given on the vertical axis.**

2. **Read across to the line.**

3. **Read down to the horizontal axis and the value you find is the value you're after.**

For example, if you want the value 35 students scored less than, you read across from 35 on the vertical axis and down to the horizontal axis: 35 students scored less than 57.

If you're asked for the value a certain number of observations are *higher* than, you need to think a little bit: you can find out how many observations are *lower* than that particular value by taking the number away from the total. So, if you have 50 observations and want to find the value 30 of them are higher than, that's the same as finding the value 20 of them are lower than (or equal to).

You can also be asked to read the graph the other way: finding how many observations are lower than a particular value, which is very straightforward:

1. **Find the value you're given on the horizontal axis.**

2. **Read up to the curve.**

3. **Read left to the vertical axis and the number you find is the number you're after.**

If you want to know how many students scored less than 60 points, you read up from 60 and across to the vertical axis – 37 students scored less than 60 points.

If, on the other hand, you're interested in the number of observations higher than a particular value, you need to make a small adjustment: just take your answer away from the total number of people.

Calculating statistics

With a cumulative frequency graph, you can quite easily work out statistics such as the median and quartiles (which we describe in Chapter 9 and the earlier section 'Getting the better of box-and-whiskers plots').

Here's how to find the median:

1. **Locate the total number of observations.** If you're not given the figure, it's the highest value the curve reaches on the vertical axis. (In Figure 10-12, the number is 50 observations.)

2. **Find half of this number for the median.** For the lower quartile, find a quarter of this number. For the upper quartile, find three-quarters of the number in step 1. (In Figure 10-12, the median would be student 25; the quartiles would be 12.5 and 37.5.)

3. **Find the value that many observations are lower than.** This number is the value you're after!

In the current example, the median is 34, the lower quartile is about 13 and the upper quartile is about 60.

When you have these values, finding the interquartile range is a walk in the park: you just find the difference between the quartiles (here, 60 – 13 = 47).

For reasons best known to examiners, you don't add 1 before halving or quartering to find the quartiles when you have a cumulative frequency graph. Luckily, even if you do it the same way as for a list, your answer will be within the tolerance margin the exam allows.

Chapter 11

Trying out Your Numeracy Skills: On-Screen Practice Questions

*W*e're sure that you're itching to get started on some Numeracy tests for yourself (we certainly are . . . itching that is – that darned stray cat's sneaked into Dummies HQ again!).

In this chapter, we provide five tests of the type you can expect to see in the on-screen portion of your Numeracy test. We also give you the answers so that you can appraise your progress and perhaps identify any areas you need to work on.

Having a Go Yourself: The Tests

In the exam, you have 36 minutes to answer the 16 questions (a little over two minutes for each question, on average), and you have access to a calculator on the computer.

You can do these tests against the clock or untimed, as you prefer!

Test A

Figure 11-1 shows the results of 14 students in two separate tests (science and maths).

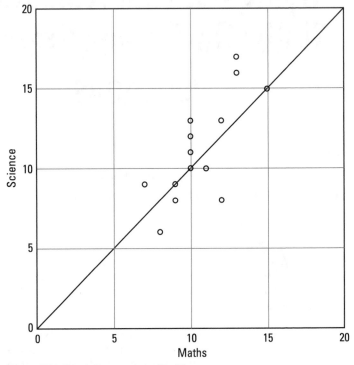

Figure 11-1: Graph for questions A1–A3.

A1. How many students scored the same in both tests?

A2. What was the maths score of the student who did best in science?

A3. What was the range of the students' maths scores?

Figure 11-2 shows the number of students in a small school achieving each grade in an exam.

	Maths	Science	English
A*	3	5	6
A	10	12	13
B	19	17	10
C	11	6	9
D	6	5	6
E	1	4	3
U	0	1	3

Figure 11-2: Table for questions A4–A6.

A4. What percentage of the students got a B or better in maths?

A5. What was the median grade in science?

A6. In which of the three subjects did most students get a C or better?

Figure 11-3 shows the number of extra tuition hours taken by a group of students in a week.

Extra hours	Students
0	5
1	8
2	4
3	2
4	1

Figure 11-3: Table for questions A7 and A8.

A7. What was the average number of extra tuition hours taken per student? Give your answer as a decimal.

A8. Students get one free hour of extra tuition, and further hours cost £35 each. How much did the extra classes cost altogether?

Look at the temperature graph in Figure 11-4.

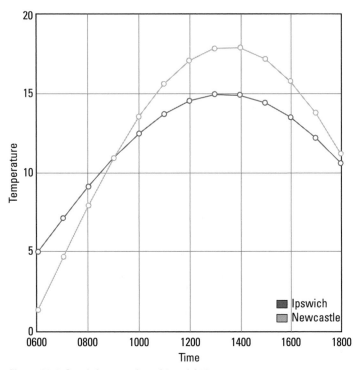

Figure 11-4: Graph for questions A9 and A10.

A9. True or false?

a) Newcastle was warmer than Ipswich all afternoon (until at least 6 p.m.).

b) The maximum difference between the temperatures in Ipswich and Newcastle was 3 degrees Celsius.

c) The range of temperatures in Ipswich was greater than that in Newcastle.

A10. At what time was the temperature the same in Newcastle and Ipswich? Use the 24-hour clock.

Questions A11 and A12 refer to Figure 11-5 which shows attendance percentages for six classes in a school.

Classes	Attendance		
	Autumn	**Winter**	**Spring**
10D	93	95	97
10E	97	96	98
10I	95	98	93
10M	94	90	93
10S	88	86	90
10U	90	96	88

Figure 11-5: Table for questions A11 and A12.

A11. True or false?

a) Class 10E had the best attendance percentage in all three terms.

b) Class 10E had the smallest range of attendance percentages.

c) Exactly half of the classes showed an improvement in attendance percentages from Autumn to Spring terms.

A12. Which class had the biggest percentage point improvement in attendance from Winter to Spring terms?

A13. Look at the box-and-whiskers plot in Figure 11-6

Which of the following are true?

a) The median time taken for students to arrive at school was 5 minutes shorter than the median time for teachers.

b) Half of the students took less time to arrive than the quickest teacher.

c) The range of times the students took to arrive was 40 minutes.

A14. What is the interquartile range of the times the teachers took to arrive at school?

A15. A teacher plans a trip to Bayeux. On the final day, the coach needs to be at Cherbourg for 2 p.m. The minibus travels at an average speed of 45 miles per hour and Bayeux is 96 kilometres from Cherbourg.

Using the approximation 5 miles = 8 kilometres, what is the latest time the bus should leave Bayeux? Give your answer in the 24-hour clock format.

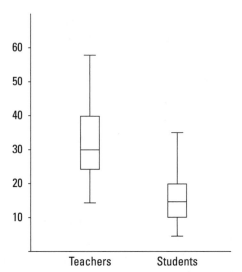

Figure 11-6: Box-and-whiskers plot for questions A13 and A14.

A16. Figure 11-7 shows mock exam and presentation scores for three students taking a course in IT. Their final grades are worked out by the formula (presentation percentage + 3 × mock exam percentage)/4. Which of the students scored more than the 70 per cent required to pass the course?

	Mock exam mark (out of 80)	Presentation mark (out of 25)
Roy	64	15
Moss	76	15
Jen	44	25

Figure 11-7: Table for A16.

Test B

Figure 11-8 shows the outcome of a Year 9 charity bake sale.

Form	Cakes sold	Cookies sold
9A	12	16
9B	15	20
9E	8	25
9G	20	10

Cookies : 50p each
Cakes : £1.50p each

Figure 11-8: Table for questions B1–B3.

B1. Which form made the most money for charity?

B2. The proceeds were split between two charities in the ratio of 3:1. How much did the first charity receive?

B3. How many more cakes would form 9E have needed to sell to have raised the same amount as form 9G?

B4. The bar chart in Figure 11-9 shows average class sizes in two local schools over three years. Which of the following statements are true?

a) In 2011, Carsville had (on average) more than twice as many students per class as Ablesborough.

b) Class sizes in all three schools increased between 2011 and 2012.

c) Ablesborough Academy had the smallest average class sizes in both years.

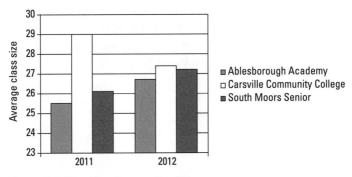

Figure 11-9: Class sizes for question B4.

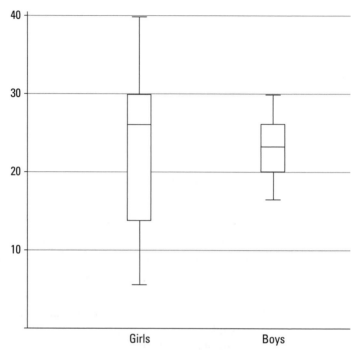

Figure 11-10: Box-and-whiskers plot for question B5.

B5. Figure 11-10 shows the performance of boys and girls in a general knowledge quiz. Which of the following statements are true?

a) Exactly 25 per cent of the boys scored fewer points than the worst girl's score.

b) Exactly 25 per cent of the boys scored more points than the median girl's score.

c) Exactly 25 per cent of the boys achieved scores between the girls' quartile scores.

Questions B6 and B7 refer to Figure 11-11.

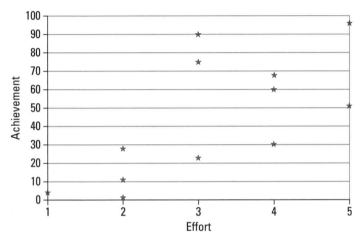

Figure 11-11: Scatter plot for questions B6 and B7.

B6. Figure 11-11 shows the effort and achievement marks awarded to a group of 12 students. Which of the following statements are true?

a) A quarter of the students were rated '2' for effort.

b) A quarter of the students scored between 50 and 70 in achievement.

c) The median achievement score was between 60 and 70.

B7. Students were allowed to go on a class trip to an amusement park if they:

✔ Scored more than 80 per cent achievement marks *or*

✔ Were rated '5' for effort *or*

✔ Were rated '4' for effort and over 65 per cent for achievement.

Tickets for the amusement park cost £15 each. How much would it cost to buy tickets for all the qualifying students?

Questions B8 and B9 refer to Figure 11-12.

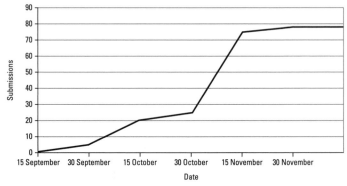

Figure 11-12: Cumulative frequency graph for questions B8 and B9.

B8. Figure 11-12 shows a cumulative frequency graph showing how many students had submitted their UCAS forms by each date. The deadline given by the school for submission was 15 October. Which of the following statements are true?

a) The median submission date was in October.

b) More than 25 per cent of the students handed in their forms late.

c) Nobody submitted their form in December.

B9. The following year, the school changed its policy, hoping to improve the number of on-time submissions. Of the 85 students in Year 13, 65 of them submitted on time. To the nearest 10 percentage points, how much did the on-time submission rate improve or decline?

B10. Figure 11-13 (a and b) shows the results of a school travel survey over two years.

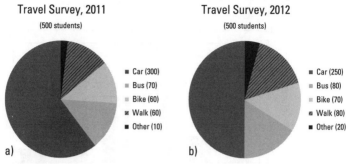

Travel Survey, 2011
(500 students)

- Car (300)
- Bus (70)
- Bike (60)
- Walk (60)
- Other (10)

a)

Travel Survey, 2012
(500 students)

- Car (250)
- Bus (80)
- Bike (70)
- Walk (80)
- Other (20)

b)

Figure 11-13: Pie charts for question B10.

The school had a target of reducing the number of students coming to school by car by 20 per cent.

a) By how many per cent did the number of students coming to school by car drop? Give your answer to one decimal place.

b) Did the school meet its target?

Questions B11 and B12 refer to Figure 11-14.

	January	March	May
DumCorps	95.87	99.85	95.89
MathsMerch	134.73	164.23	193.73
Calculators'R'Us	62.17	46.19	19.54

Figure 11-14: Historical prices, in pence, for questions B11 and B12.

An economics teacher compiles the table in Figure 11-14, showing the prices, in pence, of shares in several companies over a few months.

B11. He asks his class to consider a simulated portfolio consisting of 100 shares in DumCorps, 250 shares in MathsMerch and 500 shares in Calculators'R'Us. The class 'buys' the stocks in January and sells them in May. How much pretend profit or loss does the class make?

B12. If the price trend was consistent, how much would MathsMerch shares have been worth in April?

Questions B13 and B14 refer to Figure 11-15, which shows the number of classroom accidents requiring use of the first-aid kit in several subjects over three years.

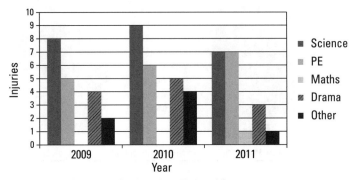

Figure 11-15: Bar graph for questions B13 and B14.

B13. In which subject did the most injuries occur over the three years?

B14. Aside from the mental and physical anguish caused to students and staff by minor medical disasters, it costs, on average, £4.50 to re-equip the first-aid kit after it has been used. How much less did the school spend on re-equipping the first-aid kit in 2011 than in 2010?

Questions B15 and B16 refer to Figure 11-16.

London Gatwick (dep)	1500	1630	1800	1930	2100
Berlin Schoenefeld (arr)	1815	2045	2115	2245	2355

Figure 11-16: A timetable for questions B15 and B16.

The timetable in Figure 11-16 shows the schedule for several flights between London and Berlin. All times are local times and Berlin is an hour ahead of UK time.

B15. Which flight has the shortest travel time?

B16. A teacher plans a school trip. She knows it takes 30 minutes to get from Schoenefeld Airport to the hotel in central Berlin, and she allows an hour to get through passport control in Germany. She also wants to get the group to Gatwick two hours ahead of departure time, and knows it will take two hours and 15 minutes to get from the school to the airport. What time must the group leave the school if it's to arrive at the hotel before 10 p.m.? Give your answer using the 24-hour clock.

Test C

The box-and-whiskers plots in Figure 11-17 show the results of a class's monthly spelling test, which contains 20 questions.

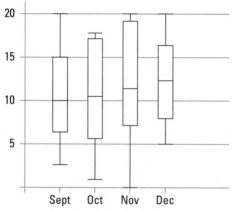

Figure 11-17: Box-and-whiskers plots for spelling test results for questions C1–C3.

C1. In which months did at least one student achieve full marks?

C2. The class's teacher notices a trend in the median score. If this trend continued, what would he expect the median score to be the following month?

C3. Which of the following statements are true?

a) The highest range of scores was in the September test.

b) At least a quarter of the students scored more than half marks in all four months.

c) The interquartile range was highest in November.

C4. A head of year is preparing programmes and tickets for the Christmas concert. She has a budget of £150 for printing and plans to print 200 tickets (see Figure 11-18). Each programme consists of two double-sided colour pages and four double-sided black-and-white pages. How many programmes can she afford to print?

	Single-sided	Double-sided
B&W	5p	8p
Colour	20p	30p

Posters (A3)	£4.50
Posters (A4)	£3.00

Ticket books (5)	£2.00
Ticket books (20)	£7.00

£10 off all orders over £100

Figure 11-18: Printing prices for question C4.

C5. Sara leaves Norwich at 8 a.m. to travel to a meeting in London. She drives the 100 miles to get there, and the meeting lasts two and a quarter hours. She then drives 50 miles to Oxford to meet a friend for coffee and a meal. After spending three and a half hours in Oxford, she drives 125 miles back to Norwich. If she drives at an average speed of 50 miles per hour, what time will she get home? Give your answer using the 24-hour clock.

C6. Figure 11-19 shows the results of a survey into students' favourite sports. What proportion of the students preferred racquet sports (tennis or squash)? Give your answer as a decimal.

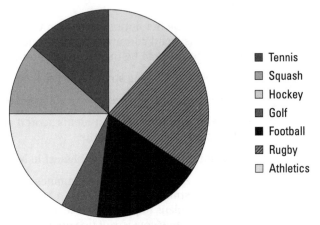

■ Tennis
▦ Squash
□ Hockey
■ Golf
■ Football
▨ Rugby
□ Athletics

Figure 11-19: Pie chart for question C6.

C7. Figure 11-20 compares a school year's exam results in geography and history. Which of the following statements are true?

a) More than half of the students achieved a B grade or better in History.

b) Less than a quarter of the students achieved a D grade or worse in Geography.

c) 30 per cent of the students achieved the same grade in both exams.

		Geography								
		A*	A	B	C	D	E	F	G	Total
History	A*	7	5	3						15
	A	8	6	9	6					29
	B	1	3	5	7	2				18
	C		3	4	7	1		1		16
	D			3	4	4	3			14
	E				4		1	1		6
	F			1				1		2
	G									0
	Total	16	17	25	28	7	4	3	0	100

Figure 11-20: Exam score comparisons for question C7.

C8. Figure 11-21 shows the reading and actual ages (in years and months) of several students. Which students have reading ages at least three months ahead of their actual ages?

Student	Reading age		Actual age	
Alex	9	7	9	10
Bob	6	5	8	11
Christine	13	9	9	10
Dawn	7	7	9	1
Elliot	9	5	8	11
Frances	9	7	9	9
Graeme	9	7	9	3

Figure 11-21: Reading ages for question C8.

C9. Figure 11-22 shows the results of a day's registration for Year 9 at a school. What values should go in the grey squares?

	Students	Percentage
Present		62%
Late	33	
Absent		16%
Total		

Figure 11-22: Registration results for Year 9 for question C9.

Questions C10 and C11 refer to Figure 11-23.

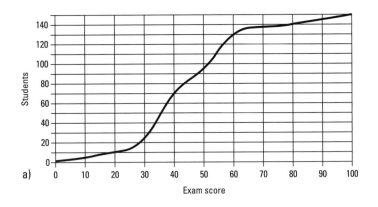

a)

Grade	Minimum Score
A	80
B	65
C	50
D	35
E	20

b)

Figure 11-23: Cumulative frequency graph for questions C10 and C11.

The cumulative frequency graph in Figure 11-23 (a) shows the scores achieved by 150 students who sat an exam, and the table (b) shows the grade boundaries.

C10. What percentage of the students achieved a grade of C or better? Give your answer to the nearest whole number.

C11. Which of the following statements are true?

a) The median score was 50.

b) The interquartile range was 55.

c) Exactly ten students achieved an A grade.

C12. In one exam, Tony scored 45 out of a possible 80 marks. In another, he scored 75 out of 120. What was his percentage point improvement between the exams? Give your answer as a decimal.

C13. A teacher is planning an experiment for her science classes. She has four classes, each with 24 students; she will have them working in pairs. Each experiment requires 15 millilitres of hydrochloric acid, and each pair will perform the experiment three times. How many one-litre bottles of hydrochloric acid should she ask the technicians to prepare?

C14. A teacher takes her history class on a field trip to a ruined castle. The minibus costs £40 to hire for the day, plus 25p per mile. The castle is 25 miles away. Entry to the castle costs £5.50 per person. Ten students pay £12 each to go on the trip. How much surplus or deficit is there from the trip?

Questions C15 and C16 refer to Figure 11-24, a stacked-bar graph showing the grade level accomplished by percentages of students in different years in a music exam.

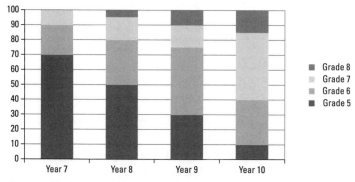

Figure 11-24: A stacked-bar graph for questions C15 and C16.

C15. Which of the following statements are true?

a) If the trend continued, 20 per cent of Year 11 students would have accomplished grade 8.

b) The same percentage of Year 8 and Year 10 students achieved grade 5.

c) The modal grade was different in all four years.

C16. Year 7 has 150 students, Year 8 has 120 students, Year 9 has 100 students and Year 10 has 80 students. How many students achieved grade 7?

Test D

Questions D1 to D3 refer to Figure 11-25, which shows the grades achieved by eight students in a mock exam and a final exam.

Candidate	Exam scores			Grade boundaries	
	Mock	Final		A*	90 or above
A	62	67		A	80-89
B	8	40		B	70-79
C	72	64		C	60-69
D	87	91		D	50-59
E	25	16		E	40-49
F	49	65		U	39 or lower
G	90	94			
H	13	15			

Figure 11-25: Exam scores and grade boundaries for questions D1–D3.

D1. Which candidates achieved better grades in their final exam than their mock?

D2. What was the modal grade of the students who took the final exam?

D3. True or false?

a) All nine students improved their scores between the mock and the exam.

b) The mean improvement in scores was more than 5 points.

c) The range of scores in the mock exam was greater than that in the final.

| | | Term | | | |
		Autumn	**Spring**	**Summer**	**Total**
9D	Boys	88	90	97	92
	Girls	81	85	97	88
	Total	84	87	97	89
9M	Boys	80	84	83	82
	Girls	78	82	82	81
	Total	79	83	83	82
9S	Boys	85	84	85	85
	Girls	85	80	81	82
	Total	85	82	83	83
9U	Boys	96	92	93	94
	Girls	90	89	96	92
	Total	94	91	94	93

Figure 11-26: A table showing attendance rates for question D4.

D4. Figure 11-26 shows the attendance percentages for four classes over a school year, split up by gender and term. Which of the following statements are true?

a) Class 9D had the highest percentage of absences in all three terms.

b) The attendance percentage of boys in class 9S improved with each term.

c) Class 9U was the class with the highest percentage of girls attending in the Spring term.

Questions D5 and D6 refer to Figure 11-27.

Supermarket	1150	1205	1220	1235
Blandford Rd	1210	1225	1240	1255
High St	1240	1225	1310	1325
Central Station	1245	1300	1315	1330
George St	1305	1320	1335	1350
St Mary's Church	1320	1335	1350	1405
Parkway Station	1335	1350	1405	1420

Figure 11-27: Bus timetable for questions D5–D6.

D5. A teacher is organising a school trip to a museum. The group has a tour booked for 2 p.m. It will take 15 minutes for the group to walk from the bus stop in George Street to the museum. The teacher plans to arrive at least five minutes early. What time should the group catch the bus from Blandford Road? Give your answer in the 24-hour clock format.

D6. Tickets to the museum cost £7.50 for adults and £5.50 for students. The museum offers a 10 per cent discount for groups of ten or more. The bus fare is £1.80 per adult and £1.50 per student. The department has budgeted £50 for the trip. How many students can go with the teacher?

D7. Figure 11-28 gives data about the number of students who travel to school by particular modes of transport. Which of the following statements are true?

a) More than a quarter of the students come to school by car.

b) The modal method of travelling to school is walking.

c) Fewer than 100 students cycle to school.

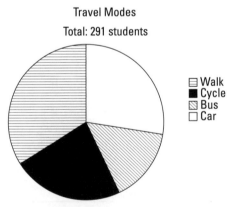

Travel Modes

Total: 291 students

Figure 11-28: Pie chart showing students' modes of transport to school for question D7.

D8. A student's predicted exam score is given by the following formula:

(mock exam score × 0.7 + coursework score × 0.3) × final term attendance proportion

A student scores 64 in her mock exam and 75 in her coursework. In her final term, she attends 97 days out of 100.

What is her predicted final exam score, to the nearest whole point?

D9. Figure 11-29 shows the actual ages and reading ages of five students. Which students have a reading age more than six months behind their actual age?

Student	Actual age		Reading age	
	Years	Months	Years	Months
A	12	1	12	2
B	11	8	11	10
C	12	0	10	9
D	12	2	11	3
E	11	10	12	9
F	11	11	11	1
G	12	4	11	9

Figure 11-29: Reading ages for question D9.

Questions D10 and D11 refer to Figure 11-30.

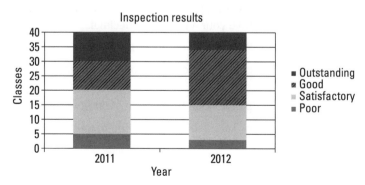

Figure 11-30: Inspection results for questions D10–D11.

D10. Figure 11-30 shows a school's results in two different inspections. Which of the following statements are true?

a) The ratio of good classes to satisfactory classes in 2011 was 3:2.

b) The proportion of classes rated outstanding in 2012 was 0.2.

c) The number of classes rated poor decreased by more than 50 per cent between 2011 and 2012.

D11. The school had a target of having 75 per cent of its classes rated good or outstanding in 2012. By how many classes did it exceed or fall short of its target?

Questions D12 and D13 refer to Figure 11-31.

Class	Students	Assignments	Total submitted on time
8G	25	15	300
8M	31	12	279
8Y	23	11	221

Figure 11-31: Homework submission for questions D12–D13.

D12. A teacher records the number of homework assignments she set for three of her classes, the number of students in each class and the total number of assignments submitted on time. Her results are in Figure 11-31. What is class 8M's proportion of on-time submissions? Give your answer as a decimal.

D13. Which of the following statements are true?

a) The proportion of on-time submissions in Class 8G was 0.8.

b) The total proportion of on-time submissions was 0.8.

c) The median proportion of on-time submissions was 0.8.

Questions D14 to D16 refer to Figure 11-32, in which you can see a graph showing the results of eight students in two tests: an initial test taken in March and a final exam taken in June.

D14. What was the June score of the student who showed the biggest improvement between March and June?

D15. What fraction of the students showed an improvement between March and June?

D16. Which of the following statements are true about Figure 11-32?

a) The range of marks in the March exam was 51.

b) The median score in the June exam was 51.

c) The modal score in the March exam was 51.

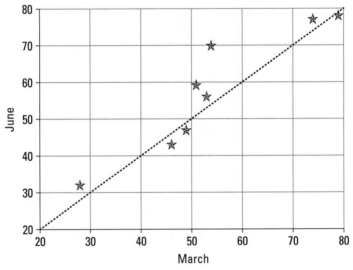

Figure 11-32: Scatter graph of results for two exams for questions D14–D16.

Test E

Questions E1 to E3 refer to Figure 11-33, which shows three schools' medal tallies at the county athletics meetings over five years.

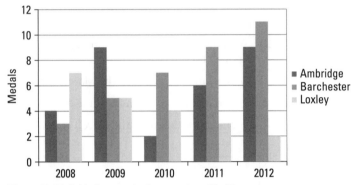

Figure 11-33: Athletics results for questions E1–E3.

E1. Which school had a mean of six medals over the five years?

E2. If Barchester School's trend of medal-winning continues, how many medals can it expect to win in 2014?

E3. Which of the following statements are true?

a) Loxley's medal tally fell each year.

b) The three schools together gained more medals in 2012 than any other year.

c) The range of the number of medals won by Ambridge was nine.

E4. On a school skiing trip, the bus leaves Calais at 9 a.m. on Monday morning, and travels the 1,000 kilometres to Val d'Isère at an average speed of 50 miles per hour. The bus stops after every three hours of driving for a 30-minute break. What time does the bus arrive at Val d'Isère? Use the 24-hour clock.

Five miles is about the same as eight kilometres.

Questions E5 and E6 refer to Figure 11-34 (a) and (b).

For a physics class, a teacher rates each student's effort as excellent, good, fair, poor or unacceptable. Figure 11-34 shows his results for the spring term (top) and the summer term (bottom).

E5. What was the percentage point increase in students rated 'excellent' or 'good' between the two reports?

E6. How many fewer students had an effort grade of 'poor' or 'unacceptable' in the summer than in the spring?

Questions E7 and E8 refer to Figure 11-35.

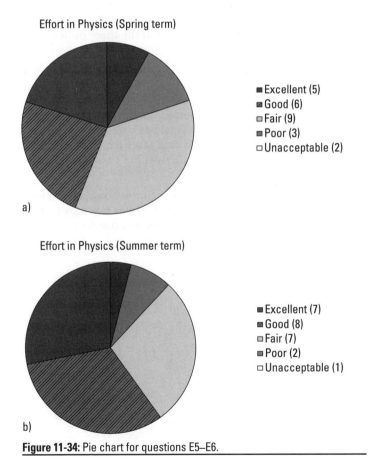

Effort in Physics (Spring term)

■ Excellent (5)
▨ Good (6)
▢ Fair (9)
▨ Poor (3)
▢ Unacceptable (2)

a)

Effort in Physics (Summer term)

■ Excellent (7)
▨ Good (8)
▢ Fair (7)
▨ Poor (2)
▢ Unacceptable (1)

b)

Figure 11-34: Pie chart for questions E5–E6.

	Basic	Educational	Professional
Number of users	10	25	100
Technical support	None	Email	Phone
Price (monthly)	£7.99	£15.99	£25.99
Extra users (each, per month)	£2.50	£1.50	£0.75

Special offer!
Educational and Professional packages include a one-month free trial.

Figure 11-35: Software prices for questions E7–E8.

E7. A teacher wants to test a new software system for her class of 30 students over a school year of ten months. The prices offered by the company are given in Figure 11-35. Which of the three options would be the best value?

E8. After the trial is completed successfully, it's extended to the whole school. This requires 750 users. The teacher suggests buying eight separate Professional packages, whereas the headteacher suggests buying a single Professional package and paying for extra users. How many per cent more expensive is the headteacher's idea than the teacher's? Give your answer to one decimal place.

Questions E9 and E10 refer to the box-and-whiskers plots in Figure 11-36, which show the times taken by three classes of 28 students each to finish a set of puzzles.

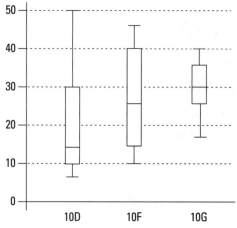

Figure 11-36: Box-and-whiskers plots for questions E9–E10.

E9. Which of the following statements are true?

a) Class 10D had the largest range.

b) Class 10D had the largest interquartile range.

c) Class 10D had the highest median time.

E10. The teacher decides to give gold stars to students who finished the puzzles more quickly than 75 per cent of class 10F. How many students altogether receive gold stars?

Questions E11 and E12 refer to the two-way table in Figure 11-37, which shows a breakdown of students by year, gender and the foreign language(s) they study.

		No language	French only	German only	French and German	Total
Boys	Year 12	31	7	7	5	50
	Year 13	12	9	4	3	28
Girls	Year 12	9	7	6	2	24
	Year 13	11	4	8	5	28
	Total	63	27	25	15	130

Figure 11-37: A two-way table for questions E11–E12.

E11. How many Year 12 boys study at least one foreign language?

E12. Which of the following statements are true?

a) In this sixth form, French is a more popular option than German.

b) Three-quarters of the Year 13 students study no foreign language.

c) More girls study two languages than study none.

Questions E13 and E14 refer to Figure 11-38, which shows a scatter graph relating students' scores in a half-term exam and an end-of-term exam.

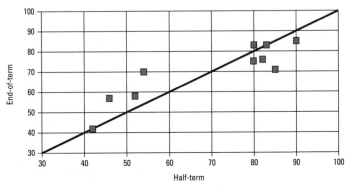

Figure 11-38: A scatter graph for questions E13–E14.

E13. What percentage of students scored higher in the end-of-term exam than in the half-term exam?

E14. The teacher calculated each student's final grade for the course using the formula:

(3 × end-of-term exam score + half-term score) ÷ 4

What was the final grade for the student who showed the biggest improvement between the half-term and end-of-term exams?

Questions E15 and E16 refer to Figure 11-39, which shows the times of a selection of trains from London to Banbury in the evening.

Departure	From	To	Arrival	Duration	Changes	Fare
20:37	London Marylebone	Banbury	21:45	1h 08m	0	£24.90
21:07	London Marylebone	Banbury	22:13	1h 06m	0	£24.90
21:37	London Marylebone	Banbury	22:42	1h 05m	0	£24.90
22:07	London Marylebone	Banbury	23:03	56m	0	£24.90
22:37	London Marylebone	Banbury	23:38	1h 01m	0	£24.90

Figure 11-39: Train times for questions E15–E16.

E15. Anji is planning her way home from a conference in central London. It will take her 40 minutes to walk from the conference venue to Marylebone, and she wants to be back in Banbury before 11 p.m. What's the latest time she can leave the conference venue to get home on time? Give your answer using the 24-hour clock.

E16. Anji has a railcard that entitles her to 1/3 off all rail fares. She'll be travelling to and from Marylebone every day for six days, and buys a single ticket for each journey. The tickets are the same price at all times. How much will she spend on rail tickets?

Checking How You Did: Test Answers

If you want to work out your score from these tests, remember that you need to answer all parts of a question correctly to get the mark: for instance, if the question asks you which of three questions are true or false, you need to get all three correct to get the point. Sorry, we know that's harsh, but we don't make the rules!

On the plus side, particularly with graph questions, you usually get a margin-of-error allowance, and so if you get an answer that's tolerably close to the correct answer, you *do* get the point even if you don't have exactly the right answer.

Test A

A1. **Three.** These students are on the line!

A2. **13.** The best science score was the highest point on the graph, which corresponds to a science score of 17 and a maths score (along the bottom) of 13.

A3. **8.** The range is the difference between the highest score (15) and the lowest (7).

A4. **64.** Thirty-two out of 50 is 64 per cent.

A5. **B.** You're looking for the grade of the 25th and 26th-best students.

A6. **Maths (43), better than Science (40) and English (38).**

A7. **1.3 hours.** The mean is the total number of hours divided by the number of students. The total number of hours taken was $(0 \times 5) + (8 \times 1) + (4 \times 2) + (2 \times 3) + (1 \times 4) = 0 + 8 + 8 + 6 + 4 = 26$. With 20 students, the mean is $26 \div 20 = 1.3$.

A8. **£385.** The five students who took no extra classes paid nothing. The eight students who just took the one free class paid nothing. The four who took two classes paid £35 each, making $4 \times 35 = £140$. The two who took three classes paid £70 each, making £140. The one who took four extra classes paid £105. Altogether, that's $140 + 140 + 105 = £385$.

A9. a) **True.** The line representing Newcastle is higher than the Ipswich line from 12:00 to 18:00.

   b) **False.** The maximum difference is 4 degrees Celsius, at 06:00.

   c) **False.** The range of temperatures in Newcastle was $(18–1) = 17$ degrees Celsius; the range in Ipswich was only $(15–5) = 10$ degrees Celsius.

A10. **09:00.** When the curves cross.

A11. a) **False.** 10I had the best attendance in the Winter term.

   b) **True.** Their range is 2 percentage points, the smallest of all.

   c) **True.** The attendance for 10D, 10E and 10S increased and the other three fell.

A12. **Class 10S.** It increased by 4 percentage points.

Percentage points are easier to deal with than 'proper' percentages – all you have to think about is the difference between the numbers rather than use the Table of Joy.

A13. a) **False.** The median time for students is 15 minutes and the median time for teachers is 30 minutes.

   b) **True.** Half of the students arrive more quickly than the median by definition. The quickest teacher arrives in 15 minutes, which is the median for the students.

   c) **False.** The students' range is 30 minutes; 40 minutes is the range for the teachers.

A14. **15 minutes.** The upper quartile is 40 and the lower quartile is 25, and so the interquartile range is 40 – 25 = 15.

A15. **12:40.** The distance from Bayeux to Cherbourg is 96 kilometres, which works out to be 60 miles. At 45 miles per hour, that takes 60 ÷ 45 = one and a third hours, or one hour and twenty minutes. To arrive for 2 p.m., the bus would need to leave at 12:40 p.m., which is 12:40 using the 24-hour clock.

A16. **Roy and Moss.** The exam percentages worked out to be for Roy: 64 × 100 ÷ 80 = 80 per cent; for Moss: 76 × 100 ÷ 80 = 95 per cent; and for Jen: 44 × 100 ÷ 80 = 55 per cent. The presentation percentages were for Roy and Moss: 15 × 100 ÷ 25 = 60 per cent; and for Jen, 100 per cent.

So, Roy's overall mark was (60 + 3 × 80) ÷ 4 = 300 ÷ 4 = 75; Moss's mark was (60 + 3 × 95) ÷ 4 = 86.25, and Jen's was (100 + 3 × 55) ÷ 4 = 66.25. Roy and Moss both scored more than 70 per cent, while Jen didn't.

Test B

B1. **9G made the most money.** Here's how to work it out:

9A: 12 cakes × £1.50 = £18; 16 cookies × £0.50 = £8; total = £18 + £8 = £26.

9B: 15 × 1.50 = 22.50; 20 × 0.50 = 10; 22.50 + 10 = 32.50.

9E: 8 × 1.50 = 12; 25 × 0.50 = 12.50; 12 + 12.50 = 24.50.

9G: 20 × 1.50 = 30; 10 × 0.50 = 5; 30 + 5 = 35 – the highest of the four totals.

B2. **£88.50.** The total raised was 26 + 32.50 + 24.50 + 35 = 118. The Table of Joy sum is 118 × 3 ÷ 4 = 88.50.

B3. **7.** The difference 9E would have to make up is 35 – 24.50 = 10.50. The number of cakes needed is 10.50 ÷ 1.50 = 7.

B4. a) **False.** Although it looks that way, the graph is misleading because the axis doesn't start at 0. Ablesborough's class size was 25.5 and Carsville's 29.

b) **False.** Carsville's class sizes decreased.

c) **True.**

B5. a) **False.** The worst girl's score was 5, and no boy scored fewer than 15.

b) **True.** The upper quartile of the boys' scores is 25, the same as the girls' median.

c) **False.** All the boys achieved scores between the girls' quartile scores.

B6. a) **True.** Three of the 12 students were rated '2'.

b) **True.** Three of the 12 students were in this range.

c) **False.** The median is between the 6th and 7th highest marks, which would be around 40.

B7. **£60.** Two students qualify through effort, one more qualifies through achievement and a fourth scored four for effort and 68 for achievement, and so qualifies as well. $4 \times £15 = £60$.

B8. a) **False.** With 78 students, the median is around the 38th and 39th student, who submitted early in November.

b) **True.** Only 20 students (about 25 per cent) handed in their forms on time.

c) **True.**

B9. **50.** The percentage of on-time submissions in the following year is $65 \times 100 \div 85 = 76.5$ per cent, compared to about 25 per cent this year. The percentage point difference is 51.5 per cent, which is 50 to the nearest 10 percentage points.

B10. **16.7 per cent and no.** In 2011, 300 students came to school by car, while in 2012, that number dropped to 250 – a decrease of 50 students. The percentage drop was $50 \times 100 \div 300 = 16.7$ per cent (to one decimal place), and so the school didn't meet its target.

B11. **Loss of £65.63.** In January, the shares in each company would have been worth $100 \times 95.87\text{p} = £95.87$ for DumCorps, $250 \times 134.73\text{p} = £336.83$ for MathsMerch and $500 \times 62.17\text{p} = £310.85$ for Calculators'R'Us, making a total of £743.55. Using the May prices, the DumCorps shares are worth £95.89, the MathsMerch shares £484.33 and the Calculators'R'Us shares £97.90. The May total is £677.92, and the class's loss is £743.55 − £677.92 = £65.63.

B12. **£178.98.** MathsMerch's price is increasing at a rate of £29.50 every two months, or £14.75 per month. To work out the April price, you calculate £164.23 + £14.75 = £178.98.

B13. **Science.** Science had a total of 24 accidents, PE had 18, Drama had 12, Maths had one (a nasty affair involving a protractor) and other subjects 7.

B14. **£22.50.** In 2010, the school had a total of 24 accidents, costing £108. In 2011, the school had a total of 19 accidents, costing £85.50. The difference was £108 – £85.50 = £22.50.

B15. **The 21:00 flight.** Taking into account the time difference, all the flights land two hours and fifteen minutes after taking off, except the second one (which takes three hours and fifteen minutes) and the final one that takes one hour and 55 minutes. (The time zones don't make a difference to this question.)

B16. **10:45.** The group needs to land before 8:30 p.m. if it wants to be on time at the hotel, and so it needs to catch the 15:00 flight. Everyone needs to leave the school four hours and 15 minutes before the departure time, which is 10:45 a.m.

Test C

C1. **September, November and December.**

C2. **12.** It's going up by half a point each month.

C3. a) **False.** The range in September was 17 whereas it was 20 in November.

b) **True.**

c) **True.** It was 12, against 11 in October, 8 in December and 7 in September.

C4. **97.** The 200 tickets would be cheapest as 10 books of 20, costing £70. She plans to spend all the money, so she will get the £10 discount, meaning she has £90 for programmes. Each programme costs (2 × 30p + 4 × 8p) = 92p and that means she can print 90 ÷ 0.92 = 97.82 programmes – but obviously, 0.82 of a programme is very little use! She'll be able to print 97 programmes.

C5. **19:15.** Sara drives a total of 275 miles at 50 miles per hour, taking 275 ÷ 50 = 5.5 hours. Her meetings take five and three-quarter hours, making 11.25 hours altogether before she gets home. Eleven and a quarter hours after 8 a.m. is 7:15 p.m.

C6. **0.25.** The racquet sports are the sectors in the top left of the graph, which make up a quarter of the graph.

C7. a) **True.** Sixty-two out of 100 students achieved a B or better in History.

   b) **True.** Fourteen of 100 students achieved a D or worse.

   c) **False.** Thirty-one of 100 students got the same grade in both exams – the numbers on the diagonal.

C8. **Christine, Elliott and Graeme.** They all have reading ages at least three months ahead of their actual ages.

C9. **Top row, left: 93. Second row, right: 22; third row, left: 24; bottom row, left: 150 and 100** The percentage column must add up to 100 per cent. You already have (62 + 16) = 78 per cent there, and so the final percentage is 22 per cent. This corresponds to 33 students, and so you can use the Table of Joy to work out the answers. (Alternatively, you can say that 2 per cent is 3 students and work from there.)

C10. **37 per cent.** Reading up from the exam score of 50, 95 students scored 50 or worse and so 55 students scored C or better. As a percentage of 150, that's 36.7 per cent – or 37 to the nearest whole number. 36 or 38 would also be acceptable.

C11. a) **False.** The 75th and 76th students scored about 42.

   b) **False.** The lower quartile is about 32 and the upper quartile is about 54, so the interquartile range is about 22.

   c) **True.**

C12. **6.25 per cent.** Tony's percentage score in the first exam was 45 × 100 ÷ 80 = 56.25 per cent. In the second, he scored 75 × 100 ÷ 120 = 62.5 per cent. His percentage point improvement was 62.5 – 56.25 = 6.25 per cent.

Make sure that you know the difference between a *percentage improvement* and a *percentage point improvement*. The percentage point improvement is simply the difference between two percentages.

C13. **Three one-litre bottles.** Each class has 24 ÷ 2 = 12 pairs; with four classes there will be 12 × 4 = 48 pairs altogether. Each pair's experiments require 3 × 15 = 45 millilitres of acid – so the total amount of acid needed is 48 × 45 = 2,160 millilitres. That means she would need three one-litre bottles of hydrochloric acid.

C14. **£7.00 surplus.** Entry to the castle for 11 people costs £60.50. The minibus costs £40 + (50 × 0.25) = £52.50, and so the total cost is £113.00. The students pay 10 × 12 = £120, resulting in a surplus of £120 – £113 = £7.00.

Common mistakes in question C14 include forgetting the return journey (the round trip is 50 miles, not 25) and not including the teacher's entrance fee.

C15. a) **True.** Year 7 has no grade 8 students, Year 8 has 5 per cent, Year 9 has 10 per cent and Year 10 has 15 per cent.

b) **False.** Year 8 has 50 per cent of students achieving grade 5 and Year 10 has only 10 per cent.

c) **False.** Year 7 and Year 8 both have a mode of grade 5.

C16. **84.** Ten per cent of 150 Year 7 students is 15; 15 per cent of 120 Year 8 students is 18; 15 per cent of 100 Year 9 students is 15 and 45 per cent of 80 Year 10 students is 36. That's a total of 15 + 18 + 15 + 36 = 84 students.

Test D

D1. **Candidates B, D and F improved their grades.**

D2. **C.** More students achieved a C than any other grade.

D3. a) **False.** Candidates C and E's scores declined.

b) **True.** The mean improvement is (5 + 32 – 8 + 4 – 9 + 16 + 4 + 2) ÷ 8 = 46 ÷ 8 = 5.75.

c) **True.** The range of the mock is (90 – 8) = 82; the range of the final is (94 – 15) = 79.

D4. a) **False.** 9S had a higher percentage in Autumn.

b) **False.** It declined between Autumn and Spring.

c) **True.**

D5. **12:40.** To be at the museum for 1:55 p.m., they must be at George Street for 1:40 p.m. They can get the third bus on the timetable, which leaves Blandford Road at 12:40 p.m.

D6. **Five.** Without the discount, the cost of the teacher's tickets would be £9.30, leaving £40.70 for the students. Without the discount, each student would cost £7 and so £40.70 ÷ £7 = 5.81. Five students can go with the teacher.

How do you know the discount doesn't apply? To have ten people in the group for £50, the average cost would need to be less than £5, and it would cost more than that for each student even with the discount applied.

D7. a) **True.** The angle in the centre for the car sector is bigger than 90 degrees.

b) **True.** More students walk than anything else.

c) **True.** 100 students would be roughly a third of the total, and the cycling sector is much less than a third.

D8. **65.** $(64 × 0.7 + 75 × 0.3) × (97 ÷ 100) = (44.8 + 22.5) × 0.97 = 65.281$, which rounds to 65.

D9. **C (15 months), D (11 months), F (10 months) and G (7 months).**

D10. a) **False.** The ratio of good to satisfactory was 2:3, not 3:2.

b) **False.** Six of the 40 classes $(6 ÷ 40 = 0.15)$ were rated outstanding in 2012.

c) **False.** The number dropped from 5 to 3, a decrease of 40 per cent.

D11. **5 classes short.** 25 of the 40 classes were rated good or outstanding. To achieve 75 per cent, that would need to be 30 classes, and so the school is five classes short of its target.

D12. **0.75.** In total, Class 8G was assigned 31 × 12 = 372 pieces of homework, of which 279 were on time and 93 missing or late. The ratio 279:93 cancels down to 3:1.

D13. a) **True.** 300/375 = 0.8.

b) **True.** The total of assignments was 1,000, of which 800 were on time, and 800/1,000 = 0.8.

c) **True.** The proportions are 0.8 for 8G, 0.75 for 8M and about 0.874 for 8Y. The middle number is 0.8.

D14. **70.** It's the observation farthest from the line.

D15. **5/8.** Five of the eight stars are above the line.

D16. a) **True.** The highest score was 79 and the lowest 28.

b) **False.** The median score of eight students is midway between the fourth and fifth scores, 56 and 59 (so 57.5).

c) **False.** No two students achieved the same score, and so the data have no mode.

Test E

E1. **Ambridge.** Its total medal tally was 30, and 30 ÷ 5 = 6.

E2. **15.** Barchester has consistently won two more medals each year. In 2013, it can expect to get 13, and in 2014, 15.

E3. a) **True.**

b) **True.**

c) **False.** It was 9 – 2 = 7.

E4. **23:30.** The distance from Calais to Val d'Isère is 1,000 kilometres, which is the same as 1,000 × 5 ÷ 8 = 625 miles. At 50 miles per hour, that would take 625 ÷ 50 = 12.5 hours. The bus would need to take four breaks, making a total of two more hours, and so the journey takes 14.5 hours altogether. The coach would arrive 14 and a half hours after 9 a.m., which is 11:30 p.m.

E5. **16 percentage points.** In spring term, 11 students out of 25 were rated 'excellent' or 'good', which is 11 × 100 ÷ 25 = 44 per cent. In summer term, 15 out of 25 were rated 'excellent' or 'good', making 60 per cent. The percentage point increase was 60 – 44 = 16.

E6. **2.** The number of 'poor' or 'unacceptable' effort grades dropped from 5 to 3.

E7. **The Educational package is the best value of the three.**

The Basic package would cost £7.99 a month for ten students, plus (£2.50 × 20 = £50) for the 20 extra students. That would be £57.99 per month for ten months, or £579.90.

The Educational package would cost £15.99 a month for 25 students, plus (£1.50 × 5 = £7.50) for the 5 extra students. That would make £23.49 per month for nine months (because one month is free), or £211.41.

The Professional package would cost £25.99 per month for nine months, making a total of £233.91.

E8. **147.0 per cent more expensive.** The teacher's suggestion will cost 8 × 25.99 × 9 = £1,871.28. The headteacher's suggestion will cost (25.99 + 0.75 × 650) × 9 = £4,621.41. To work out the percentage increase, you do (4,621.41 − 1,871.28) × 100 / 1871.28 = 2,750.13 × 100 ÷ 1,871.28 = 146.965 per cent.

A common mistake in question E8 is to forget to take away the original price.

E9. a) **True.** 10D's range was 45, 10F's 35 and 10G's 23.

b) **False.** 10D's range was 20 whereas 10F's was 25.

c) **False.** Class 10G had the highest median time.

E10. **21.** The target time for a gold star was 15 minutes. Nobody in class 10G finished that quickly, a quarter of class 10F beat that time (7 students) and half of class 10D (14 students) also finished more quickly.

E11. **19.** Year 12 has 50 boys, of whom 31 study no foreign language: 50 − 31 = 19.

E12. a) **True.** 42 students study French, against 40 for German.

b) **False.** 23 out of 56 Year 13 students study no foreign language, which is less than half.

c) **False.** Seven girls study two languages and twenty study none.

E13. **40 per cent.** Four out of ten students scored more in the end-of-term exam than the half-term exam. They're the ones above the line.

E14. **66.** The most improved student scored 54 in the half-term exam and 70 in the end-of-term paper. Her final score would be: $(3 \times 70 + 54) \div 4 = 264 \div 4 = 66$.

E15. **20:57.** Anji needs to catch the 21:37 to get to Banbury before 11 p.m. (23:00). She'll need to leave the conference 40 minutes before, at 20:57.

E16. **£199.20.** Anji will make 12 single journeys, which would normally cost $12 \times 24.90 = 298.80$; however, she gets a discount of 1/3 of the price of each, which is 99.60, and so she ends up paying £199.20. Alternatively, each journey will cost £16.60 and £16.60 × 12 = £199.20 as well.

Part IV
Timed Practice Tests

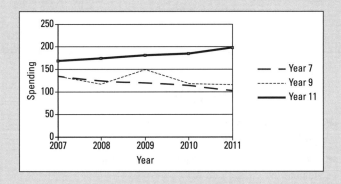

In this part . . .

✔ Prepare yourself for the real thing by getting used to working under exam conditions.

✔ Test your ability and knowledge in both literacy and numeracy.

✔ Be sure you're on the right track by checking your answers.

Chapter 12

Practising Literacy Tests under Timed Conditions

• •

In This Chapter

▶ Working on your literacy skills under test conditions

▶ Checking and reviewing your answers

• •

*T*he ability to communicate all sorts of information clearly and efficiently is an essential part of the successful teacher's skills set. This is especially true when it comes to written communication. In fact, every subject relies on you knowing how to use English properly in order to teach it: no point in a geography teacher knowing where Timbuktu is if he can't spell it; and a history teacher can't set an assignment on King Ethelred the Unready if she's not ready to use capital letters properly!

In this chapter, we present sample questions (and answers) in the four fundamental areas of spelling, punctuation, grammar and comprehension. The content of these tests is different from the trial tests in Chapters 4 to 7, and their purpose is different, too.

We cover these four literacy sections in detail in Chapters 4 (spelling), 5 (punctuation), 6 (grammar) and 7 (comprehension).

Putting Your Literacy Skills to the Test

Having worked through the types of questions you face in the tests at your own pace, it's now time to face the music and dance. You should try doing these tests in the actual time allocation you have on the test day – so you should allow yourself 45 minutes and no more. Before you begin, think carefully about how long you want to allow yourself for each section of the test. Remember that the pass mark for these tests is approximately 64%, so that's what you're aiming for.

Spelling questions

In this section of the test you will be asked to listen to and spell a sequence of words that fit into the sentences that follow. Remember, you can come back to the words while you're in the spelling section of the test when you do it for real, but once you move on to the punctuation section, you cannot come back!

Ask a friend to read out the sequence of words (which can be found in the answers section at the end of this chapter) or visit www.dummies.com/go/teachersskillstests to access an audio version of these questions.

1. He reported the recent developments in the project to his line _____.

2. Every member of the class was required to complete an _____.

3. The Science department ensured every class did one _____ per week.

4. The teacher explained the major _____ of the topic.

5. She encouraged her pupils _____.

6. Ensure you always wear clothing that is _____ for the work you have to do.

7. Geography was being taught in a _____ classroom.

8. The girl was given a three-day _____ for her behaviour.

9. Smoking on the school grounds is strictly _____.

10. The school day always _____ at 3:30 p.m.

Punctuation questions

The passage that follows has been punctuated incorrectly. Your task is to identify the deliberate mistakes and to correct them. It contains ten errors for you to correct.

The Key Skills tests ask you to deal with only one kind of punctuation – omissions. In other words:

> ✔ You're never asked to take away punctuation marks or capital letters that shouldn't be present;
>
> ✔ You're asked only to insert punctuation marks or capital letters that need to be present.

Here's the passage:

The world of information Communication Technology (ICT) is constantly developing with this increase in classroom technology comes an ever-increasing field of exploration for teachers who wish to examine and utilise the potential of these technologies in their teaching for the benefit of their students. as ICTs become increasingly a part of students day-to-day lives it is self-evident that these have a role to play in the classroom, both as pedagogic tools and, in some cases, as sources of cognitive content in their own right. It cannot and should not however, be accepted automatically that technology equates to improvement (see Simpson & Oliver, 2007) In some cases technology leads to specific and identifiable pedagogic and cognitive advances (e.g. creative use of the internet with its potential to engage students deeply and critically in the reception and production of multimedia text, but in others it provides nothing genuinely new in the way of pedagogy, representing a simple shift of medium, whilst on still other occasions the technology itself may prove actually limiting in its impact on the classroom. 'Too frequently,' Green (2005) observes, PowerPoint is simply a way of off loading lesson content, which reduces the requirement for pupils to think and which can lead to repetitive and passive classrooms.'

Grammar questions

In the following tests you need to select the best available option from the four alternatives offered to fill the gaps in the written text.

Test A

This is an extract from a letter to the parents of a child who has been excluded from school for his behaviour.

Dear Mr & Mrs Gurr,

Here at Bigtown School we take pride in the pleasant and positive learning environment we have created. Staff and pupils generally work very well together so that all pupils can fulfil their potential. _____

_____.

    A) Occasionally, however, there is incidents of misbehaviour.

    B) Occasionally, however, there are incidents of misbehaviour.

    C) Occasionally, however, there is incident of misbehaviour.

    D) Occasionally, however, there are incident of misbehaviour.

Your son, Robert, has unfortunately been involved in such an incident this week. As the headteacher of Bigtown School, ___

_____.

    A) I take the learning of all pupil very seriously.

    B) I takes the learning of all pupil very seriously.

    C) I take the learning of all pupils very seriously.

    D) I takes the learning of all pupils very seriously.

For the third time this week, Robert has been sent to me for repeatedly interrupting teaching and for failing to show the respect he _____ to his peers and his teachers.

    A) should of

    B) could have

    C) could of

    D) should have

Under these circumstances, I have no choice. A meeting of the senior staff_____ in agreeing that Robert should be temporarily excluded until next Monday.

A) was unanimous

B) are unanimous

C) were unanimous

D) was unanimity

Test B

This is an extract from a notice inviting pupils to take part in a school writing competition.

This term, as usual, Littleschool Comprehensive _____ its annual writing competition.

A) are running

B) is running

C) will run

D) will ran

There is no cost to enter, and pupils from across the school are encouraged to take part. _____ _____ _____.

A) There are categories for all year groups.

B) There are category for all year groups.

C) There is a category for all year groups.

D) There is categories for all year groups.

All entries must be between 300–500 words in length and must be _____.

A) the unaided work of the entrant.

B) the unaided work by the entrant.

C) the unaided work for the entrant.

D) the unaided work with the entrant.

The deadline for submitting entries _____.

   A) is last week.

   B) are last week.

   C) is next week.

   D) are next week.

Comprehension questions

Read the following passage and respond as directed to the questions that come after. As indicated, in the actual test you may be required to 'drag and drop' your answers into the correct spaces, but for the purposes of this book, simply tick the boxes that correspond to your answers.

Passage

We know that to effectively deliver sanctions the message needs to be simple, clear and non-negotiable; in practice it is easy to get caught up in a lengthy argument or confrontation. Focus on moving in, delivering your sanction as discreetly as possible and then moving out quickly. Choose a phrase that you will withdraw on 'I need to see you working as well as you were in yesterday's written task, thank you for listening' or 'I will come back and give you feedback on your work in five minutes'.

Avoid waiting around for the student to change their behaviour immediately; they may need some time and space to make a better choice. Engage another student in a positive conversation or move across the room to answer a question and only check back once the dust has settled. No one likes receiving sanctions and the longer the interaction, the more chance of a defensive reaction or escalation. Get in, deliver the message and get out with dignity; quickly, efficiently and without lingering.

A good technique for getting the attention of the whole class is to use a 'countdown' from 5 or 10 to allow students the time to finish their conversations (or work) and listen to the next instruction. Explain to the class that you are using a countdown to give them fair warning that they need to listen and that it is far more polite than calling for immediate silence. Embellish your countdown with clear instructions so that students know what is expected and be prepared to modify it for different groups: 'Five, you should be finishing the sentence that you are writing. Three, excellent Marcus, a merit for being the first to give me your full attention. Two, quickly back to your places. One, all pens and pencils down now. Half, all looking this way. Zero, thank you.'

Some students may join in the countdown with you at first; some will not be quiet by the time you get to zero at first but persevere, use praise and rewards to reinforce its importance and it can become an extremely efficient tool for those times when you need everyone's attention. You may already have a technique for getting everyone's attention, e.g. hands up. The countdown technique is more effective as it is time-related and does not rely on students seeing you.

Prefacing requests with 'Thank you' has a marked effect on how the request is received: 'Thank you for putting your bag on the hook' or 'Thank you for dropping your gum in the bin'. The trust in the student that this statement implies, combined with the clarity of the expectation, often results in immediate action without protest. It is almost a closed request which leaves no 'hook' to hold onto and argue with.

A similar technique can be applied to requests for students to make deadlines or attend meetings that they would rather ignore; salesmen would call it an assumed close. Say, 'When you come to see me today get as close to 3:30 as you can so we can resolve this quickly and both get home in good time' as opposed to, 'Meet me at my room at the end of school'. Say, 'When you hand in your coursework next Monday, meet me by the staff room so that I can store it securely' as opposed to, 'I want your coursework in on Monday'. You are assuming and encouraging a positive response; making it awkward for the student to respond negatively.

Perhaps your greatest contribution to managing behaviour around the school site is your presence. If you have your coffee in the playground, your lunch with the students (what % of your students eat at a table with an adult every day?) and are ever-present in the corridor outside your classroom, students will see consistency in your expectations for behaviour both in and out of class. They will grow used to your interventions in social areas and your presence will slowly have an impact on their behaviour.

Questions

1. Select the best heading for the article. (In the actual Key Skills test you have to drag a tick into the box corresponding to your selection.)

   ❏ Pupils out of control

   ❏ Manage your behaviour

   ❏ Develop your behaviour management

   ❏ Teachers take charge

2. From the list below select three points that accurately convey information about calling classes to silence given in the text.

   ❏ Pupils respond better to being called instantly to silence.

   ❏ Talk to the class while you are using a countdown to explain what you want to happen.

   ❏ Develop a fixed and repeated set of instructions.

   ❏ Accompany your requirements with praise.

   ❏ Vary your instructions to reflect the needs of different groups.

   ❏ Rewards do not help.

   ❏ If pupils join in with countdowns, abandon the strategy.

3. From the list below select the two options closest in meaning to the following phrase as it appears in the context of the passage you have read. (In the actual Key Skills test you have to drag a tick into the boxes corresponding to your selections.)

   Prefacing requests with 'Thank you' has a marked effect on how the request is received.

   ❏ Assume co-operation when you ask something of a class.

   ❏ Insist that pupils speak politely at all times.

   ❏ Talking politely to pupils increases the likelihood that they will co-operate.

   ❏ Always say 'thank you' when you ask pupils for something.

❏ Talking politely to pupils ensures that they will co-operate.

4. Re-read the final paragraph of the passage. Select three phrases from the list below that best complete the following statement.

It is worth being seen around and about the school by pupils because:

❏ they will begin to relate to you in different ways.

❏ they will pick up on your inconsistencies.

❏ they will accord you more authority to intervene in their behaviour.

❏ this will help the lunch supervisors.

❏ it will ensure they behave.

❏ they will see that you are consistent in your expectations of them in and out of the classroom.

❏ they enjoy spending time talking to their teachers.

5. Read the statements below and decide whether:

✔ The statement is **supported** by the text (**S**).

✔ The statement is **implied** by the text or is implicitly supported by the text (**I**).

✔ The text provides **no evidence** or information concerning the statement (**NE**).

✔ The statement is **implicitly contradicted** or implicitly refuted by the text (**IC**).

✔ The statement is **contradicted** by the text (**C**)

❏ It is important to allow pupils time and space to comply with instructions.

❏ When you have delivered an instruction, wait to ensure it is complied with.

❏ Pupils enjoy developing good relationships with their teachers and this helps in behaviour management.

❏ Girls are more likely to be compliant than boys.

❏ Teachers' presence around school does not have an impact on behaviour in class.

Checking Your Answers

Here we give answers to the preceding section's questions – something oddly omitted in the actual test; wonder why!

Spelling answers

1. MANAGER: Build from the root word MANAGE, remembering that the 'J' sound can be made using the letter 'G', and then add the final letter 'R' to make MANAGER.

2. ASSESSMENT: Remember that the hissy 'S' sound in English is made by doubling the letter 'S', and after you've constructed the root word ASSESS, simply add the common suffix 'MENT'.

3. PRACTICAL: The root word PRACTICE gets you most of the way, and then you need to remember that the hard 'K' sound is often made in English by the letter 'C' before adding the 'AL' ending.

4. PRINCIPLES: A tricky one. To start, you make the central hissing 'S' sound with the letter 'C'.

Vowels appearing in the consonant-vowel-consonant construction are short in sound.

You then need to know the difference in meaning between PRINCIPLE (something you believe in or the basis for something) and PRINCIPAL (the most important thing or the head of a school); context is important in establishing the spelling here.

5. REPEATEDLY: Start with the root word REPEAT, remembering that 'EA' is a common way in English of making the long 'E' sound, and then add the suffix 'ED' and the further suffix 'LY' to construct the adverb.

6. SUITABLE: The root word here, SUIT, is one of those words that's simply easiest just to learn; then add the common 'ABLE' suffix.

7. TEMPORARY: Sounding the word out is a good strategy here, because the word is constructed in a straightforward way; the trickiest part is to remember that you make the final vowel sound (the 'E' in 'ARY') using an 'A'.

8. EXCLUSION: The prefix 'EX' is common and is well worth learning in helping to construct the root word EXCLUDE; then you build the new word.

9. FORBIDDEN: The thing to remember here is that you need to double the final 'D' of the root word FORBID before adding the suffix in order to retain the short 'I' sound.

10. CONCLUDED: This word is clearly related to the word CONCLUSION, and so you have a lot of help here.

The hard 'K' sound in English is often made using the letter 'C' and the long central vowel sound is made with the letter 'U'.

Don't double the final 'D', because you need the long 'U' sound.

Punctuation answers

The world of Information **[capital letter needed for proper noun]** Communication Technology (ICT) is constantly developing; **[a semi-colon is needed here to demonstrate the connection between the opening statement of the article and the information that follows]** with this proliferation of classroom technology comes an ever-increasing field of exploration for teachers who wish to examine and utilise the potential of these technologies in their teaching for the benefit of their students. As **[a capital letter is required for the word 'As', because it's the beginning of a new sentence]** ICTs become increasingly a part of students' **[possessive apostrophe required – the 'day-to-day lives' belong to the students – because the 'owning' word (students) ends with an 's', the apostrophe goes after it]** day-to-day lives, **[the comma is required in order to mark off the initial subordinate clause from the main clause of the sentence]** it is self-evident that these have a role to play in the classroom, both as pedagogic tools and, in some cases, as sources of cognitive content in their own right. It cannot and should not, **[the word 'however' should be in parentheses and so the initial comma is required to complement the one that follows the word]** however, be accepted automatically that technology equates to improvement (see Simpson & Oliver, 2007). **[a full stop is required in order to mark the end of the sentence]** In some cases technology leads to specific and identifiable pedagogic and cognitive advances (e.g. creative use of the internet with its potential to engage students deeply and critically in the reception and production of multimedia text) **[this is the end of the parentheses, and so the closing bracket is required]**, but in others it provides nothing genuinely new in the way of pedagogy, representing a simple shift of medium, whilst on still other occasions the technology itself may prove actually limiting in its impact on the classroom. 'Too frequently,' Green (2005) observes, 'PowerPoint **[a quotation mark is required before the word PowerPoint, because this is where the writer continues with direct quotation from Green]** is simply a way of off-loading **[a hyphen is required here to connect 'off' and 'loading' in order to create the compound noun]** lesson content, which reduces the requirement for pupils to think and which can lead to repetitive and passive classrooms.'

Grammar answers

Test A

This is an extract from a letter to the parents of a child who has been excluded from school for his behaviour.

Dear Mr & Mrs Gurr,

Here at Bigtown School we take pride in the pleasant and positive learning environment we have created. Staff and pupils generally work very well together so that all pupils can fulfil their potential._____

_____.

B is the correct answer.

A) Occasionally, however, there is incidents of misbehaviour.

   This can't be correct, because the singular verb form 'is' can't go with the plural noun 'incidents'.

B) Occasionally, however, there are incidents of misbehaviour.

   This is correct. The plural noun 'incidents' and the plural for the verb 'are' agree.

C) Occasionally, however, there is incident of misbehaviour.

   This can't be correct. To work, this sentence would require the insertion of the indefinite article 'an' before 'incident'.

D) Occasionally, however, there are incident of
misbehaviour.

**This sentence is incorrect because the plural form of
the verb 'are' can't go with the singular form of the
noun 'incident'.**

Your son, Robert, has unfortunately been involved in such an
incident this week. As the headteacher of Bigtown School, ___

_____

_____.

C is the correct answer.

A) I take the learning of all pupil very seriously.

**This is incorrect, because the word 'all' makes clear
that there must be more than one 'pupil'.**

B) I takes the learning of all pupil very seriously.

**This sentence is wrong for two reasons. First, the
subject of the sentence ('I') doesn't agree with the
verb ('takes'). Second, the word 'all' makes clear that
there must be more than one 'pupil'.**

C) I take the learning of all pupils very seriously.

**This is right – the subject ('I') agrees with the singu-
lar form of the verb ('take'). The plural 'pupils' also
matches the word 'all'.**

D) I takes the learning of all pupils very seriously.

**This is wrong because the subject of the sentence ('I')
doesn't agree with the verb ('takes').**

For the third time this week, Robert has been sent to me for
repeatedly interrupting teaching and for failing to show the
respect he _____ to his peers and his teachers.

D is the correct answer.

A) should of

**'Should of' is never grammatically correct. It's an
inaccurate rendition of the conditional form of the
verb 'should have'.**

B) could have

> **Although the conditional form of the verb is correct in using 'have' rather than 'of', the implication of the sentence is that Robert hasn't displayed the behaviour he ought to. The 'could' conditional form is, therefore, not appropriate.**

C) could of

> **In this instance, neither the 'could' form of the conditional nor the 'of' is correct.**

D) should have

> **This is right. The 'should' form of the conditional for the verb is used correctly.**

Under these circumstances, I have no choice. A meeting of the senior staff _____ in agreeing that Robert should be temporarily excluded until next Monday.

A is the correct answer.

A) was unanimous

> **This is correct. The meeting has evidently already taken place, and so you need to use a past tense form of the verb 'to be'. The singular form of the verb is also correct, because although the word 'staff' includes many people, it's nevertheless a singular collective noun.**

B) are unanimious

> **This is incorrect. The meeting has already taken place, and so the present tense form of the verb 'to be' can't be appropriate.**

C) were unanimous

> **The noun 'staff' is a singular collective noun, and so the plural past tense form 'were' is incorrect.**

D) was unanimity

> **Although the singular past tense form 'was' is correct, 'unanimity' is a noun, and therefore it's the wrong word class to explain the decision of the senior staff.**

Test B

This is an extract from a notice inviting pupils to take part in a school writing competition.

This term, as usual, Littleschool Comprehensive _____ its annual writing competition.

B is the correct answer.

A) are running

> **Because Littleschool Comprehensive is singular, the plural continuous form of the verb is wrong.**

B) is running

> **This is correct. The singular form of the verb is required.**

C) will run

> **This may seem a reasonable answer at first, but the context of the passage makes clear that the competition is taking place now, whereas 'will run' is a future tense verb and implies that the event is to happen at some future time.**

D) will ran

> **This is wrong for two reasons. The future tense ('will') is wrong as we explain in point C and the simple past tense of the verb 'to run' has been incorrectly used instead of a verb participle.**

There is no cost to enter, and pupils from across the school are encouraged to take part. _____
_____
_____.

A is the correct answer.

A) There are categories for all year groups.

> **The verb form 'are' agrees with the plural 'categories' and the passage makes clear that each year group has its own category in the competition.**

B) There are category for all year groups.

> **The verb form 'are' doesn't agree with the singular 'category', and so this can't be correct.**

C) There is a category for all year groups.

> **This option may at first seem a reasonable answer, but look carefully. The wording means that the competition has only one category and that it's for all year groups.**

D) There is categories for all year groups.

The singular 'is' doesn't agree with the plural 'categories' and so the sentence doesn't make sense.

All entries must be between 300–500 words in length and must be _____.

A is correct.

A) the unaided work of the entrant

This is the only answer that can be correct, because the word 'of' demonstrates possession.

B) the unaided work by the entrant

C) the unaided work for the entrant

D) the unaided work with the entrant

In B, C and D, no word appropriately demonstrates possession.

The deadline for submitting entries _____.

C is right.

A) is last week

Although the present tense of the verb 'to be' is correct and agrees with 'the deadline', 'last week' makes no sense.

B) are last week

'Are' doesn't agree with the singular 'deadline' and 'last week' makes no sense.

C) is next week

This is right. The verb form agrees, and 'next week' makes sense in terms of the timeframe for the competition.

D) are next week

This can't be right because the verb form doesn't agree.

Comprehension answers

1. Select the best heading for the article. (In the actual Key Skills test you have to drag a tick into the box corresponding to your selection.)

   Develop Your Behaviour Management

   Given the general tone of the article, this is the title that best captures the spirit of the piece. The 'your' makes clear that the audience of the article is teachers, and that the thrust of the piece is about developing strategies to manage classrooms more effectively.

2. From the list below select three points that accurately convey information about calling classes to silence given in the text.

   ❑ Pupils respond better to being called instantly to silence. **No: paragraph 3 explicitly contradicts this view.**

   ❑ Talk to the class while you are using a countdown to explain what you want to happen. **Yes: this is recommended and examples are given in the text of how it can be done.**

   ❑ Develop a fixed and repeated set of instructions. **No: it's clear from the text that instructions and teacher talk should be modified to meet the needs of different classes.**

   ❑ Accompany your requirements with praise. **Yes: the article states that using praise and rewards for compliance with instructions raises compliance levels.**

   ❑ Vary your instructions to reflect the needs of different groups. **Yes: it's clear that teachers need to vary their talk and instructions to reflect the needs of different classes.**

   ❑ Rewards do not help. **No: the article is explicit that using rewards is a good strategy.**

   ❑ If pupils join in with countdowns, abandon the strategy. **No: The article implies that persisting with this strategy is important to familiarise pupils with it.**

3. From the list below select the two options closest in meaning to the following phrase as it appears in the context of the passage you have read. (In the actual Key Skills test you have to drag a tick into the boxes corresponding to your selections.)

Prefacing requests with 'thank you' has a marked effect on how the request is received.

❑ Assume co-operation when you ask something of a class. **Yes: the prefacing of requests in this way assumes that the pupils are compliant.**

❑ Insist that pupils speak politely at all times. **No: the article says nothing about this at all.**

❑ Talking politely to pupils increases the likelihood that they will co-operate. **Yes: when the statement says this strategy has 'a marked effect', this is being implied.**

❑ Always say 'thank you' when you ask pupils for something. **No: the article says nothing about this.**

❑ Talking politely to pupils ensures that they will co-operate. **No: whatever happens in classroom management, there are no guarantees, and the article doesn't claim any!**

4. Re-read the final paragraph of the passage. Select three phrases from the list below that best complete the following statement.

It is worth being seen around and about the school by pupils because:

❑ they will begin to relate to you in different ways. **Yes: this is certainly implied by the final paragraph.**

❑ they will pick up on your inconsistencies. **No: If teachers are inconsistent in their behaviour, this may well be the case, but the article says nothing about it.**

❑ they will accord you more authority to intervene in their behaviour. **Yes: this is what the final paragraph states.**

❑ this will help the lunch supervisors. **No: the article says nothing about this aspect.**

❑ it will ensure they behave. **No: as before, there are no guarantees, and the article doesn't claim any.**

❏ they will see that you are consistent in your expectations of them in and out of the classroom. **Yes: this is what the article claims, assuming that the teacher's behaviour is, indeed, consistent.**

❏ they enjoy spending time talking to their teachers. **No: this is, perhaps, implied, but it's not stated.**

5. Read the statements below and decide whether:

✔ The statement is **supported** by the text (**S**).

✔ The statement is **implied** by the text or is implicitly supported by the text (**I**).

✔ The text provides **no evidence** or information concerning the statement (**NE**).

✔ The statement is **implicitly contradicted** or implicitly refuted by the text (**IC**).

✔ The statement is **contradicted** by the text (**C**).

❏ It is important to allow pupils time and space to comply with instructions. **(S – paragraph 2 explicitly states that teachers need to allow pupils 'take up' time.)**

❏ When you have delivered an instruction, wait to ensure it is complied with. **(C – paragraph 1 tells teachers to deliver the instruction and then quickly withdraw.)**

❏ Pupils enjoy developing good relationships with their teachers and this helps in behaviour management. **(I – see the final paragraph where this is implied, even though it's not directly stated.)**

❏ Girls are more likely to be compliant than boys. **(NE – the text makes no distinctions about behaviour according to gender.)**

❏ Teachers' presence around school does not have an impact on behaviour in class. **(IC – the final paragraph implicitly contradicts this idea, suggesting that what happens outside the classroom does have an impact on what happens inside.)**

Chapter 13

Tackling the Timed Numeracy Test

Sometimes when you're hungry, you want a full, rich meal, with every sauce and garnish on the menu and all the trimmings – and that's fine. But at other times, a simple, straightforward meal just hits the spot. Well, in this chapter, we give you a plain-old, no-messing-around, exam-style Numeracy test: all the meat and none of the gristle.

The test is in two parts: a mental arithmetic section, in which you have a total of about 30 seconds to work out each question, and an on-screen section, where you have 36 minutes to answer as many of the 16 questions as you can.

It's designed for you to use as a practice exam – so feel free to set yourself up as if you're in the test centre, with a felt-tip pen and a countdown timer!

For added authenticity, go to www.dummies.com/go/ teachersskillstests to access the audio questions that go with this practice test.

Practising Numeracy Questions

In the mental arithmetic section, you have as long as it takes someone to read a question, clearly, twice – plus an extra 18 seconds – for each question. Once your time's up, you have to go on to the next question; you can't go back to change your answer later. Check out Chapter 8 if you struggle – or if you want more tests to practise on!

Mental arithmetic questions

1. In a class of 25 students, 19 are right-handed. What percentage of the students are not right-handed?

2. What is $145 \div 0.1$?

3. A school has 120 teachers. One week, because of a flu virus, a sixth of the teachers were absent. How many teachers were present?

4. A teacher's car travels 10 miles on a litre of petrol. Petrol costs £1.50 per litre. How much would a journey of 40 miles cost? Give your answer in pounds.

5. A coach holds 48 people. Two classes of 28 students each, three classes of 25 students each, eight teachers and five parents are going on a trip. How many coaches are needed?

6. A student lives 3.5 miles from school. If she cycles to and from school each weekday, how many miles does she cover in a week?

7. A school has 800 students, of whom 20 per cent are in Year 7. How many students are in Year 7?

8. A parents' evening begins at 5 p.m. A teacher has to see the parents of 35 students. Each appointment lasts five minutes. Assuming he takes two ten-minute breaks for coffee, at what time will he finish? Use the 24-hour clock.

9. An exam is scheduled to start at 9:30 a.m. and last an hour and a half. A student is entitled to 10 per cent extra time after injuring his writing hand in a rugby match. When will the exam finish for the student? Use the 24-hour clock.

10. A student scores 47 per cent in one practice exam, and 42 out of 75 in a second practice paper. By how many percentage points did her score improve?

11. Fifteen members of a basketball squad do a sponsored free-throw competition for charity. Each player is sponsored £1.50 for each basket she scores. If the players score an average of eight baskets each, how much money do they raise?

12. 62.5 per cent of a drama class are involved in the school play. What fraction of the class is *not* involved in the play? Give your answer in its lowest form.

On-screen questions

The bar graph in Figure 13-1 shows the number of students registered as present, late and absent in each year of a school on a particular day.

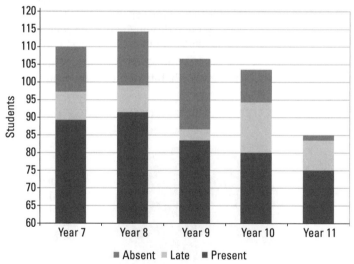

Figure 13-1: A stacked-bar graph for questions 1 and 2.

1. How many students in the whole school were registered late on that day?

2. Which of the following statements are true?

   a) Year 7 was the year with the highest number of absences.

   b) Year 11 had a higher percentage of students marked present than Year 9.

   c) Year 8 has 15 more students in it than Year 10.

Figure 13-2 shows a train timetable.

Warrington Bank Quay	0840	0940	1040	1140
Crewe	0900	1000	1100	1200
Wolverhampton	0930	1030	1130	1230
Birmingham New Street	0950	1050	1150	1250

Figure 13-2: A timetable for questions 3 and 4.

3. A teacher is planning a trip to a conference in Birmingham. The group needs to be at the conference before 12:30 p.m. The conference centre is a 20-minute walk from New Street Station and the teacher would like to allow 10 extra minutes in case of delays. Which is the last train the group can catch in Warrington to be on time? Use the 24-hour clock.

4. The distance from Warrington to Birmingham is 80 miles. What is the average speed of the 9:40 a.m. train from Warrington to Birmingham? Give your answer to the nearest mile per hour.

The pie chart in Figure 13-3 shows information about the exercise habits of the students in a school.

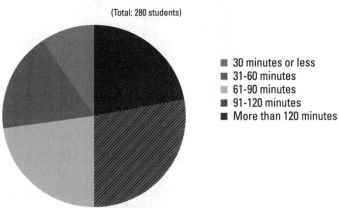

Exercise times per week

(Total: 280 students)

- 30 minutes or less
- 31-60 minutes
- 61-90 minutes
- 91-120 minutes
- More than 120 minutes

Figure 13-3: A pie chart for questions 5 and 6.

5. Which group is the modal group?

6. Young adults are recommended to exercise for at least 90 minutes per week. How many students exercise for less than the guidelines recommend? Round your answer to the nearest ten students.

The two-way table in Figure 13-4 shows the number of students working at different maths achievement levels in different years.

		Achievement level					
		6	7	8	9	10	Total
Year	7	80	86	25	9	0	200
	8	1	24	93	30	2	150
	9	0	1	45	76	28	150
	Total	81	111	163	115	30	500

Figure 13-4: A two-way table for questions 7 and 8.

7. Which of the following statements are true?

a) At least half of the Year 7 students are working at level 7 or better.

b) Less than a quarter of the Year 8 students attained level 9 or better.

c) Exactly a tenth of the Year 9 students are working at level 7 or worse.

8. The achievement levels represent students working near the target standard for the numbered year – so an achievement level of 7 means that a student is working near the standard of an average Year 7 student, and so on. How many students are working at around the target level for their age?

The box-and-whiskers plot in Figure 13-5 shows the size of classes in a school over five years.

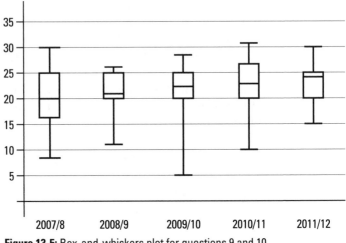

Figure 13-5: Box-and-whiskers plot for questions 9 and 10.

9. Which of the following statements are true?

 a) No class ever had more than 30 students.

 b) The biggest range in class sizes was in 2007–8.

 c) The smallest class size was in 2010–11.

10. The headteacher expects the trend in the median class sizes to continue for the foreseeable future. What would he expect the median class size to be in 2013–14?

The line graph in Figure 13-6 shows the results of an annual survey into the amount parents spend on school uniforms and supplies.

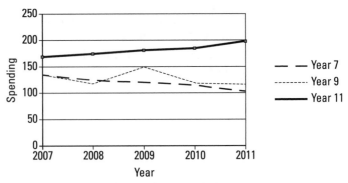

Figure 13-6: Line graph for questions 11 and 12.

11. In the year with the biggest difference between the average spend on a Year 11 student and a Year 7 student, how much would the parent of a typical Year 9 student have spent on supplies and uniform? Give your answer to the nearest £5.

12. Which of the following statements are true?

    a) In all five surveys, the average spend on a Year 11 student was highest.

    b) The average spend on a Year 9 student fell each year.

    c) The average spend on a Year 7 student fell each year.

13. A group of students puts on a play to raise money for charity. The play runs for three nights. They spend £35 on costumes and £45 on props. Tickets cost 10p each to print, and programmes cost 70p to print. They print 200 tickets for each night and 300 programmes altogether. They sell a total of 550 tickets at £2 each and 170 programmes at £3 each. How much profit do they make for charity?

14. The play is due to begin at 7:30 p.m. and consists of two acts of 45 minutes each with an interval of 25 minutes. However, the start of the play is delayed by quarter of an hour due to a fire alarm. What time does the play end? Give your answer using the 24-hour clock.

Figure 13-7 shows a cumulative frequency graph of the time taken for 200 students to write an essay.

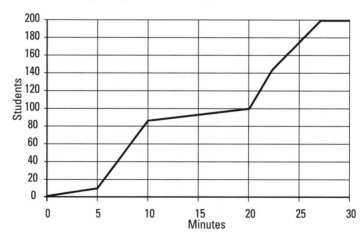

Figure 13-7: Cumulative frequency graph for questions 15 and 16.

15. Which of the following statements are true?

    a) 90 per cent of the students finished within ten minutes.

    b) The median time was around 20 minutes.

    c) The longest time taken was around 27 minutes.

16. What was the interquartile range of the times? Give your answer to the nearest five minutes.

Checking Your Answers

The pass mark for Numeracy tests is now around 63 per cent, which means that you need to get a total of 18 marks out of a possible 28 to pass this test.

But don't worry too much if you don't get that many marks on these practice tests – just take note of the ones you struggled with and review the relevant sections in the book before trying again.

Mental arithmetic answers

1. **24 per cent.** Six of the 25 students are not right-handed. Each student represents 4 per cent of the total, making 24 per cent who are not right-handed.

2. **1,450.** If you multiply both numbers in the sum by 10, you get $1,450 \div 1 = 1,450$.

3. **100.** One-sixth of 120 is the same as $120 \div 6 = 20$. If 20 teachers are off sick, 100 are present.

4. **£6.** A 40-mile journey requires $40 \div 10 = 4$ litres of petrol, which costs $4 \times £1.50 = £6$.

If you're listening to the question rather than reading, make sure that you take down – and label – all the information as quickly as you can.

5. **3.** There are $2 \times 28 = 56$ people in the first two classes and $3 \times 25 = 75$ people in the next three classes, plus 13 adults. That adds up to 144 people, who would fit on $144 \div 48 = 3$ buses.

Instead of doing the long division, writing out your 48 times table is probably easier – 48, 96, 144 – and then seeing how many coaches you'd need.

6. **35 miles.** The student travels seven miles each day, five days a week: 5 × 7 = 35.

7. **160.** 10 per cent of 800 is 80 students, and so 20 per cent is twice as much.

8. **20:15.** The teacher spends a total of 35 × 5 = 175 minutes talking to parents and 2 × 10 = 20 minutes drinking coffee, making 195 minutes, or 3 hours and 15 minutes altogether. Three hours and 15 minutes after 17:00 is 20:15.

9. **11:09.** The exam lasts 90 minutes normally, and so the student has 99 minutes (or 1 hour and 39 minutes). This will take him to 11:09 a.m.

10. **9.** The student's score in the second paper is 42 out of 75, which is the same as 14 out of 25 or 56 per cent. She has improved by 9 percentage points.

11. **£180.** The sum is 15 × 1.5 × 8. The easiest approach is to work out 1.5 × 8 = 12 first, and then 15 × 12 = 180.

12. **3/8.** 12.5 per cent is one-eighth, and so 62.5 per cent is an eighth more than a half (which makes 5/8). Therefore, 3/8 of the class remains.

On-screen answers

1. **42.** 8 students were late in Year 7, 8 in Year 8, 4 in Year 9, 14 in Year 10 and 8 in Year 11, making a total of 42. Anything between 40 and 45 is acceptable.

2. a) **False.** Year 9 had more absences.

   b) **True.** Year 11 had 75 out of 85 students marked present, or 88.2 per cent. Year 9 had 83 out of 107, which is 77.6 per cent.

   c) **False.** The difference is only 11.

3. **10:40.** The teacher needs to be at New Street before midday, and so the 10:40 from Warrington is fine; it arrives at 11:50 a.m.

4. **69 miles per hour.** The train travels 80 miles in 70 minutes, and the sum is 80 ÷ 70 × 60 = 68.57: to the nearest mile per hour, that's 69.

5. **91–120 minutes.** This is the biggest sector.

6. **140.** The three groups (30 minutes or less, 31–60 and 61–90) make up half of the total, and there are 280 students altogether.

7. a) **True.** 120 of the 200 Year 7 students are at level 7 or better, which is more than half (half of 200 is 100).

   b) **True.** 32 out of 150 Year 8 students are at level 9 or better, which is less than a quarter (quarter of 150 is 37.5).

   c) **False.** Only one Year 9 student out of 150 is working at level 7 or worse, which is less than a tenth (a tenth of 150 is 15).

8. **255.** There are 86 Year 7 students working at level 7, 93 Year 8 students working at level 8 and 76 Year 9 students working at level 9: 86 + 93 + 76 = 255.

9. a) **False.** A class in 2010–11 had 31 students.

   b) **False.** The range in 2009–10 was (29 – 5) = 24, against (30 – 9) = 21 in 2007–8.

   c) **False.** The smallest class was in 2009–10.

10. **26.** The medians are 20, 21, 22, 23 and 24 (in 2011–12). For 2012–13, the trend predicts 25 and for 2013–14 it would be 26.

11. **£115.** The biggest difference between the Year 11 spend (solid line) and the Year 7 spend (dashed line) is in 2011 – and the Year 9 spend in that year is £120. To the nearest £10, that's £120.

12. a) **True.** The solid line is highest in all five surveys.

    b) **False.** The Year 9 spend (dotted line) rose from 2008–9.

    c) **True.** The Year 7 spend (dashed line) fell every year.

13. **£1,260.** The costumes and props cost a total of £80. The 600 tickets cost £60 and 300 programmes cost £210, making a total outlay of £350. As for income, the group makes £1,100 from ticket sales and £510 from programme sales, a total of £1,610. The profit is £1,610 – £350 = £1,260.

14. **21:40.** The play lasts a total of 45 + 45 + 25 = 115 minutes, or one hour and 55 minutes. The play started at 7:45 p.m. and so would finish at 9:40 p.m.

15. a) **False.** 90 students out of 200 finished within 10 minutes, which is 45 per cent.

    b) **True.** 100 students finished in 20 minutes.

    c) **True.** The 200th student took 27 minutes.

16. **15 minutes.** The lower quartile is around 7.5 minutes. The upper quartile is 23 minutes. The interquartile range is 23 − 7.5 = 15.5 minutes. To the nearest five minutes, that's 15.

Part V

The Part of Tens

Go to www.dummies.com/go/teachers professionalskillstests for free bonus content.

In this part . . .

✔ Get your head in the right place: revise, focus and breathe your way to exam success.

✔ Learn to manage your time, work neatly and re-read the question in order to find those final marks that could make the difference you need.

Chapter 14

Ten Top Tips for Keeping Your Head

*W*e know what getting overwhelmed feels like — such as when words and numbers start jumping around on the page in front of you – but we're also aware that getting panicked about it doesn't help.

Therefore, we provide ten ways to stay calm when you're studying and during the exam. These tips help you to help yourself when you're faced with those horrible, ugly questions. Just remember that it's okay; the questions don't bite. Honest!

Breathing Well

Your brain runs on oxygen (among other things) and so breathing properly is one of the best weapons in your anti-panic arsenal. Colin knows this fact well, because when he used to get regular panic attacks his counsellor recommended *diaphragmatic breathing* to help get them under control.

When you feel like you're starting to lose the plot – your breathing's shallow, your heart's racing and you want to run away – the thing to do is to acknowledge it and breathe deeply. Here's how to do diaphragmatic breathing:

1. **Put one hand on the top of your chest and the other hand on your stomach.**

2. **Breathe in as deeply as you can, trying not to move your upper hand; your lower hand should move out as your lungs fill with air.**

3. **Breathe in for a count of seven, but don't hold your breath.**

4. **Breathe out very slowly for a count of 11.**

Don't worry if you can't manage all the way up to 11 – just breathe out for as long as you can and make a note to breathe more slowly next time.

5. **Repeat this breathing in and out for a minute or so and you start to feel your heart rate drop and your head start to clear.**

A clear head makes working on maths questions in particular a lot easier. And it doesn't hurt with tricky spellings, grammar and comprehension either!

Sitting up Straight

You can get a quick psychological boost by sitting up straight. It's true. Have you ever noticed how people with good posture usually look like they're in complete control? Well, there's a good reason for that.

Your brain speaks fluent body language. If you sit up straight, with your shoulders back, your brain understands that you're in a strong position. But if you're slumped forward with your head in your hands, your brain gets the message that things are hopeless.

Sitting up straight also makes breathing well and getting air to your brain easier (see the preceding section). Plus, it helps you to avoid back pain, which is a great bonus.

Talking Kindly To Yourself

 Think for a moment about your friends: are they people who build you up, encourage you and cheer you on every step of the way? If your friends aren't supportive, maybe you need to find some better friends!

Most people are quite nasty to themselves much of the time. They say things that they'd never dream of saying as a good friend, the kinds of things that would be insulting if anyone else said them, such as 'Oh, I'm no good at that' or 'I could never do that' or 'I'm not smart enough to'. Yet getting good at something is much easier if you *don't* put yourself down all the time.

For example, instead of saying 'I'll never be any good at maths', which runs the risk of becoming a self-fulfilling prophecy, say 'I've struggled with maths, but I'm getting better at it'. Instead of saying 'I don't like literacy', say 'I'm working on my literacy skills'; or if you're stuck on a problem, try saying 'I don't see how this works yet, but I'll figure it out'. You may be pleasantly surprised at the difference it makes to how you get on.

 A good friend suggests changing your passwords to something positive: for example, Ir0ck@Maths would do the trick! (Don't use exactly that, of course, because it's the first thing hackers will try now!)

Making Studying a Habit

Here's a tip from American comedian Jerry Seinfeld on motivating yourself: buy a calendar, put it above your desk and cross off the days when you do what you need to do (in this case, your numeracy and literacy studies). Watch the crosses increase and resolve not to break the chain!

When Jerry was a young, up-and-coming comic, he found he was hampered by not having enough material and so he resolved to write something every single day. To motivate himself, he got hold of a cheap calendar and every time he wrote a joke, an observation or anything work-related, he put a cross on the date.

He quickly noticed that the crosses on the calendar were forming a nice chain – and that he didn't want to break it! This approach helped give him the impetus to write something every day, even if he didn't feel like it.

Knowing What's Coming

You know the cliché: forewarned is forearmed. If you know what's likely to happen, you can prepare for it.

Obviously we can't tell you exactly what questions are going to be in your test (otherwise the book would be a lot shorter and a lot more expensive), but the example tests in Chapters 12 and 13 are based on past exams. You can also visit the government's Skills Tests website at `http://www.education.gov.uk/schools/careers/traininganddevelopment/professional/` to work through even more practice tests.

The more you practise, the better you can focus your studies – and the better you do in the tests!

Using a Last-Minute Cheat Sheet

The last few minutes before an exam can be the difference between passing and failing. You can use them productively if you take an hour or two before the test to make a last-minute cheat sheet.

On your cheat sheet, place all the fiddly things you know you need to remember but that you sometimes forget: maybe some tricky spellings, perhaps some formulas you need.

You can then read through this cheat sheet in the last few minutes before the exam, using your short-term memory as well as your long-term memory, and the fresh facts in your brain are relatively easy to recall!

Don't put too many things on your last-minute cheat sheet – five or six is about as many as you can expect to remember.

Thinking Creatively

You may think that exams are absolutely not the place for creative thinking, and that the last thing you want to do under test conditions is come up with wacky new ideas. But sometimes doing so is a good idea – especially for a question you don't recognise.

In that kind of situation, you have two options: you can leave the question blank or try to find a sensible answer. And doing the latter without a little bit of creative thinking is pretty difficult. Ask yourself questions such as:

✔ **What can I think of that's like this?**

For example, if you see an unfamiliar-looking graph that's a bit like a line graph, see what happens if you treat it like a line graph! If you've got a question that talks about something per hour, try using your speed formulas and see how you get on – it's certainly a better idea than leaving it blank! In the wonderful world of literacy, think carefully about where to go creative! Brilliant and imaginative new spellings will not be appreciated, nor will the invention of a new, one-size-fits-all punctuation mark! (How great would that be!!!) But always be on the lookout for words and situations you've encountered – or similar words and situations – and use the information to help you out of a hole.

✔ **What should my answer look like?**

If you've got to give a number as an answer, have a think about what you'd expect it to be. If it's asking about the length of a school day and your sums say '15 minutes' or '96 hours', you know those aren't sensible answers and something has gone wrong. And when you're doing your literacy the same rules apply. If you've brushed up on your phonics, you should know within a limited range of possibilities how to spell the words you face. If you've worked through your verb tenses, you should know that if you're talking about tomorrow you shouldn't be using the past tense.

✔ **How can I combine the information I've been given?**
In the numeracy part, you may be given several numbers. Would it make sense to add two things together? Divide

them? Comprehension is all about combining information – that's what making meaning from reading is. So, always be looking for how the words in a sentence and the sentences in a text combine to create the meaning you're looking for.

If you're in part of the test where you can flag a question and return to it later, do so. Aim to pick up as many marks as possible from the questions you *do* know how to answer than from the harder ones!

Keeping Your Notes Neat

Although anyone who's seen the chaotic scribbling in the notebooks scattered around our houses may accuse us of hypocrisy, in an exam (or whenever you have to work things out) having untidy, disorganised working makes getting the right answer much harder than necessary.

But if you keep your notes labelled neatly and write in a way that's easy to read back, you minimise the chances of making a sloppy mistake.

Pressing the Reset Button

Almost everyone has had some kind of exam-related meltdown. You can easily fall into the trap of thinking 'I don't know this thing, so I don't know *anything*'. It happens to the best of candidates.

If it starts to happen to you, you need to act fast. Remember the following process with A, B, C:

- ✔ **Acknowledge:** That your brain is trying to sabotage you.

- ✔ **Breathe:** Deeply and reassure yourself that you can still do well.

- ✔ **Calm down:** Start from scratch with the next question.

Don't let one bad question turn into a disastrous exam.

Focusing on the Result

Every summer, when the GCSE and A-level results come out, newspapers across the country run feel-good stories with a handful of delighted students jumping for joy after getting excellent grades.

Take a moment and picture being in their shoes: you just heard the news that you got the marks you needed to get into your teacher training course and start your new career. Imagine it vividly: feel the paper in your hand and think about calling your best friend to share the news.

Whenever you're struggling during your exam preparation, think back to this image and remind yourself why you're bothering to learn all this stuff: it's so that you can experience that scenario of success for real.

Chapter 15

Ten Tricks for Acing Your Numeracy Test

*O*kay, we get it: you're facing your Numeracy test and you're in a hurry! Here are ten tricks you can use to get the best results as efficiently as possible.

Reading the Exam Question Properly

Doing the sums is only half of the work in any maths test, but especially in computerised ones. The other half is giving the answer you're asked for.

Few things are more demoralising than doing almost all the work correctly and then slipping up at the last stage and losing the mark – just as if you'd left the answer blank.

Get around this problem by making sure that you read the question very carefully: check that the answer you're giving answers the question the paper asks!

Approaching a Question in a Different Way

Although each question in the numeracy portion of the test has only one answer, there's usually more than one way to reach it.

We know that you don't have a lot of time in the exam, and sometimes finding even *one* way to work out the answer in time can be a struggle. But if you're getting stuck, or you're not sure of your answer, and you have a few moments to play with, consider seeing whether you can think of another, less obvious way to work things out.

For example, if you have to work out 3/8 as a decimal and if you haven't memorised your conversions from eights to decimals, you might try working out 3 ÷ 8 using long division, or saying 'it's half of three-quarters, and half of 75% is 37.5% – so the answer is 0.375.'

Managing Your Time Effectively

One of the good things about the software you use in the on-screen portion of your Numeracy test is that it gives you the ability to manage your time. You get to spend as long as you like on each question (as long as you don't exceed the total time) and you get to come back and review your answers afterwards if the clock allows. Believe us, these options are very useful.

Here are a few ways to manage your time:

- ✔ If you don't see how to get started on a question, click on the flag at the top of the screen and go on to the next one. You always have a chance to come back to it at the end.

- ✔ Don't spend too long on a question: you only have about two minutes per question. If you're close to going over that allowance, click on the flag and come back to the question later; you don't want to miss out on any questions you may find easier later in the test! (The questions aren't necessarily in order of difficulty – and in any case, what's easy for you might be difficult for another student.)

- ✔ Use any time you have at the end of the test to review the questions you flagged.

Guessing Quickly When All Else Fails

Just to be clear: this tip is an *absolute last resort.*

When you're running short of time, or when you genuinely don't have a clue about a question, guessing quickly is better than leaving the answer blank.

If at all possible, try to work out the answer accurately. But obviously, under time pressure, this isn't always possible. The next best thing is an educated guess, where you come up with the simplest answer that looks about right. After that, guessing wildly makes sense, because you've more chance of being right if you guess than if you don't answer at all.

The Numeracy test isn't negatively marked. A wrong answer and a missed-out answer both score zero points and so you don't lose a point for guessing.

Writing Down What's Important

When you have a complicated graph or table in front of you, you can all too easily get information overload and have all the numbers start to swim in front of your eyes!

For this reason, writing down only the *relevant* information you're given is really important. Make notes of every number referred to in the question and label it with what the number is: a price, a speed, something else?

Then read through the text again to make sure that you have everything down right first time. After that, you're prepared to attack the question properly.

Making Things Simple

You're going to have to do some dividing – possibly lots of dividing – in your Numeracy test, and so you need to spend some time getting good at division.

One of the most powerful tools for dividing quickly is *simplifying:* quickly dividing or multiplying the top and the bottom of a fraction by the same easy number, most often 2, 3, 5 or 10. Check out Chapter 8 to discover more about simplifying dividing sums.

Keeping on Track

If you're not careful, a tricky question can easily turn into a disaster. We've heard many stories of students who decide that because they didn't get the first question right, they must be rubbish at maths and give up.

Please don't do that.

While researching this book, Colin sat the online test to see how it was. He had a bit of a fluster over one question and didn't get the answer down in time. It can happen to anyone. The best response is to take a deep breath and do your best to get the next question right.

The pass mark for the test is around 60–70 per cent: even if you get a few questions wrong, you can still pass the exam.

Reading Your Answers Again

One thing you always, always need to do is read your answer before you go on to the next question and make sure that it was what you meant to type.

Common mistakes include:

- ✔ **Missing out a decimal point:** A pretty big difference exists between, say, '144' and '1.44'!

- ✔ **Transposing digits:** For example, writing '132' instead of '123'.

- ✔ **Answering the wrong question:** For instance, if you misread or mishear 'the number of students who are *not* left-handed' as 'the number of students who are left-handed', you'll get the answer wrong even if you did all the working correctly.

Laying Your Work Out Neatly

Without doubt, you're under time pressure in the test and have only a small whiteboard to work with, but nonetheless if you're interested in getting the answer right in an exam, you *have* to set out your work neatly.

In the Numeracy test, you're marked *only* on whether your final answer is correct. You can do ten steps of the question right and then lose the mark just because you become mixed up between the columns you're adding up or misread a '0' as a '6' (something one of us does all the time – no names, no shame!).

Setting out your work in a neat, logical way is one of the best habits you can develop. It gives you the best chance of picking up as many marks as possible.

Doing the Most Obvious Thing

The human brain is much better at processing pictures than dealing with numbers, which is why graphs are so popular. People have been seeing and interpreting shapes for thousands of generations, whereas the number system is only a few centuries old.

Many of the Numeracy test questions use graphs. If you're ever not sure what's going on with one, try the most obvious thing! Even if you've never seen the type of graph before, you can have a decent stab at it. Check out Chapter 10 for more on working with graphs.

An educated guess is much, much better than no answer at all. ('Pass' is probably only the right answer if they ask 'What should you do if you have the ball and can't shoot?')

Index

• U •

About the Authors

Colin Beveridge is a maths tutor, writer and speaker from Weymouth, Dorset.

After a PhD in mathematics from St Andrews, he spent several years in Bozeman, Montana, working on NASA's Living With A Star program. He came home in 2008 and discovered that tutoring maths was much more fun than proper work.

He splits his spare time between running and looking after his young son.

He tweets at @icecolbeveridge and blogs at http://flyingcoloursmaths.co.uk/blog/

Andrew Green is a senior lecturer in Education and English, a writer and speaker from London.

After many years as a teacher and as a lecturer, he still loves anything to do with English and English teaching.

Three children and his wife keep him busy in his free time.

Dedications

This book is fondly dedicated to William Beveridge Russ: may all your teachers be enthusiastic students.

—**Colin Beveridge**

For Nat, Ollie and Bethi, with love. You never know, you might need this one day.

—**Andrew Green**

Authors' Acknowledgements

I would like to thank the many students I've helped through the Numeracy test, helping me discover what works and what doesn't.

The Little Red Roaster in Parkstone's regular supply of coffee and cake is largely responsible for the numeracy section being written at all.

And, as always, I'm grateful to my family for their unflagging support.

—Colin Beveridge

I would like to thank the students I've worked all these lessons out on over the years and the colleagues who have shared their own helpful ways of doing things.

I also want to thank my wife and children for their encouragement in writing this book.

—Andrew Green

We'd both like to thank the team at *For Dummies* Towers for getting our book out into the world; special thanks to our editors Jo Jones and Mike Baker, and to the technical editors for their helpful comments.

Publisher's Acknowledgements

We're proud of this book; please send us your comments at `http://dummies.custhelp.com`. For other comments, please contact our Customer Care Department within the U.S. at 877-762-2974, outside the U.S. at (001) 317-572-3993, or fax 317-572-4002.

Some of the people who helped bring this book to market include the following:

Project Editor: Jo Jones

Commissioning Editor: Mike Baker

Assistant Editor: Ben Kemble

Development Editor: Andy Finch

Technical Editors: Sunita Babbar and Chloe Orchin

Copyeditor: Kate O'Leary

Proofreader: Helen Heyes

Production Manager: Daniel Mersey

Publisher: Miles Kendall

Cover Photo: © nicole waring / iStockphoto

Take Dummies with you everywhere you go!

Whether you're excited about e-books, want more from the web, must have your mobile apps, or swept up in social media, Dummies makes everything easier.

FOR
DUMMIES
A Wiley Brand

BUSINESS

978-1-118-73077-5

978-1-118-44349-1

978-1-119-97527-4

MUSIC

978-1-119-94276-4

978-0-470-97799-6

978-0-470-49644-2

DIGITAL PHOTOGRAPHY

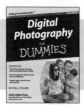

978-1-118-09203-3

978-0-470-76878-5

978-1-118-00472-2

Algebra I For Dummies
978-0-470-55964-2

Anatomy & Physiology
For Dummies, 2nd Edition
978-0-470-92326-9

Asperger's Syndrome For Dummies
978-0-470-66087-4

Basic Maths For Dummies
978-1-119-97452-9

Body Language For Dummies,
2nd Edition
978-1-119-95351-7

Bookkeeping For Dummies,
3rd Edition
978-1-118-34689-1

British Sign Language For Dummies
978-0-470-69477-0

Cricket for Dummies, 2nd Edition
978-1-118-48032-8

Currency Trading For Dummies,
2nd Edition
978-1-118-01851-4

Cycling For Dummies
978-1-118-36435-2

Diabetes For Dummies, 3rd Edition
978-0-470-97711-8

eBay For Dummies, 3rd Edition
978-1-119-94122-4

Electronics For Dummies
All-in-One For Dummies
978-1-118-58973-1

English Grammar For Dummies
978-0-470-05752-0

French For Dummies, 2nd Edition
978-1-118-00464-7

Guitar For Dummies, 3rd Edition
978-1-118-11554-1

IBS For Dummies
978-0-470-51737-6

Keeping Chickens For Dummies
978-1-119-99417-6

Knitting For Dummies, 3rd Edition
978-1-118-66151-2

FOR
DUMMIES

A Wiley Brand

SELF-HELP

978-0-470-66541-1 978-1-119-99264-6 978-0-470-66086-7

LANGUAGES

978-0-470-68815-1 978-1-119-97959-3 978-0-470-69477-0

HISTORY

978-0-470-68792-5 978-0-470-74783-4 978-0-470-97819-1

Laptops For Dummies 5th Edition
978-1-118-11533-6

Management For Dummies,
2nd Edition
978-0-470-97769-9

Nutrition For Dummies, 2nd Edition
978-0-470-97276-2

Office 2013 For Dummies
978-1-118-49715-9

Organic Gardening For Dummies
978-1-119-97706-3

Origami Kit For Dummies
978-0-470-75857-1

Overcoming Depression
For Dummies
978-0-470-69430-5

Physics I For Dummies
978-0-470-90324-7

Project Management For Dummies
978-0-470-71119-4

Psychology Statistics For Dummies
978-1-119-95287-9

Renting Out Your Property
For Dummies, 3rd Edition
978-1-119-97640-0

Rugby Union For Dummies,
3rd Edition
978-1-119-99092-5

Stargazing For Dummies
978-1-118-41156-8

Teaching English as a Foreign
Language For Dummies
978-0-470-74576-2

Time Management For Dummies
978-0-470-77765-7

Training Your Brain For Dummies
978-0-470-97449-0

Voice and Speaking Skills
For Dummies
978-1-119-94512-3

Wedding Planning For Dummies
978-1-118-69951-5

WordPress For Dummies, 5th Edition
978-1-118-38318-6

Think you can't learn it in a day? Think again

The *In a Day* e-book series from *For Dummies* gives you quick and easy access to learn a new skill, brush up on a hobby, or enhance your personal or professional life — all in a day. Easy!